BRINGING A GUN TO A KNIFE FIGHT

BRINGING A GUN TO A KNIFE FIGHT

Steve Tarani

P.O. Box 491788, Los Angeles, CA 90049

Disclaimer
Please note that the author and publisher of this book are NOT RESPONSIBLE in any manner whatsoever for any injury that may result from practicing the techniques and/or following the instructions given within. Since the physical activities described herein may be too strenuous in nature for some readers to engage in safely, it is essential that a physician be consulted prior to training.

First published in 2007 by Empire Books
Copyright © 2007 by Empire Books

All rights reserved. No part of this publication may be reproduced or utilized in any form or by any means, electronic or mechanical, including photocopying, recording, or by any information storage and retrieval system, without prior written permission from Empire Books.

First edition
06 05 04 03 02 01 00 99 98 97 1 3 5 7 9 10 8 6 4 2

Printed in the United States of America.

Empire Books
P.O. Box 491788
Los Angeles, CA 90049

Library of Congress Cataloging-in-Publication Data

ISBN-13: 978-1-949753-11-0

Tarani, Steve,
  Bring a gun to a knife fight / by Steve Tarani. -- 1st American ed.
      p. cm.
  ISBN 978-1-933901-38-1 (pbk. : alk. paper)
  1. Knife fighting--Training. 2. Firearms--Use in crime prevention. 3. Self-defense. I. Title.

  GV1150.7.T36 2007
  796.8--dc22

2007040580

Editor: John Spezzano

Contents

Foreword 10
Acknowledgements 16
Disclaimer 18
Acronyms 20

Part I—Solid Foundation

Skill Levels 21
Background 22
Depth and Credibility 31
DT versus Martial Arts 34
Frequently Asked Questions 38
Training Methodology 40
Winning versus Fighting 41
28 Real World Reasons 44
Taking the Shot 50
Safety Rules 53
DTI and SAI 57
Tale of Two Worlds 58

Part II—Building Blocks: SAI

Secrets of the Handgun 61

Hardware and Software 62

Defensive Mindset 64

    Conditions of Awareness 65

    Scale of Injury 68

Handgun Manipulation 69

    Presenting the Handgun 69

    Ready Positions 86

    Holstering the Handgun 90

Marksmanship 91

    Aiming the Handgun 92

    Holding the Handgun 95

    Handgun Stances 96

    Gripping the Handgun 102

Threat Engagement 103

    Standard Defensive Response 103

    SDR Failure Response 105

    Non-Standard Response (NSR) 106

    Multiple Threat Engagement 107

Sighted and Unsighted Fire 109

The Two-Second Rule 110

PART III—BUILDING BLOCKS: DTI

Secrets of Defensive Tactics 111

Hardware and Software 112

Defensive Mindset 113

    Violence of Action 113

    Forward–Aggressive–Effective 115

    Fightin' Ain't Easy 116

Action-Reaction 117

    The Power Curve 118

    Gross and Fine Motor Skills 119

    Pain Compliance versus Mechanical Compliance 120

Cycles and Gaps 121

    OODA Cycle 122

    Reactionary Gap 125

    Liability Gap 125

Position, Range and Mobility 128

    Control of Position 129

    Control of Range 131

    Control of Mobility 133

Stable Fighting Platform 135

    Hands and Feet 136

    Moving the Stable Fighting Platform 137

    Pivots 141

Soft and Hard Targets 145

Committed and Uncommitted Attacks 146

PART IV—BRINGING A GUN TO A KNIFE FIGHT

Combining Both Worlds 147

View from Above 148

Scenario 1—OAE at NCR and N/S 152

Scenario 2—OAE at NCR 155

    The 21-Foot Rule 159

    Reverse Tueller Drill 162

Scenario 3—CAE at NCR 165

    Weapon Retention Position 171

    Weapon Retention Live Fire Drill 175

Shot Placement Cycle 177

    Presentations While Moving off LOA—Strong Side 182

    Live Fire off LOA—Strong Side Drill 189

    Presentations While Moving off LOA—Support Side 194

    Live Fire off LOA—Support Side Drill 199

Changing Range and Firing Position 202

    Live Fire Range Position CQB Drill 202

Low Line Attack 207

Scenario 4—Low Line Attack at CAE and CR 211

    Speed and Surprise 217

    Hands versus Hands 217

    Down and Away 218

    Push Back 221

    Grabbing the Knife Hand 224

High line Attack	225
Scenario 5—High Line Attack at CAE and CR	229
Quick Shield	234
Quick Shield Push Back Live Fire Drill	241
Highline Attack at CR in CAE—"Get In" Option	250
Condition of Preparedness	258
Perishable Skills	261
Glossary	265
About the Author	270

Foreword

Steve and I met some years ago. The first time he came to my home, he glanced at my African mounts and headed straight for a World Championship trophy based on a Kris dagger asking "Where did you get this?" I started to tell him about the match, but was interrupted by Steve saying something along the lines of "Please tell me about your pre-match training regimen!" You cannot help but feel Steve's enthusiasm for training and his strong drive to bring reality-based training to his students.

We tend to trade email these days as we travel from place to place working with elite men and women stepping into harm's way. We exchange ideas on training, say we need some time off (but both love the hectic schedules we keep) and share the desire that we help to bring our warriors home alive and well to their family and friends.

Our most common ground (among other things) is training. We both share the same exact philosophy that the terminal objective of all hard skills training is to develop *reactive response*. In today's sound-byte age, most students expect to hammer out a few repetitions and figure that's good enough, practice makes perfect right? What's missing from the equation is perfecting technique—*perfect* practice makes perfect. Now take that perfected technique, apply controlled stress and out comes true performance capability. One of the greatest training aids which both develops technique *and* makes it work under pressure is competitive stress otherwise known as "competition."

Whether against the clock, another person or in a structured match, competition is critical to personal growth. It is every bit as essential as attitude, conditioning, good instruction, sound training and the need for mission success.

Having won National and World championships with rifle, carbine, shotgun and handgun, my area of expertise is shooting. These championships were won on square ranges where a very narrow skill set was tested as well as over miles of rugged terrain where skill selection was just as important as implementation. The pressure of competition rapidly develops skill selection and implementation in a timely manner.

Currently I am proudly serving a second term as President of the United States Practical Shooting Association and have competed and won in IPSC, USPSA, NRA, NSSA, NSCA, IHMSA, IDPA, IMG, ITRC and many other forms of competition over the past twenty plus years. The alphabet soup list of organizations is not as important as the various challenges they present to the competitor. These challenges further develop and encourage the shooter to reach beyond their current level of skill.

Over the years I have worked with firearm manufacturers as consultant, shop foreman and owner. Additionally, I have worked within the shooting industry for companies producing optics, ammunition, holsters, suppressors, lights, nylon gear, holsters, etc. Having been around the block a couple of times and as a senior-level shooting instructor it's my job to share this volume of knowledge and experience with others. Based on this experience, one of the most important concepts that I pass along to my students world-wide is that there is no substitute for training. What you're about to read in this manuscript further crystallizes this importance.

It has been and is a continued privilege and honor for me to instruct elite military and law enforcement operators in shooting principles and skills based on my personal experience for the past fifteen plus years. The skills imparted and the principles that make them work have been proven both in the field of competition as well as by operators on the battlefield.

Typically a student goes through several phases of learning and growth.

1. Instruction is where skills are taught and rehearsed under an instructor's eye for a specified amount of time. This first phase establishes a basic of understanding and familiarization.

2. Competitive stress is introduced and tests these skills and the student's ability to use them, but still under the watchful eye of an instructor.

3. Training missions (dynamic high-stress simulators) are set up to test ability and reactive response while under duress.

All of the above ensures the shooter has met a standard of skill requirements and has the ability to apply them. You will find that this vetted training methodology is also used in the following chapters.

Competition is a very healthy training tool. Open competition tests your skills against all other competitors within a certain set of parameters. A competition that gives the scenario and you are fairly free to come up with the best solution is fantastic. Rules are necessary to identify the goals of the competition and to make the results relevant. Your results in the competition are based on your knowledge of skills, the ability to choose the proper skill and the level you perform the chosen skill—against all others! Not against the person most closely matched to you. Not against the better skilled—until the instructor stops the competition to explain why you are losing. Not against others with only your training… but against ALL.

If you are planning to drive a Humvee in hostile territory, you need to know about driving through obstacles, navigating in unfamiliar territory as well as evasive maneuvers. Off road rally driving is a fantastic form of competition to test your driving and navigation skills and learn to hone those skills through interaction with great drivers. Indoor Go Karting will certainly teach you driving skills, but may be a little too specialized for your immediate needs. Choose your competition to test the practical skills you desire to hone.

If you want to learn to shoot in the most rapid and accurate manner, USPSA competition is for you. There are handgun divisions for everything from stock pistols to the most highly modified handguns on the planet. Do not be put off by the Open division "race guns," when I started this type competition in the late 1970s... a 100% custom pistol did not have as many features as a box stock Kimber!

Checkering, ambidextrous thumb safeties, beveled magazine wells, throated barrels and rugged high visibility sights all came from USPSA. USPSA is the best place to learn high speed gun handling, period. AR15s and shotguns have gone through a similar process of modifications. All of the competition modifications are tested by shooters across the country with a tremendous volume of ammunition. Because of the "no alibi" nature of practical competition, reliability is essential.

Accuracy, multiple shots on a target, engaging multiple targets, draw, reloading, shooting around obstacles and then all of the afore mentioned skills done on the move are tested every weekend at 350 USPSA clubs across the USA. And that is just the handgun divisions. USPSA has shotgun, carbine and precision rifle matches. We have MultiGun and Three Gun matches where competitors use handgun, carbine and shotgun in the same match and sometimes on the same course of fire. USPSA currently has over 16,000 members. If you want to test your practical shooting skills, USPSA is the place! You can find a local match by entering your zip code in our "club finder" at www.uspsa.org. Major matches are listed on our website as well as Area, State, Sectional and local events.

Critics of competition tend to cite the specialized nature of the tests and fail to appreciate the lessons learned by watching someone compete at the highest levels of human performance. If your job responsibilities include the carry and handling of a firearm, then compare the skills of someone who performs your same job and further develops their shooting skills as opposed to the other guy who does not further develop or even *maintain* his shooting skills. If the paint chips start to fly for real, which of these two shooters would you want to cover your back?

Specialized competitions such as NRA highpower rifle use shooting coats, iron sights and slow time limits. The wind reading, sight adjustment and shooting positions learned in highpower can certainly be employed with an M4. A USPSA or IMG competition that uses multiple targets and shooting locations, uses natural terrain as well as doorways, vehicles and other props, rewards both accuracy and speed; encouraging shooting on the move on close targets, shooting from braced positions on longer targets and allowing various optics seems a little more relevant to typical M4 work.

Competition teaches a shooter to perform under stress. I have witnessed real-world operators who do not hesitate to close contact with an armed enemy, get jittery when a timer is pulled out. They like to joke about this, but they understand and learn to perform at THEIR level instead of attempting to match someone else's.

One of the most important lessons from competition is to compete at the best of your ability at all times. I have lost competitions thinking I was ahead. I have lost competitions try to "match" another competitor's speed. Competition will teach you that your best performance will be to execute your skills at your highest level. Competition will allow you to hone a specific skill to a razor's edge. Competition will help you use skills at a very high level without conscious thought or effort. Competition will allow you to make aggressive decisions concerning the situation.

You alone must decide if you have the time and spirit to enter the arena of competition. To do this you must know that you will lose and have your weaknesses exposed. You will also grow tremendously in your ability to hit your target in the most rapid manner possible.

Purchasing a book on training indicates that you have a desire to learn. Acquiring *this* book means you have a desire to learn from one of the best and are willing to work to succeed. Study the techniques and principles following, practice the training drills as if your life depends upon it, hone your skills and then finally test them in competition— one of the best training tools available to develop operational readiness.

—Michael Voigt

President United States Practical Shooting Association
IPSC Regional Director US Region
United States Practical Shooting Association www.uspsa.org
National Rifle Association www.nra.org
International Practical Shooting Confederation www.ipsc.org
International Defensive Pistol Association www.idpa.org

Acknowledgements

Regarding Small Arms Instruction: Special thanks to Brent Alexander, Jimmy Blount, Randy Cain, Ken Campbell, Chris Dwiggins (deceased), George Harris, Steve Hendricks, Mark Lyons, Bill Maughan, Jim Morgan, Andy Moody, Bill Murphy, Fred Platt, Bob Reed, Pat Rogers, Tom Rovetuso, Ed Stock, Mike Voigt, Chris Weare and Jimmy Woods for their continued input, support and contributions over the years to this expanded body of small arms instruction and firearms tactical knowledge.

Regarding Defensive Tactics Instruction: The author acknowledges: Antonio Diego, Leovigildo M. Giron (deceased), Dan Inosanto, Ted Lucaylucay (deceased), Christopher Ricketts, Edgar G. Sulite (deceased) and Herman Suwanda (deceased) for their sharing of defensive tactics knowledge over the decades and priceless contributions to the world of edged weapons training.

Regarding Bridging the Gap: A special thank you to Lt. Col. Dave Grossman (US Army, Ret.), Bill Hall (USBP), SSA Tom Petrowski (FBI), and Lt. Dennis Tueller (SLCPD, Ret.) for their continued support and generosity in allowing inclusion of their well-researched training materials to be included in this manuscript, to Brad Ahrensfield (APD), Mark Babyak (FBI Ret.), Tom Bjerke (PCSO), Greg Dossey (LAPD Ret.), Jerry Huffman (SAPD), Chris Lutrell (NMSP), Jim Morgan (SBSD) and Cardo Urso (USMC Ret.) for their contribution of skills and knowledge over the years, their gracious assistance in developing and beta-testing these proven techniques for bridging the gap between the worlds of DT Instruction and Small Arms Instruction.

Regarding support documentation: The author further acknowledges: Jonas Cortes (SCPD), Jeremy James (DPD), Moe Morales (CDCR) and Dylan Fletcher (CDCR) for their written contributions herein, Barry R. Shreiar for his continued project support, John Spezzano for his most generous offer of time and effort in the mind-bending task of editing, and, Paul "Ted" Bubba Grybow and Tim Egberts for assisting with illustrations and the folks over at 10-8 Consulting for their donation of training materials; all of whom without their support this project would never have made it to the bookshelves.

Disclaimer

All of the material in this program of instruction is derived from direct feedback from the field (by way of operators who work directly in the environment) as well as actual training courses (delivered to various agencies throughout the professional training community) for more than sixteen years. As such, this material is intended for members of the professional community as well as informed law-abiding citizens.

The gun is nothing more than a problem-solving tool. It can be utilized to uphold the law, save the lives of teammates, partners, and family members and of course for personal defense. However, any tool is only as good as is the operator's ability to use it.

Simply having the tool at hand is not good enough. A tool requires a level of familiarization and proficiency to render it useful. Of what use to the military is an Apache Helicopter if nobody knows how to fly it? The same applies to the gun—especially with regards to its use in a high-stress-demand requirement such as effective response in a close quarters life-and-death scenario. The exact purpose of this material is to provide a familiarity and level of proficiency with a handgun so as to solve the problem of being attacked without warning while in confined areas of operation with little or no time to respond.

The first thing that comes to the mind of experienced law-enforcement professionals regarding this training is, "What about the bad guys? Can't this valuable information be used by them?" Nothing in this material is designed for bad guys. In fact, although presented as a training aid to the untrained gun-owner, the material is also structured in such a way as to build upon previous training in either small arms or defensive tactics at the academy level or advanced officer training (AOT). It is also cryptically written to allow those who currently train to "read between the lines" to see an additional layer of instruction here that will make sense when assimilated.

Rest assured that this is very carefully selected training material and represents only highlights of more complete programs of instruction. Those of us that know, it's no secret; books and videos are a great source for reference, but there is absolutely no substitute for a real live instructor providing hands-on training. In fact if you are one of the good guys, then visit www.opskillsgroup.com to find out more information on how this training can be brought to your agency or department.

Again, there's nothing in this material that you can't find on the web, in a local bookstore or your neighborhood library. There are no trade secrets being given away here whatsoever to either enemies of the state or your friendly neighborhood gang banger. All of the training materials in this program are of a *defensive* nature only.

Acronyms

If you're in any way involved in the professional training arena with the government (military, federal agencies, etc.) there is no way around the alphabet soup universe of acronyms. All of us in every aspect of our job run into acronyms at one time or another and some of us complete entire sentences all in acronyms (with a few adjectives). In response to a wide variety of students from all levels of the training community and specifically for the sake of non-military, non-law enforcement, defense-minded civilians all acronyms will be spelled out at least once for clarity throughout the body of the text and again defined in a glossary provided at the back of this book.

Over the years teaching professionally, it is my observation that acronyms are part and parcel of all training packages regardless of agency. They are unavoidable in this line of work and in fact are a necessity. As this manuscript is intended for all levels of interest, including law-abiding citizens with little or no prior experience in these areas, a complete list of acronyms has been provided at the back of this manuscript as part of the glossary for convenience of reference.

PART I
SOLID FOUNDATION

SKILL LEVELS

In the world of personal defense, there exists an extreme range of skill levels. On one end of the spectrum stands the battle-seasoned special-operations veteran with more than sixteen years on the job and trained by senior-level instructors to the very edge of perfection. This individual has many years of hands-on, real-world operational experience coupled with the best training available to modern high-profile operators. If this is you and you're reading this manual you may find the material an excellent refresher with tremendous emphasis on the critical basics, especially with regards to Part IV. As a seasoned professional there's no need to stress the life-and-death importance of honing the basics as you have first-hand experience and subjective knowledge that there's no such thing as a "beyond-the-basics" gun fight.

If life's experiences up to now have placed you at the opposite end of the spectrum with no prior military, law enforcement, federal or formal (or any) training in firearms or defensive tactics (or even martial arts), then just about every concept and drill in this manual will be brand new and chock full of extremely useful information. If you happen to fall somewhere in between the edge of technical perfection and having never held a gun in your hand before, then the information in this book will prove to be of tremendous value. Regardless of where your life's experiences have placed you along this vast gamut of knowledge and skill levels, it is my intent that this manuscript be utilized to develop critical basics and provide vetted combative concepts and techniques useful to those seeking to increase their skills in personal safety and to gain increased familiarity and proficiency with an effective problem-solving tool.

BACKGROUND

Most folks would say: "Bringing a gun to a knife fight? Well, that's pretty darn self explanatory isn't it? You just take your blaster, point it at the idiot who brought his knife to a gunfight and press the trigger—problem solved! What the heck do you need a training book for when it's as simple as point and shoot? The gun (as the more technically superior weapon) wins every time right?" Tell that to the families of numerous officers and agents (and also civilians) who have tested this theory at the cost of their lives or severe and debilitating injury. The need for this training information is borne of these numerous real-world incidents where simply *having* a gun *did not* in fact solve the problem based on a number of conditions which will be analyzed in extreme detail later on in this study.

FBI records for 2004 alone show there where 1,121 incidents where a peace officer (or officers) brought a gun to a "knife fight" and were either killed or injured. While no statistics are currently available as to the severity of these injuries, suffice it to say that said injuries warranted reporting.

According to the US FBI UCR Law Enforcement Officers Assaulted by Region, Geographic Division, and State by Type of Weapon, 2004 (see Table 68), a sum total of 1,121 officers were assaulted with a knife or "other cutting instrument." Other dangerous [hand-held] weapons (other than a gun) made up 8,598 assaults and an additional 47,459 assaults with Personal Weapons (hands, feet, etc.). Keep in mind that is what was *reported*. It is a proven fact that what is reported on official government records is not an accurate representation of what really happens on the street. These numbers do not include other law enforcement professionals such as correction officers and federal agents working abroad nor does it include any civilian incidents.

It is also interesting to note that even these reported statistics of 1,121 knife assaults on police officers plus 8,598 assaults on police officers with "other dangerous weapons" (other than a knife or gun)—again these are attacks at close quarters with an attacker wielding a contact weapon in his hand, a total of 9,719 assaults exceeds those assaults on police officers for the same time period with a firearm (listed as 2,109)—by nearly *five times* that number.

The following are just a sampling of actual incidents which have been provided as background as well as the impetus for this manuscript. The names of the officers involved in these incidents (if not published openly) have been purposefully changed out of respect to their families.

Suffolk County, New Jersey, August 14, 2006

A Suffolk County police officer and a police dog were stabbed with a box cutter during a struggle with an emotionally disturbed man. Authorities said the incident started at about 5:15 p.m. Sunday, when Officer William Krolikiewicz and his canine partner, Ike, responded to a report of a suicidal, disturbed man who had fled his house on Stony Hollow Road in Ridge.

Krolikiewicz spotted the man in nearby Brookhaven State Park and began to track him through the woods, police said. The man brandished a box cutter and threatened to stab Krolikiewicz and Ike, authorities said. When the man advanced on Krolikiewicz, the officer released Ike to apprehend him, police said. There was a struggle, and the man stabbed Ike in the paw, police said. When Krolikiewicz went to the dog's aid, he was stabbed in the right hand, police said.

Krolikiewicz and the dog eventually subdued the man, who was taken to Stony Brook University Hospital for psychiatric evaluation. Krolikiewicz and Ike were treated for their injuries and released.

New York Police Department, New York, July 27, 2007

A man who was being issued a summons for smoking on a subway platform in the East New York section of Brooklyn, Hugo Hernandez, sliced and stabbed a police officer in the head. Officer Angel Cruz had asked

Hernandez, 30, and another man if they had any weapons. His companion, Andrew Battiste, 21, handed the officer his ID and a knife.

Hernandez pulled out a hunting knife with a 6-inch blade and sliced Officer Cruz on the left side of his head, a police spokesman, Deputy Commissioner Paul Browne, said. Officer Cruz stumbled backward and fired three times at Hernandez, who again attacked him, this time stabbing the knife into the officer's skull and fracturing it. Officer Cruz fired two more times. Hernandez was hit twice in the elbow, but fled down into the subway. During the melee, Mr. Battiste fled back to Freeport, N.J., where the two men live.

Officer Cruz chased the man onto the platform, where responding officers arrested him. Both men were in stable condition yesterday. Officer Cruz went through multi-hour surgery, officials said. "Nobody should think that he's out of the woods yet," the mayor warned. Another officer broke his arm during the scuffle with Hernandez.

Hernandez, who hails from Guatemala, has a lengthy criminal record that includes two charges of assaulting a police officer in New Jersey, Mr. Browne said.

He was charged with attempted murder of a police officer in the first degree, assault in the first and second degrees, aggravated assault of a police or peace officer, and criminal possession of a weapon, a spokesman for the Brooklyn district attorney's office said. On the attempted murder charge he faces 25 years to life in prison if convicted.

"I just think it's another example of the kinds of risks that the men and women who work in our police department endure every day," Mr. Bloomberg said. "They want to go home to their families."

Part I: Solid Foundation

Saratoga Springs, New York, September 5, 2007

A city police officer was listed in fair condition Wednesday night after being slashed in the neck earlier in the day as he attempted to arrest a mental health patient on Jefferson Street, police said.

Officer Adam Baker, 30, was taken by helicopter to Albany Medical Center Hospital. He underwent surgery for a severed carotid artery in midair, Chief Edward Moore said. Two other officers arrested Seth M. Dawson, 19, of Shushan, after the attack.

Police had received a call at about 2:52 p.m. from the Four Winds Hospital to pick up Dawson after he was brought there by his mother for treatment. An incident occurred in the facility's parking lot, according to Moore and Saratoga County District Attorney James A. Murphy III, and Dawson fled.

He apparently wandered up Crescent Avenue and onto Jefferson Street, where he was confronted by Baker at the corner of East Broadway.

"The officer approached the individual and asked him to show his hands—he had one of his hands in his pocket—and at that point in time this individual came out with a razor and sliced the officer in the jugular (artery)," Moore said.

Baker approached Dawson alone, the chief said, but Officers John Kehoe and John Carey were responding as backup when they saw the attack, called for help and arrested Dawson. Moore said the razor was recovered.

Moore said several residents of Jefferson Street witnessed the attack. One teenage girl rushed with towels to aid the wounded officer, which Moore said helped save Baker's life. The stabbing scene is located near the backstretch of the Saratoga Gaming and Raceway harness track.

Baker joined the Saratoga Springs police in January 2004 and normally worked an evening shift, Moore said. "I was able to speak with him, he was still conscious when he was taken from the scene," Moore said. "We're hoping for the best." Dawson, who is charged with aggravated assault upon a police officer, is in Saratoga County Jail without bail.

Suffolk County Police Department, August 2007

ROCKY POINT—A bloody brawl early Saturday morning hospitalized a police officer and a man he was trying to arrest, and put a police dog in an emergency animal hospital with multiple stab wounds.

What began as a domestic dispute evolved into what Det. Sgt. William Lamb of the Suffolk County Police Department's Seventh Precinct termed "a tumultuous scene," which eventually included "numerous police officers."

Initial calls reporting a "disturbance" in Rocky Point came in around 3 a.m. Saturday, the detective sergeant said. John Anzalone, 41, had allegedly assaulted his female companion at 56 Sycamore Road and then fled the scene before officers arrived.

"We always send a team of two to deal with domestic cases," Det. Sgt. Lamb said. Officers searched for Mr. Anzalone before a decision was made to call in a K-9 unit, consisting of Officer John Mallia and his dog, Boomer, a 9-year-old German shepherd.

The unit quickly did its job and discovered Mr. Anzalone hiding in bushes in front of a residence on Tulip Road, the detective sergeant said. "When the dog went in to get him, he stabbed the dog multiple times with a knife," Det. Sgt. Lamb said.

When Officer Mallia tried to subdue Mr. Anzalone—and protect his dog—he was slashed on the hand by Mr. Anzalone, according to police reports.

Backup was requested as Mr. Anzalone continued "to fight with officers," Det. Sgt. Lamb said. "He didn't want to be arrested."

Part I: Solid Foundation

The suspect was eventually subdued, arrested and taken to John T. Mather Memorial Hospital in Port Jefferson. He was treated for "numerous dog bites," and released into police custody, spending the night at the Seventh Precinct stationhouse, Det. Sgt. Lamb said. Officer Mallia was also taken to John T. Mather Memorial Hospital in Port Jefferson, treated and released, according to the Suffolk County Police Department's Public Information Office.

Boomer was taken to Animal Emergency Service, a 24-hour Selden facility, and examined by Matthew Kearns, a veterinarian on duty Saturday morning, according to Mindy Mullins, Dr. Kearns' colleague at the animal hospital.

"Boomer was treated for multiple stab wounds, including those to his shoulders, neck, thorax and above his left eye," Dr. Mullins said, adding that X-rays revealed the stabbings didn't penetrate the body cavity of the dog, so no vital organs were affected.

"His wounds were thoroughly cleaned and surgically sutured," Dr. Mullins said. "He had lost enough blood to make him mildly anemic, but not enough to require a transfusion."

According to Det. Sgt. Lamb, there was no indication that Mr. Anzalone was intoxicated or under the influence of drugs. He has been in trouble with the police before, the detective sergeant added, including a charge of criminal contempt and various motor vehicle infractions. Mr. Anzalone was arraigned Sunday in First District Court in Central Islip on charges of assault, injuring a police animal, aggravated cruelty to an animal, resisting arrest and harassment. Bail was set at $200,000, which he didn't make, according to Det. Sgt. Lamb.

After two days spent getting back to eating regularly, Boomer was released on Monday with the expectation of a full recovery, Dr. Mullins added. "He's a beautiful dog," she said.

Bringing a Gun to a Knife Fight

Chicago Police Department, IL, December, 2006

Officer Robert Smith, was off-duty when dropping off his son at school observed a white male exiting a pickup truck and entering a vehicle which was parked on the North side of the lot of the school. Smith walked up to the vehicle and identified himself as a police officer, at which time the defendant exited the vehicle and stabbed Smith with a screwdriver directly into his dominant hand and began to struggle as Smith repeated commands to stop.

Smith then pushed the defendant against the truck as he attempted to reach for an object in the bed of the truck. The defendant then swung using his left hand when Smith observed a 5-inch knife blade in the left hand of the defendant, which he used to strike Smith in the neck. Defendant then ran through a residential area and in between houses. Smith was fortunate enough to flag down a fellow officer (Office Gregory Jones) in the vicinity who assisted him in searching for the defendant which Smith found under a truck hiding with the knife in his right hand.

Jones (the assisting officer) happened to be in the area when he was flagged down by Smith. Jones later indicated in a report that Smith attempted to detain the subject in the school parking lot, and the subject attempted to stab Smith even after Smith identified himself as a police officer. Smith (again, off duty) gave brief chase but lost subject in a nearby yard. Smith searched area for several minutes when he observed the subject under a truck in the yard.

The suspect then left his hiding location and fled north over fence and continue north between the buildings. Smith jumped over fence in yard adjacent to where the suspect was hiding and as Jones followed the suspect in his vehicle Smith ran west in alley to the end where Smith observed the suspect running south thru the fenced lot with a knife in his hand pointed towards Jones.

Smith drew his department approved revolver from the holster, pointed it at the suspect and ordered suspect to drop the knife, which suspect refused to do. Smith crouched through a hole in fence at rear of location, still pointed revolver at suspect and continually ordering suspect to stop and drop the knife. Suspect refused to comply and turned west and climbed another fence in an attempt to flee. Smith exited lot through the same hole he entered and ran down the alley until he noticed suspect sitting atop fence he climbed, still armed with knife. Suspect then climbed down back into the first lot and fled to a fence on another street and climbed same, still armed with knife in his hand. Smith reentered lot through hole in fence and ran toward suspect, again pointing his revolver at suspect and ordering him to drop the knife. As he approached suspect he dropped the knife but refused to come off fence.

Smith grabbed suspect pulling him off the fence and to the ground. Smith kept suspect face down on ground with arms out until Jones entered fenced lot and assisted with cuffing and brief search of the suspect. Smith received injuries to his hands and neck which were bleeding and came into contact with suspect's hands, which were also bleeding. Later, Supervisor orders Smith off scene to go to medical section to check on injuries/exposure.

Incident report lists observations of cuts to the hands of the officer and a cut to the left side of his neck caused by the knife attack.

Detroit Police Department, Michigan, February 12, 2002

Police Officer Joseph Michelson was stabbed to death after making a traffic stop in Redford Township at about 2150 hours. Officer Michelson was working traffic detail in the 8th Precinct when he observed a vehicle make an illegal turn on to Six Mile Road. He followed the vehicle into Redford Township where he initiated a traffic stop on Beech Daly Road. During the stop he removed the driver from the vehicle and began a cursory weapons search.

During the search the suspect attempted to flee and was tackled by Officer Michelson. During the ensuing struggle the suspect stabbed the officer in the neck and back nine times. While trying to defend himself Officer Michelson shot the subject in the chest, seriously wounding him. The round unfortunately also stuck Officer Michelson in the arm. The suspect then stole Officer Michelson's patrol car and service weapon and drove himself to the hospital, where he was taken into custody. Another suspect in the vehicle with the driver fled the scene. Officer Michelson passed away at the age of 35 with seven years on duty. The weapon utilized in taking the life of this officer was an edged weapon—a knife.

The above incidents are provided as a small sampling of actual real-world examples to illustrate what really happens out there with regards to guns versus knives and from various perspectives—and these are only the ones that are reported. There are numerous incidents which go unreported and that is only within the *professional* community.

In my many years of teaching professionally, there have been at least one or two students in each class (I'm talking about well over a thousand documented classes delivered throughout the US Professional L/E Training Community in my career to date), who either shared their edged weapon attack incidents with the entire class at the time or with me apart from the students after class.

There's no way to tell or track to what extent these incidents occur in the civilian community. Suffice it to say that there are unfortunately a substantial number of these real-world incidents (both reported and unreported) which run contrary to the common "I saw it in the movies so it must be real" belief that having and possibly using a gun will always make you win a "knife fight."

DEPTH AND CREDIBILITY

Where did the information in this book come from? No doubt that many of us have been to a class where we were very under-impressed with the instruction, the training material, the background and support information—the exact reason why part of this briefing section is devoted to depth and credibility.

The Operational Skills Group, LLC (OSG) (click on www.opskillsgroup.com for more info) began back in the mid-1990's (in the State of California) reaching out into the local law enforcement training community and delivering small arms and defensive tactics classes to officers seeking additional training skills—most of these classes were AOTs (Advanced Officer Training) and were very well received. In fact they were so well received, that the individual departments notified neighboring departments of the value of these programs and over time word spread from California to Nevada to Arizona, New Mexico, Texas and so on all the way out to Virginia. All the while delivering classes, the OSG mobile training team staff was exposed to various training methodologies, performance requirements and of course industry standard practices from coast to coast.

As time went on those agencies invited field office agents from their respective States (State of California, State of Nevada, State of New Mexico, State of New Jersey, etc.) and with further acceptance, the state agencies went on to invite agents from the federal field offices of the US FBI, US DEA, US FAMs, DOD, etc. which in turn eagerly adopted and recommended this training to their headquarters in Virginia and elsewhere.

All the while, on the training side of the house we worked with the top trainers in the industry and our programs of instruction were forced to meet very high standards and performance requirements. It was a byproduct of providing training services to local, state and federal agencies, that these programs of instruction were borne from a unique blend of industry standards from the best shooting schools, top level federal academy training and drawing upon the military, American professional law enforcement, US, federal training academies and respectable civilian shooting schools as well as professional firearms instructors including top competitive shooters—several of whom have offered input for this training material. All of this information was meticulously synthesized and presented in an easily digestible delivery format.

The material contained herein is a composite of two separate divisions of study—Small Arms and Defensive Tactics. The small arms material was developed specifically for the operational side as well as the training side with regard to CQB. The same goes for the defensive tactics—with regards to application of defense specifically against edged weapons.

On the operational side of the house, this training material has been vetted through numerous agencies based squarely on the recommendations of real-world operators whose entire careers were devoted to the usage of small arms and at extreme close quarters. Each of these stellar individuals were (and some of them still are) merciless (and for this brutal honesty we owe them a great debt) when it comes to calling the BS flag on something that doesn't (or wouldn't) work in the field which leaves only what has been battle-proven. In other words if a particular tactic or technique works and continues to be proven in the field over and over again, then it ended up in this manuscript. If it was found not to work (i.e. bravo sierra), then it won't be found in these pages.

Hailing from the small arms operational arena we were most fortunate to have the opportunity to draw upon the expertise and gracious input of several combat veterans of both Desert Storm and Operation Iraqi Freedom from each branch of the military. Additionally, experienced operators currently (as of this writing) in command of overseas on-the-ground counter-terrorism operations run by various federal agencies have also significantly contributed to this material.

Hailing from the professional training arena in the private sector, senior-level instructional staff at Gunsite Academy (AZ) and also of the Sig Arms academy (NH) has also substantially contributed to this training material. You will notice more than one reference to Gunsite Academy.

Part I: Solid Foundation

Also included as part of the private sector are professional competitive shooters who were gracious enough to include their input as well.

Referencing the edged weapons roots of the defensive tactics material, almost all of the defensive techniques were derived from prominent and very-well respected edged weapons masters hailing from the blade-oriented cultures of the Philippines and Indonesia.

Throughout this manuscript, with reference to edged weapons, you may from time to time run into the terminology—"The Masters say"—well who exactly are these "Masters?" Very long story, but in fifty words or less, I devoted almost a quarter-century of my adulthood ensconced in the study of edged weapons training. As a direct disciple of several of the most respected experts in the field, the likes of Guro Dan Inosanto of Stockton California, perhaps the greatest conservator of the traditional Filipino weapon arts alive today, Grandmaster Leovigildo Miguel Giron (US Army ret. Deceased)—World War II special operations veteran who utilized elements of this material in his covert activities during the recapturing of the Philippines under General Douglas MacArthur, Punong Guro Edgar Sulite, founder of the LAMECO system—one of the most highly respected weapons experts of our generation, Pendekar Herman Suwanda—Pencak Silat Master and co-founder of the famed Mande Muda system (West Java, Indonesia), among others. All of this material was synthesized over the decades into a comprehensive presentation of viable defensive tactics which are now accepted as industry standard in a number of state and federal training programs of instruction.

Combining this vast wealth of knowledge from real-world operators, senior-level military, law enforcement and federal agency training staff, as well as the private sector (professional competitive shooters), both from the Small Arms side of the house and the Defensive Tactics side of the house, allows the reader to utilize this manuscript as a "one-stop shop" vetted training resource.

The Masters say, "Without roots the tree falls down." The reason for sharing this background information is to demonstrate that this tree has roots. You, of course, can go out there and look up the individual pieces (building blocks) all on your own and are certainly encouraged to do so. However, one would be hard-pressed to find them carefully integrated and synthesized into a single instructional manuscript.

As with any quality training material it needs to qualify (and it certainly does) against some very rigid standards: verifiable source-reference material, reliable expertise, direct real-world application, direct feedback from the field, updates and revisions based on a living body of knowledge, keep-up with latest technology (gear), litigation (laws), changes in Rules of Engagement (ROE), Use of Force (UOF) and of course compliance with departmental or agency policy. All from which the reader may directly benefit.

DT VERSUS MARTIAL ARTS

The term 'Martial Arts' conjures up images of Bruce Lee, Chuck Norris and Jackie Chan flying through the air with spinning monkey-kicks to the head of a movie-land opponent and Karate-chops to the neck while yelling at the top of their lungs and grimacing. Well, you can delete that mental image picture from your brain-box right now as the material in this book has NOTHING to do with Karate chops, flying kicks, breaking bricks or wearing a black belt whatsoever. Nothing disrespectful implied or insinuated here, however, such components of the Martial Arts simply do not directly apply to the operational world.

The Martial Arts is exactly that—art. Similar to any art, it takes an entire lifetime to master and is therefore solely a private sector pursuit. Defensive Tactics (DT) on the other hand, is specifically designed to be disseminated to a group of individuals with zero background for a required terminal learning objective and in such a manner as to be assimilated in an extremely abbreviated amount of time—usually a matter of hours.

The difference between Martial Arts and Defensive Tactics can be compared to the body of knowledge about your entire background and career. If you were tasked with teaching a brand new student every single aspect of your job including your years of personal discovery, hard-earned skills and understanding through personal experience how long would it take to transfer all of that to your new student? Depending upon the depth of your background, that individual would probably need to spend a very long time (possibly years) as your apprentice in order to come fully up to speed to be able to perform at *exactly* the same level as yourself.

Now what if you were tasked with teaching that same student as much as you possibly could about that entire body of your life's experience and hard-earned knowledge in about four hours? (Similar to the task of Defensive Tactics) How would you know what to include in your class and what to leave out? As an instructor, how would you prioritize those items and create a performance test and training drills? These same hard-hitting questions apply to the world of Defensive Tactics.

Although the Martial Arts are considered a distant cousin of Defensive Tactics, there are tremendous differences between the two worlds. Some of those differences may be cultural and some may be technical but the bottom line is *applicability*. Are these techniques applicable in the real-world operational environment given the current gear, tactics, case law, department policy, and numerous other considerations?

What are some of the real-world considerations utilized by the professional training industry to segregate DT from the Martial Arts? The real answer to this question would take up an entire manuscript (and probably have you fighting for consciousness), however, suffice it to say that in order for a specific technique to make it over to the DT side of the house (directly from the Martial Arts with no modification) it must survive a fire-test series of requirements. Following is a mere sampling of some of these requirements. In order to pass through this crucible, a technique must:

1. be directly applicable to the officer's/ agent's/ operator's job.

2. be able to execute in less than 2 seconds.

3. be of less than three total movements—usually only one or two simple steps.

4. be easily assimilated—not memorization—and delivered in a matter of hours

5. require no prior training whatsoever.

6. meet current UOF and ROE requirements

7. meet or exceed departmental or agency policy

8. meet or exceed current industry training standards

9. fall within the parameters of academy training requirements

10. be directly compatible and integrate w/ all firearms instruction

11. be able to stand alone or work in unison with pre-existing training (modular)

12. be easy to understand and presented in a layered foundational approach

13. be compatible with existing agency doctrine and philosophical perspective

14. be presented in an accepted delivery format (lesson plans, hourly distribution, specific performance objectives, written / physical testing, TLOs, etc.)

15. be beta-tested on a variety of students over extended time periods to work out the kinks in delivery and hourly distribution.

16. be battle-tested or combat-proven to truly work in the field.

Again, this is a small sampling of the torture tests that it takes for a specific Martial Art technique to make it all the way over and across the barbed-wire fence to the DT side. In other words if a Martial Arts technique cannot minimally pass through the gauntlet of all of the above (and depending upon the specific agency or department may be as many as a dozen or more beyond what is listed above), then it cannot qualify as a defensive tactic. All of the techniques presented in *this* manuscript have successfully passed all of the above plus far more imposed by various US agencies and departments over no less than the past fifteen years.

The first question usually posed on day one of a DT instructor's training course to a room full of instructor-trainers is "Can any one in this room demonstrate the one DT technique that will work every single time?" Can you guess how many instructors raise their hand? You guessed it—none. The reason being—there is no magic bullet. If there *was* one then we'd all know it. The reality of the situation is that similar to a game of football or baseball or any professional sport for that matter, there is a counter-technique for every technique. There is no one play in football, or baseball or basketball that will work *every single time*.

Another important aspect of the presentation of this material is that we don't want to run off the handle with a counter to the counter to the counter to the counter. Yes, of course there is a counter for everything, but the objective of this training is to account for realistic and practical scenarios and not to wander too far in a fruitless game of hypothetical "what-if's." For purposes of clarity and study focus we will limit these only to what is relative to the topic at hand—bringing a gun to a knife fight.

The materials in this manuscript are focused squarely upon DT and *not* the Martial Arts—again, nothing personal against the Martial Arts (as I have been for decades and am to this day an avid student), but if it does not minimally match the above criteria, then it doesn't belong in this skill-set of training. Any further reference to any technique throughout the remainder of this book will be purely of DT in nature.

Each of the techniques and concepts contained herein are considered "tools in the toolbox." These methods are further considered "**A** way" and not "**The** way." Don't ever let an instructor tell you to "throw away everything you know because my way is the only way." Any instructor (including the author of this book) aspiring to deliver gold-standard quality instruction, will advise you to seek out training on your own, train in different systems and with different instructors, keep adding to your tool kit, cross-train and take what fits your profile, don't be encumbered by what doesn't fit and don't throw away anything that you know already works for you.

FREQUENTLY ASKED QUESTIONS (FAQS)

As a by-product of delivering numerous classes throughout the professional training community since the mid 1990's, a set of frequently asked questions (FAQs) almost always pop up. Since these directly apply to this body of training materials I would like to share these with you in the event that you may have the same questions about the training material before we get started into the meat and potatoes.

Question: Well, if he's got a knife, then why not just shoot him?
Answer: Determine that his actions warrant lethal force application, then shooting may be a justifiable solution. However, that is assuming that you are armed and can answer questions such as: is the gun accessible? Is it loaded? Do you have the time? Can you truly make the shot? Do you have *immediate* access to your firearm? Are you capable of safe and functional deployment? Does your environment and physical position allow for accurate shot placement? In fact there are more than two-dozen considerations that will be covered in more detail. A significant amount of training material will be devoted later to this important and common inquiry.

Question: What about techniques that I've already learned?
Answer: Any quality instructor will never tell you to throw away anything you've already learned. This course is designed to give you the reactive skills needed for you to take the next step in your training. You can think

of these as additional tools in your tool-kit. Keep in mind that our goal here is to elicit both familiarization and proficiency.

Question: Is this another one of those crazy wazoo kung-fu martial arts courses with too many complex karate moves to memorize?
Answer: Martial arts and memorizing techniques are not part of this program. This course provides dynamic, interactive training that develops appropriate *reactive response* and NOT memorization of complex movement. Comprised of simple gross-motor defensive tactics and small arms skills this training is specifically designed to meet and exceed real-world operational application.

Question: Well, I'm not very athletically inclined and have no martial arts background whatsoever. Can I still learn this stuff?
Answer: Yes. The objective is to get the situation under control as quickly and as efficiently as possible—again Defensive Tactics and *not* the martial arts. These exercises are based upon familiar everyday movements such as closing a car door, reaching for a cup of coffee and picking up a set of keys. If you can perform the minimum physical requirements listed by your department or agency then you are good to go.

Question: I saw this great technique in a movie. Can I use that one?
Answer: Fight scenes are choreographed for film. The camera angle is the most important element. In real life there is no need for exaggerated or complex movement (or drama). Your objective is to get the situation under control as quickly as possible using the most efficient means available. The exercises in this program are not pretty. This program does not teach "flying-monkey-spinning-back-kicks" and it will not impress a martial artist by any stretch of the imagination, but by the end of this training manuscript, an interested reader will take home an understanding of battle-proven "bread and butter" defensive skills that work.

Training Methodology

As with any practical study, there must be a systematic method of presentation. Such a method must be based on the fundamentals of basic instructional technology. Keep it simple and deliver the material in a sound foundational, layered (one building block built upon another building block) approach. The simple delivery concept of "first crawl, then walk, then run" directly applies to this training methodology.

Beginning with "strong roots" (as per above), a concrete foundation is built piece by piece—training block of instruction meticulously placed upon training block of instruction in a layered manner by which this material can either stand alone (work all by itself) or be integrated with other training (pre-existing tools in the tool box).

When providing ongoing training services throughout the professional training community it is critical to the acceptance of programs of instruction (POIs) by various agencies that a sound training methodology is incorporated in all aspects of training. The Operational Skills Group (OSG) [click on www.opskillsgroup.com for more info] developed a methodology which was universally accepted and is still utilized by the group in its professional deliveries to varying agencies to this very day—Familiarization, Proficiency and Sustainment. Let's take a look at each of these and the importance that this approach plays in the delivery and assimilation of this material.

"Familiarization" means the student is introduced to a technique or a concept for the very first time. It's similar to being handed a tool that you've never seen or held in your hand prior. The instruction allows a look, feel, smell, and taste of the new tool just as a cursory introduction or basic familiarization. This is known throughout the training community as a "Fam Drill"—short for "familiarization drill." *Crawl.*

Following familiarization phase of instruction is the development of proficiency. Here, the training is further delivered in such a manner as to develop both a deeper understanding and is brought to elicit a certain level of proficiency with the technique or concept. *Walk.*

Later on in the training, the final step is to isolate the technique and run it standalone, then run it with a compliant role-player and then run it against a non-compliant role-player. As with all training of this professional caliber, a sustainment drill is included as part of the lesson which is provided for the purpose of maintaining your newly acquired proficiency as all physical (hard) skills are perishable. *Run.*

In summary, the reader is provided the opportunity here to gain knowledge and skills based on Depth and Credibility (strong roots) and a proven training methodology.

Keep it simple—*crawl, walk, run.*

WINNING VERSUS FIGHTING

One important item that needs to be addressed right away is the phrase "Knife Fight." Ok, you may ask—what exactly is a "Knife Fight?" Based on my two and one-half decades (as of this writing) of training and experience working with the highest-grade level of instructors available, the term "Knife Fight" is one of the most misunderstood terms in the world of defensive shooting and in the world of defensive tactics.

As was passed down to us from ancient times, two fighters were connected with a rope tied around their waists (about plus or minus three feet apart) and each handed a knife. The idea was to see who had the greater skill. Unfortunately, it was a death sentence as both fighters got their stabs and slashes in on the other guy and 100% of the time—both died.

Later on, instead of tying ropes to connect each fighter (never any fun when both fighters die as it's difficult to place bets) the new rules were to dig out a pit and put both of them in a pit in the ground—from which the original saying "two men in—one man out" came. Although a little better, the "one man" who "came out" usually expired within a matter of minutes to a matter of hours. The term, "knife fight" again equaled the term "death sentence."

Much later in history (around the 15th-16th century), the game was changed from "fighting to the death" to "fighting to first blood." In other words, instead of a death sentence, two fighters armed with knives (or swords) would only fight until one drew first blood upon the other, thus ending the bout. Unfortunately, even "first blood" would usually end the career (and most of the time the lives) of both fighters.

Historically, the term "knife fight" came to be synonymous with the term "suicide." The odds on surviving a "knife fight" are slim to none. There's no "fighting" involved. Other than the movies or action-adventure novels, when was the last time you either witnessed with your own eyes, read it in the paper, saw it on the news or even heard second hand (or even third-hand) of two guys squaring off to each other FOR REAL attacking each other with *real* knives?

Outside of the movie theater and outside the pages of action-adventure novels, let's say in the yards of federal penitentiaries, state prisons, county jails and nasty parts of the inner-city, the complexion of the game is a little different. Yes, the attacker may have a blade in his hand, but usually the victim does not. An attack may last anywhere from a second and a half to four or five seconds. There's no *fighting* involved whatsoever. It's purely a matter of the victim (already cut and bleeding) trying to get away from the guy with the knife.

As was my personal experience training in the Far East, the most highly-respected blade cultures of the Philippines and Indonesia *do not* train to maim or to cut their opponent with a knife—they train to kill them. The entirety of training at that level is based on accessibility and placement of the blade at specific "rapid termination targets" on the human body. It's a completely different mindset.

Here is a clear example of the difference in mindset. We (alpha males) here in the West go to a bar, have a few drinks, get in a fist fight with another alpha male and within a short time, alpha male A knocks alpha male B to the ground, beats both closed fists upon his chest in victory, helps the guy up and buys him a beer. In the P.I. or Indo, you get into a hassle, the fastest man with the concealed blade wins. A typical scenario would be a little stink eye (mutual challenge-glare of the eyes) followed by an eight-inch ragged edged blade shoved deep into your opponents rectum all the way to the hilt and turned clock-wise to ensure a deep enough debilitating cut (what they call a "distraction") and then clipping the femoral arteries on the way out—aka "knife fight."

The moral of the story here is that two people squaring off each holding a knife in hand is ludicrous. It may look good in the movies and is certainly the stuff of action adventure novels, but a "knife fight" has no place in the real world. If you're close enough to another human being and either of you have a knife with the intent on truly using it, then guess what—it's too late, you will be cut. Neither of you will walk away without severe internal or external bleeding, loss of a limb, an eye or even your life. Minimally you will need stitches and you may never recover.

A physical altercation involving getting cut up with a knife at close quarters is truly nasty business. Let's keep it all in perspective here—you can get a paper cut from the edges of this page. We can cut ourselves shaving, picking up pieces of broken glass, etc. But I'm talking about an intentional and nasty series of brutal stabs and slashes—not just a situation that will send you home with a few stitches across your face, but a scenario that you won't be able to walk away from…at all.

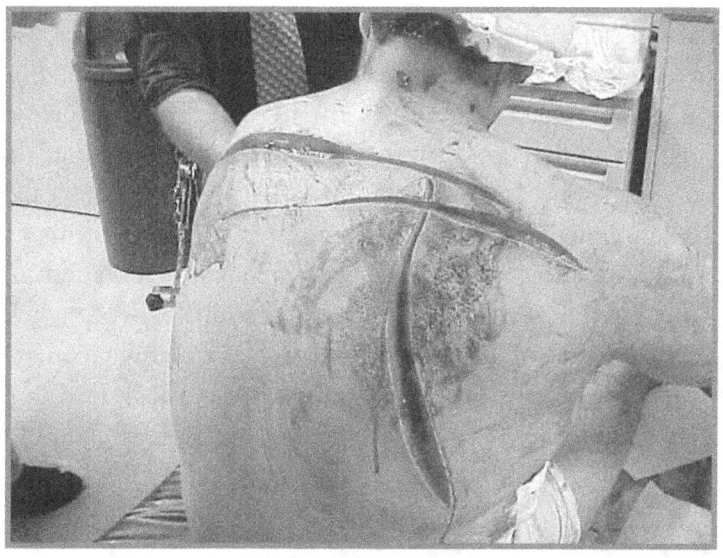

Example of a "warning" with an edged weapon.

This crap about magically taking a knife away from somebody or shooting it out of your opponent's hand is also fictional—movie material. If you want to know what it feels like to fight a guy with a knife and you only using your bare hands, then go get a lawn mower, place it on its side, crank the motor and go ahead and crash both your hands into the spinning blades. Another example of "empty hands" versus knife is to activate your garbage disposal in the sink and shove your right hand deeply into the spinning blades as hard and fast as you can.

Bringing a gun to a "knife fight" is a matter of *winning* versus *fighting*. There is no "fighting" with regards to a knife—only winning or losing. If you get cut or killed with a knife, then you lose. Something maybe George Lucas might write into a movie script involving guns and knives—"Win or lose—there is no fight."

The purpose of this manuscript is not to teach how to "*knife fight*" but, should you be fortunate enough to carry a loaded gun (and trained in its use), how to effectively utilize your firearm and consequentially walk away the victor.

28 REAL WORLD REASONS

On staff at Gunsite Academy (prominent civilian small arms school located in Paulden, AZ and founded by Col. Jeff Cooper (USMC Retired—Deceased)) since the late 1990's to date I was fortunate enough to participate in golden opportunities to interact and share knowledge with other instructors. The group of Gunsite instructors comes from varying backgrounds (all branches of the military, federal agents, intelligence community, urban and rural law enforcement, etc.) and was (and still is) a melting pot of priceless information and experience (click on www.gunsite.com for more information). In fact I highly recommend if you're a gun owner and have never trained at Gunsite Academy— you need to get out there and experience world-class instruction from the very best.

Part I: Solid Foundation

Some hard-hitting questions such as "In real-world civilian law-enforcement application, what percentage of your career have you placed hands-on versus rounds down range?" "Regardless of application, is a firearm ALWAYS the optimal response to a close-quarter threat?" "Why may I not be able to employ my firearm to effectively stop a threat at contact ranges?" were posed both in professional classes by many students and at numerous round-table discussions with various instructors.

These questions (originating from the instructors at agencies in Virginia (federal), California, Arizona, New Mexico, Georgia, etc. (state) and Gunsite Academy, Sig Arms Academy, etc. (civilian) and other credible sources were also asked of the instructors by their students, many of whom are instructors themselves. The responses were recorded for posterity by yours truly and are presented here as a cornerstone for the bridge connecting the worlds of firearms training and defensive tactics training.

The following list of 28 real world reasons why a firearm may not be the first response to a "*knife fight*" drawing upon the input of literally hundreds of experienced operational students and more than fifty-seven of these highly respected and experienced senior-level veteran firearms instructors over a span of ten years.

1. You don't have a gun on your person or in your immediate vicinity.

2. You cannot easily access your gun (out of reach, too deeply buried under, gear, safety levels, etc.)

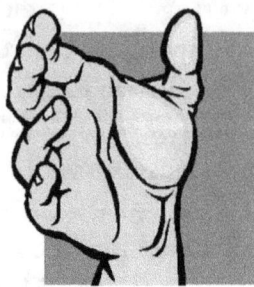

You don't have time to respond:

3. The average attack occurs in less than 2.5 seconds.

4. The average human *mental* reactive response time is nearly 1 second.

5. The average full presentation of an open-holster firearm (for most cops based on a 2002 national average) is over 2.5 seconds.

6. The average full presentation of a concealed firearm is closer to 4.5 seconds.

You're unsure of your decision:

7. Is this a shoot? Given the litigious nature of the society in which we live, most trained professionals realize that their entire career, house mortgage, kids future and their retirement, go along for the ride on the nose of each round fired from their muzzle.

8. Is this a no-shoot? Just as important a question, this can put your mind on the fence and soak up valuable time that could otherwise be put to good use.

You are unable to make the shot because of:

9. Physical reasons (stress, adrenaline, shock, loss of fine motor skills, etc.)

10. Legal reasons (this may not in fact be a justifiable shooting, etc.)

11. Emotional reasons (personal fear, anger, terror, shock, etc.)

12. Religious reasons (personal beliefs)—interestingly enough there are certain individuals who carry a gun for a living that have already made the mental decision that they will not take the life of another human being regardless of the situation as a matter of personal belief.

You have no ammunition:

13. There is no round in battery. As difficult as it is to believe and I know of course it has never happened to any shooter reading this manuscript who has walked up to that line and executed a perfect trigger press straight to the rear of the trigger guard only to hear the soft painful "click" of the strike of the firing pin against an empty chamber.

14. You ran out (shot to slide/bolt-lock, have only one magazine, etc.) could this happen in the heat of a firefight?

Impaired visual acuity:

15. You **can't see** your target (based upon your immediate position, rapid target movement, etc.).

16. You **cannot clearly identify or are unsure** of your target and what is beyond your target (low-light, obstructions, partner or family members in vicinity of shot, etc.).

17. You move into a **Hazardous Area**—this can be something like a Methamphetamine-Lab or other area containing Flammable Liquids, and/ or Explosive Gases

Malfunctions—there are two types of malfunctions—one is Mechanical, that has to do with the mechanical function of the firearm itself. The other is human—that is operator induced malfunction. Let's take a look at each of these categories of malfunction:

Part I: Solid Foundation

Mechanical Malfunction:

18. Failure to fire.

19. Failure to eject.

20. Failure to feed.

21. Failure to return to battery.

Operator Malfunction:

22. You missed the target. As difficult as this may seem to believe, does it happen in the real world?

23. Unable to handle the firearm. What could be one reason that you may not be able to effectively handle a firearm? How about an injury to your weapon arm or hand or fingers? What other reasons may you not be able to handle the firearm?

24. The bullet failed on impact. What may be a real-world reason why a bullet may fail on impact? Maybe he's wearing a hard shirt (protective vest) or maybe he's just not impressed or maybe doesn't even know he's expired yet.

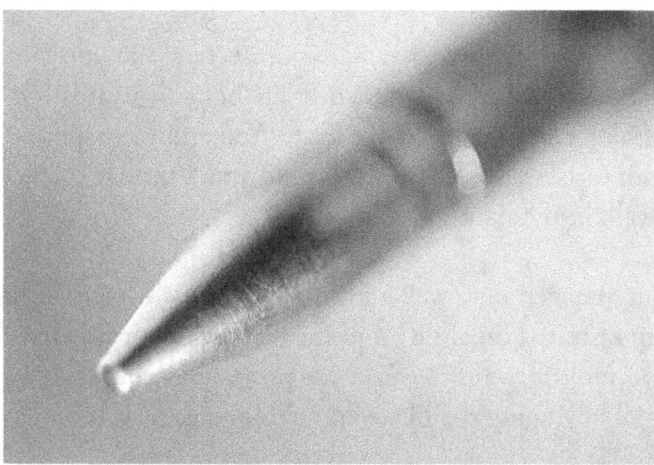

You hit the target with full impact, however, assailant is coming straight at you full force and you have:

25. No *time* to move out of the way

26. No *space* to move out of the way.

Assailant has physical/mental reasons:

27. Drugs, alcohol and/or other stimulants or depressants on board.

28. Mindset (rugged and deterministic mindset, religious extremist, suicidal, etc.)

TAKING THE SHOT

It's a beautiful spring day about middle of the afternoon. A light breeze gently pushes a colorful butterfly through the air and two bluebirds perched on a nearby tree branch are happily chirping away. You happen to have just zeroed your personal carbine out to 200 yards and are happy with your last grouping. Armed with a fully functional M4 with several magazines on standby you've got a fully loaded magazine in the mag-well with one in the tube. There's a fresh battery in your optics system which happens to be perfectly adjusted to the current lighting.

You're wearing both eye and ear protection and you are set up in stable prone position behind solid cover at about 175 yards out from your attacker coming at you with a large knife. You and your spotter have been training with carbines since you were a kid and a shot at such close distance is a walk in the park for you.

Your attacker, now well within a perfect sight picture, having already demonstrated capability and intent to rip your throat wide open, continues to vault forward toward your position at you in an aggressive manner wildly swinging the blade and closing fast.

Part I: Solid Foundation

Already set up with good protection and plenty of time you maintain good sight picture, execute superb trigger control you wait for him to reach a "no way I can miss" distance and crack a round off which of course strikes the intended target—problem solved. Gun versus a knife—well that's all there is to it—that's the appropriate ending to a no-win situation for the knife guy.

Optimal response to an attack with a knife.

Given the above situation, how many of us walk around every day (other than military and specialty teams) with all that gear and ready to go? Can you imagine what type of problems it would cause, no matter how cool it would be, to walk over to an ATM set up as per above in the middle of your neighborhood? Now what about the distance? Is that a normal everyday event—an attacker presenting a knife at greater than seven to ten yards and you have all day to take the shot?

Now, let's take that same example and instead of a carbine, now let's replace the carbine with your trusty handgun. There you are, again, very well trained, (you shoot about 1500 rounds a week and happen to be a ranked competitive shooter), in the middle of a beautiful day, the scent of flowers in the air, plenty of visibility, cool breeze in your hair, firearm pointing downrange and up on the target, you have your eye and ear protection on, a fully loaded magazine in the well, one in the tube, hammer back with your front sight dead on center mass of incoming threat. All that remains is of course to check off all 28 of those boxes above. You go rapidly through the checklist (as you have plenty of time), the decision has been made, this is in fact a shoot scenario and about 25 yards out is a good enough shot so you take it. Good sight alignment, excellent trigger control (as you have plenty of time and space to work) and a perfect trigger break of course places the round directly upon the intended target and problem solved. Gun versus a knife—well that's all there is to it—that's the appropriate ending to a no-win situation for the knife guy. He shouldn't have brought a knife to a gun fight.

If it was the case that you were most fortunate enough to have been mentally and physically prepared with all the gear, at safe distances, plenty of time, a good background, and some idiot running straight toward your muzzle (and of course it's a justifiable shoot), then why *wouldn't* you take the shot? Unfortunately, this particular set of circumstances is *not* the real world and as such is *not* what this book is about.

If this were a standard shooting program, then the entire book would be squarely focused on taking that perfect shot, in a classroom environment, on a square range with perfect shooting conditions and with ample reaction time and plenty of preparation for the shot. But, again that's *not* what this training material is geared for. The exact purpose of this material is to provide the reader with a familiarity and level of proficiency with the handgun (problem-solving tool) as to solve the problem of being attacked without warning and in confined areas of operation with little or no time to respond (problem).

In the real world most of us law-abiding citizens don't have the luxury of carrying a fully-loaded carbine slung and safe with the warm and fuzzy feeling of our weapon hand wrapped snugly around the grip with our thumb vigilantly resting on the selector switch. Even carrying a loaded handgun, for most of us (especially if carrying concealed) the weapon is safely stored in its carry position secured in a holster and in some cases with an additional retention strap, snap, Velcro® or other similar device plus any mechanical safeties that may be engaged on the weapon itself. No ear protection, no eye protection, no Rangemaster or Range Safety Officers issuing shooting commands, no early warning of any incoming threat, no time to prepare for a life-threatening attack and walking around, not on a safe firing range with vetted backstops but, in a crowded urban environment which provides little or no safe backstop.

Minding your own business and probably talking on your cell phone or your hands otherwise occupied with electronic devices and the like or maybe even a cup of coffee. You turn around the corner fumbling for your car keys as you're starting to walk through the parking lot late at night and all of a sudden you get an ominous feeling.

A predator, who has been stalking you since he noticed you not paying attention to your environment, pops out of the darkness wielding a shiny metallic object in his right hand waving a razor sharp blade edge and pointing at your throat demanding your wallet. He's so close you can smell his bad breath. Sure you've got a gun strapped to your body but can you get to it with him so close?

He's sweating profusely and is screaming at you to hand it over and although shocked and caught by surprise you can tell by the looks of his crazed bloodshot eyes that he means business and you're so far behind the power curve that there's no way you're going to get to your gun in time. If you're interested in an optimal solution to this nasty little problem—then read on.

Safety Rules

Although including equal elements of both DTI (defensive tactics instruction) and SAI (small arms instruction), this is not a pure firearms training program per se. However, this material does involve the handling of firearms and as such is subject to the exact same rules and regulations as pure firearms training program.

First off you must check with the Rangemaster at the range you plan on shooting these drills to ensure that they allow this type of training. Some ranges—especially those located out there in the People's Republic of California—barely allow bullets on the range, so be sure to double check with your range to ensure regulation compliance.

Anywhere in the world of firearms training there are two sets of rules—Firearms Safety Rules and Range Safety rules. Given that the majority of your time carrying and handling a firearm will most likely not be out on a range (unless you are a professional firearms instructor), then the more important of the two is the firearms safety rules.

Paramount to any training with a firearm is firearms safety. Firearms safety is as important during daily activities as it is during range and training activities. Those of us carrying concealed, are required to carry, handle and deploy a firearm in a safe manner, whether assigned to patrol, investigation, SRT (specialty response team) or a defense-minded citizen. Firearms safety rules are developed for training and carry situations that prepare the shooter for actual field application.

A set of industry-standard firearm safety rules were developed back in the late 1960s by Col Jeff Cooper (USMC Ret.—Deceased) and first incorporated at the American Pistol Institute in Paulden Arizona which was founded by Col. Cooper. (the name was later changed to Gunsite Academy) in the early 1970s. Since that time, those same safety rules were "borrowed" by pretty much every major department (including the US military, law enforcement, etc.), agency, state, federal and even civilian private shooting club or range. Although there may be some slight variations, the four general safety rules have not changed since that time and are as relevant today as they were in the middle of the 20th century.

The four firearms safety rules should be adhered to by the shooter regardless if he is on a range, in a public restroom or out in the field. They are universal and apply at all times and with all guns.

1. **All guns are always loaded.** No exceptions. It doesn't say "might be loaded" or "I think it's loaded" or you are to pretend or make

it up in your mind—all guns are always loaded means just that—any shooter must remain deadly serious about it.

2. **Never let the muzzle cover anything you're not willing to completely destroy.** Many of us who have been handling firearms for a long time need to be especially aware of this important rule as "familiarity breeds contempt."

3. **Keep your finger off the trigger until your sights are on your target.** Often referred to as "the golden rule" of gun safety, this is perhaps the most important of the three especially with regards to safe handling. Unless you have made the conscious decision to shoot, and it is a justifiable shoot, or you are at the range and you're 100% sure that you are up on target and your sights are aligned with the target—then stay off that trigger and keep your fingers outside of and away from the trigger guard.

4. **Be sure of your target and what's beyond.** Know exactly what the target is, what is in line with it, and what is behind it. Never point in at anything you have not positively identified and are absolutely certain of what lays behind it.

Rules vary from range to range based on the requirements of facility authorities, but for the most part they are fairly industry standard. The following list is a good sampling of general range rules that would most likely be asked of you when training—so be advised.

While on the range, it is mandatory to utilize approved eye and sound barrier-type ear protection and other protective equipment (depending upon your agency and their live-fire training policies), as required by the RSO (range safety officer). Unsafe conditions must be immediately reported to the RSO or the RM (rangemaster). All firearms shall be carried in a manner as specified by the RM or the program director.

No firearm shall be left unattended or unsecured. Fingers shall not be placed in or near a firearm's trigger or in or near the trigger guard until the firearm is pointed directly in and up on target (see Safety Rule #3). The loading and shooting of all firearms shall commence only on command of range staff (RM or RSOs). Until the firing line has been declared safe by the RM, shooters shall not bend over to pick up any gear or move forward or back of the firing line.

All shooters shall be trained and instructed on what constitutes an unsafe condition and to shout "cease fire" when such a condition is observed. Shooters shall ensure that their firearms are properly cleared, cleaned, stored and secured after training. Cleaning materials shall be properly stored or disposed. While a firearm is being cleaned, any and all live ammunition shall not be allowed in the cleaning area.

As a responsible gun owner, home firearms safety is a mandatory consideration. To ensure firearms safety at home it is recommended that the following precautions be practiced regularly: Store all firearms and ammunition separately and out of the reach of curious children. Use an acceptable trigger guard lock or locked container such as a gun safe or other secured storage location.

An often neglected scenario, control of a firearm in restrooms is deadly serious business. Although the question of what to do with your firearm while you use the restroom is a delicate subject, it must be addressed. Many real-life incidents have been reported (and many more unreported) about firearms being negligently discharged while the owners were engaged in natural bodily functions. The results can be disastrous, such as the death of a child sleeping in the next room or apartment. There are numerous cases of firearms being stolen from police officers that were careless under these circumstances. By leaving the handgun holstered, any one of the following methods will assist in deterring theft or negligent discharge of the firearm. Place the handgun (and holster) between your feet. Place the handgun and holster in your underwear, carefully sling the belt, holster and firearm over your shoulder with care that no unsecured pieces of gear fall out.

Firearms safety is *everyone's* business. There is no such thing as being "too safe" with regards to handling firearms.

Part I: Solid Foundation

DTI AND SAI

Although much improved at the time of this writing, back in the day, a firearms academy may have instructed a young cadet to do such things as stand in a certain shooting stance (Weaver, Chapman, Isosceles, Modified Isosceles, etc.), keep his weapon side back away from the threat and keep his hands above his belt and other sage advice. Whereas across the street at the DT building, the DT instructors may have issued contradicting commands such as "when utilizing the baton and for optimal impact keep your weapon hand and weapon foot forward and…" Well, it's the same student going through both schools—yet this very same student is instructed in some cases with completely contradictory instruction. How do you think that affected that cadet's performance (and confidence) in the field?

As a direct result of this training discrepancy there was a tremendous gap identified in training that could only be solved by a bridge between the two worlds—the world of Small Arms Instruction (SAI) and the world of Defensive Tactics Instruction (DTI).

Such a bridge would require a deeply compatible, "seamless progression" of training technology that would provide the student with *optimal response* capability.

The first steps toward building such a bridge across both sides is to align the building blocks so that they are at least set up in the right direction. Rather than place attention on the *differences* between the two sides (of what is considered the same coin anyway), emphasis will be placed on the common threads shared by both. The true irony of all of this "division of training" stuff is that it takes fierce and lethal combat to leach out the commonalities between both worlds. In fact such a lethal encounter involving a gun and a knife is not survivable *without* skillful usage of *both* sides of the same sword—both SAI and DTI. In subsequent chapters more attention will be placed on identification of the commonalities between the two worlds. That is, finding the *common threads* of both DTI and SAI. Enough common threads going in the same direction (toward winning a lethal encounter) focuses our studies squarely on the combined benefits that both worlds have to offer.

The reader must also keep in mind that the world of DTI, although considered a necessary evil by all agencies requiring *hard skills* of their employees, has always and always will take a second seat to SAI. The reasons for this, among many others, are that firearms present the higher liability (the biggest concern of administrators), and that most people would rather press a trigger than sweat and roll around on the ground and risk potential personal injury in training—even though every day they must put hands on the public and despite the fact that such skills have been proven beyond any doubt to increase their chances of success.

Because of this secondary status, even though throughout more than 98% of their entire careers law enforcement professionals put their hands on someone on a regular basis as opposed to sending rounds down range, the emphasis on both mandatory sustainment (time) and funding (money) rests with SAI. Not to open another can of radioactive worms here, but both SAI and DTI share the same exact impact to budgetary and time constraints. In fact, regardless of whether it's federal, state or municipalities, the very first budget to get cut during hard times is—you guessed it—training. Both SAI and DTI suffer equally when administrators instead of cutting their own (top-heavy) overhead costs, go after the training that the troops most depend upon for their daily survival—SAI and DTI training.

The similarities between DTI and SAI are numerous, (as will be covered in much more detail following), *mutually supportive* and when joined together stand far more effective combined than if divided. Throughout the remainder of this manuscript the material is presented in such a manner as to facilitate and allow the reader to take full advantage of these common and mutually supportive training technologies between the two worlds.

TALE OF TWO WORLDS

Back in the day, old school thinking was to handle everything with a gun and with a gun handle everything. In this modern age it was arduously discovered that, given how litigious a society we now live in, (as well as

Part I: Solid Foundation

the media's innate disdain for law-abiding citizens of a free republic to safely own and carry a firearm for self-defense and the protection of their loved ones), one just can't go around blasting everything that appears to be a threat. Conversely, in a situation where an attacker appears out of nowhere and with a knife in your face, you may want to retaliate by sticking your muzzle in his face, but the complexity of the reaction game changes with proximity and it's not as easy a challenge to meet as we will soon discover.

Most handguns can accurately hit a target out past one-hundred yards. In fact I know of a certain retired New Mexico state police trooper (Jimmy Woods) who can do just that—at will. General small arms training usually covers training materials from the fifty yard line on in but focus predominantly from the three yard line to the seven yard line—reason being that's the range at which most gunfights occur.

Mainstream small arms instruction (other than the very few schools which offer training in shooting from the retention position) is limited in its scope of study as it tends to shy away from contact ranges (that range where you can physically reach out and touch your threat with your hand as well as your threat can reach out and physically touch you with his hand) for a number of reasons—liability not being the least—and begrudgingly leaves this range of personal combat to the world of defensive tactics.

The world of defensive tactics deals exclusively with these physical contract ranges, specifically hand-to-hand either standup or on the ground. Specializing in dissemination of effective techniques for handling hand-to-hand engagements, defensive tactics is unparalleled in its capability to deliver.

However, aside from a small handful of weapon retention techniques and a few random "officer survival" counter-retention (gun take-aways), mainstream defensive tactics instruction (DTI) is limited in its scope of study as it tends to shy away from non-contact ranges (that range where you can shoot someone with a gun but he is literally out of reach with his hands) simply because this range of combat is fully covered over in the small arms instruction (SAI) world.

A student from the school of hard knocks (who's been there, done that, checked off all the boxes and has all the T-shirts) is acutely aware of this observable gap between the two worlds of training—the lines of demarcation being drawn by both *range* of physical confrontation and the *tools* used at those respective ranges.

In order to adequately provide the student with optimal response capability in the event of a surprise close-quarter attack with an edged weapon (knife or other cutting instrument), it is important to reconcile the world of Small Arms Instruction (SAI) and the world of Defensive Tactics Instruction (DTI).

As previously mentioned, it is the intention of this material to facilitate the *commonalities* between defensive tactics training instruction and small arms training instruction. The best approach to this seamless progression of training technology –to bridge the gap—is to take the best of what both worlds have to offer.

The first step in that process is to take a closer look at the fruit of what each of these has to offer individually—the world of small arms instruction (SAI) and the world of defensive tactics instruction (DTI). All of this material is covered in Part II (Building Blocks: SAI) and Part III (Building Blocks: DTI).

The second step is to take the best that each world has to offer by *combining* the building blocks (low-hanging fruit) of SAI and DTI in such a manner as to take advantage of these commonalities. All of this material is covered in Part IV (Bringing a Gun to a Knife Fight) which pulls it all together.

Let's go to guns first.

Part II
Building Blocks: SAI

Secrets of the Handgun

Since this is not specifically a handgun course our scope of study will be limited to the actual usage of the handgun in close-quarter battle (CQB) as it pertains to defense against an attack with a knife (or other edged weapons). The first step toward wining any fight (knife or otherwise) with a gun is to bring a gun. Sounds pedantic but it's true, you can't win a fight with a gun if you don't have one.

Step one—get yourself a handgun. A good rule of thumb when looking for the optimal handgun is to carry and own a handgun that fits your profile (body size, hand grip, skill level, department policy, state laws, etc.).

One of the things that continues to amaze me as a professional firearms instructor is the morning of day-one of a civilian handgun training course. When I look down the firing line at some beginning students pointed in on target, I occasionally find these amazing $5,000 plus guns all tricked out, all the bells and whistles, gadgets, modifications, etc. Those guns inevitably jam up about five times a day and all the extra moving parts begin to fall off and break and further disable and/ or interfere with the functionality of the gun. Standing right next to the gun with the racing stripes and computerized onboard bullet-trajectory tracking system is Joe Snuffy with a pair of well-worn baggy jeans, standing there with a stock handgun right out of the box with zero modifications maybe cost him a bout $600 and there he is hitting everything he aims at and with not a single malfunction in more than 2,000 rounds gone through his brand new blaster in five straight days (and sometimes also nights) of shooting. Moral of the story: stay away from needless modifications, add-ons and computerized onboard bullet-trajectory tracking systems.

If you're planning on bringing a gun to a knife fight, then you may want to also bring some CQB skills with you as the gun—all by itself—just won't cut it. That's like buying a brand new piano with no prior piano lessons whatsoever and expecting to sit down in front of it and play like Mozart. Most folks think, "Yeah, I'll buy a gun and that will work." Owning a gun is one thing, but what comes with owning a gun is the responsibility to know how to use it, this includes safety, storage and maintenance.

Now that you've got a quality handgun that fits your profile let's take a look at the meat and potatoes of utilizing the handgun should you be faced with a lethal threat—such as an attacker coming at you with a knife.

Hardware and Software

Overall proficiency with a handgun starts with familiarity of the gun itself and with the usage of the gun. The body of knowledge regarding the usage of a handgun is quite vast and could (and does) fill volumes. However, for purposes of our scope of study here we will focus predominantly on that aspect of handgun training dealing with winning in a fight against an attacker with a knife.

The training materials in this study block are divided into two parts—combative concepts (software) and combative application (hardware). Just like a computer, the system cannot remain functional unless both parts are working. The software won't work without the hardware and vice-versa.

Part II: Building Blocks—SAI

Software

Hardware

Step one—turn on the computer (that's your brain), get your head in the game. In a fight for your life you will need every fiber of awareness that you can muster. The key point here is awareness (software).

Three of the best kept secrets of proficiency with a handgun are *Mindset, Manipulation* and *Marksmanship*. Each one of these key training areas is a complete study on its own and could each fill an entire training manual.

However, the training material contained herein is limited in volume to fit the scope of our study as it pertains to small arms defense against an edged weapon attack. Regardless, these are the *three critical components* that are necessary to survive a lethal confrontation involving firearms, the most important of the three being mindset (software).

DEFENSIVE MINDSET

According to the book *The Tactical Edge* by Charles Remsberg, the mental skill of an officer accounts for approximately 75% of his ability to survive a lethal encounter. This leaves the remaining 25% to shooting skills, tactics and maybe even a little luck. With 75% of a favorable outcome for the officer due to "mental condition" (software), there is considerable emphasis placed on being mentally prepared for potentially mortal combat.

Any individual who has the potential of being involved in a lethal encounter, guns, knives or otherwise, must condition the mental state of mind to be prepared to survive any lethal encounter that may occur. Col. Jeff Cooper (USMC Ret.—deceased), founder of the American Pistol Institute, completed extensive studies on the subject and outlined in his programs of instruction "mental conditioning for combat." Col. Cooper concluded that, to mentally condition one's mind three phases of the conflict must be addressed: before, during and after the fact.

The first phase is prior to the attack. Before anyone gets involved in an altercation, it must be understood that conflict is an inevitable condition if there is reason for a gun owner to carry a gun in the first place. Prior to the attack it's important for the gun owner to recognize that using a gun for purposes of self-defense is dangerous business. Handling guns and knives at extreme close quarters is a recipe for death and minimally severe bodily injury and neither one of you may walk away. A gun owner must be prepared to recognize inherent dangers in a life-threatening altercation and the factors that may influence the outcome of the encounter. Such factors can include, but are certainly not limited to: threat, distance, timing, condition of threat, condition of the environment, and condition of your weapon system. We will look at each of these more in depth later in our study.

As most would agree it is better to be proactive than reactive. Instead of reacting to an incident that has already occurred, an awareness of your immediate surroundings may prevent trouble before it even happens. Most shooters are familiar with the mindset color codes, but for the

Part II: Building Blocks—SAI

sake of those who are not, many years ago (approximately early 1970's) Col. Cooper identified four *conditions of awareness* to help prepare an officer (military or law enforcement) to more effectively manage his work environment. These conditions were color-coded as an aid in identifying a particular condition of awareness.

Conditions of Awareness

Condition White—is a state of total unawareness of the events developing and occurring around you. When something occurs that requires immediate reaction, you are caught off guard, unprepared (mentally and physically) and unable to respond in a timely manner. We can observe this as folks walk around talking on their cell phones, looking at their watches or other electronic devices and since their awareness is wrapped up in their gear the mind is preoccupied off somewhere else. Walking around in this condition places you way behind the "Action-Reaction" power curve.

Condition White—Total Unawareness

Condition Yellow—is a state of general awareness or "relaxed alertness." Although you may not be expecting specific hostile activity, you are nonetheless fully aware of your surroundings—some security folks recommend 360 degree awareness in this condition—and that a threat may be possible. This condition of awareness can reduce reaction time considerably.

Condition Yellow—General Awareness

Condition Orange is a state of specific alert. You have noticed a specific threat. It may be a direct threat or an indirect threat but you have awareness of something going down and this is a direct awareness—you noticed something and it's nearby and it doesn't look right. In this condition of awareness you have identified a potential problem area or threat and are ready to act, up to and including deadly force.

Condition Orange—Specific Threat

Part II: Building Blocks—SAI

Condition Red—You're in the fight. The threat is real. He's got a knife in your grill and the fight is on. You see the threat and react to it. You are mentally and physically capable of dealing with the situation.

Condition Red—You're in the Fight

In certain training schools additional conditions and color-codes are presented. Again, to stay on track with our initial scope of study and for purposes of brevity and simplicity (always keep it simple), in my opinion these four (as they were first presented by Col. Cooper) are sufficient.

In the second phase during a lethal physical confrontation, there are varying determinant factors which greatly contribute to the outcome of the fight. These include, but are not limited to: your physical conditioning, tactics, application of your skills, manipulation of the handgun, marksmanship, equipment, the training and conditioning of your opponent(s) and lady luck.

And finally after the attack, given the reality that consequences follow every action, the moral and legal issues of use of deadly force should be squarely addressed in one's mind prior to any lethal encounter. If you are mentally prepared prior to a lethal confrontation, then you are further hardened to become a difficult target. There is nothing wrong at all with winning; however, there's a great deal wrong with losing—those of us as law-abiding citizens of a free republic who carry firearms need to keep this in mind.

Scale of Injury

Actions speak louder than words. Results speak louder than actions. In any lethal altercation the end-result of applying a specific technique or tactic is not answered in terms of "Does it work?" or "Does it not work?" the real answer is where does this technique or tactic place *me* on the Scale of Injury and where does this technique or tactic place my *opponent(s)* on the Scale of Injury.

The Scale of Injury (SOI) is simply a factual scalar representation of a degree of injury that is sustained as a result of a particular tactic or technique applied.

Scale of Injury

1. **No Injury**—walk away untouched

2. **Minor Injury**—minor bruising or scratches—nothing a band aid couldn't handle

3. **Recoverable Injury**—broken nose, broken leg, broken arm, etc.

4. **Unrecoverable Injury**—irreparable damage, loss of limb, permanent paralysis, blindness

5. **Death**—dead right there (DRT), flat lined, loss of life, no recovery possible

Many of us have personally experienced "no injury" (SOI—Level 1) in a fight. Most of us have experienced minor injury (SOI—Level 2). Some of us have experienced a recoverable injury (SOI—Level 3) and still others have unfortunately sustained an unrecoverable injury (SOI—Level 4). The very worst case personal injury scenario bar none is Level 5 on the Scale of Injury—Death.

Handgun Manipulation

The second critical element in the wide world of small arms training is *manipulation* of the handgun. Such manipulation of the handgun includes, but is not limited to loading, unloading, reloading, handling malfunctions and presenting the handgun.

Regarding loading, unloading, reloading and handling of malfunctions, it is assumed the reader has a functional understanding of these skills set and at least a good working knowledge of each. Since this is not specifically a handgun training course, again, we will remain focused on the core of our study which is the effective usage of the handgun in combination with the skills of defensive tactics versus a knife attack.

Presenting the Handgun

Second only to *bringing* a loaded gun to a "knife fight," is the ability to *use* the handgun. In order to effectively utilize a handgun it must be expediently retrieved from its carry position, pointed in an appropriate direction and prepared to fire if necessary. This critical action of removing the handgun from its carry position and pointing the muzzle toward a lethal threat is commonly referred to in industry vernacular as "presenting the handgun."

The handgun, utilized as a defensive tool in response to an unexpected deadly attack, is of no use if it cannot be easily accessed and rapidly deployed. The ability to draw the handgun from its carry position efficiently involves consistent and deliberate movements that allow the handgun to be presented to the target. The desired result of the handgun presentation is to get the handgun out of the holster and pointed at the target in a minimum amount of time (less than 1.5 seconds) in a smooth, efficient and safe manner.

The eventual goal of any firearm presentation is not only to end up on target (and on time), but should enable the shooter to engage a lethal threat from multiple shooting positions or "presentation configurations" commonly referred to as Sighted Fire (also known as Extended Firing Position) and Unsighted Fire (also known as Retracted Firing Position) which is also commonly referred to in the SAI world as Weapon Retention Position.

Sighted Fire Strong Hand Supported firing position.

Unsighted Fire Strong Hand Supported firing position.

Similar to swinging a bat at a baseball, presentation of the handgun, in practical application, is a one-step process. One smooth gross-motor skill of removing the handgun from its carry position and sequentially disengaging any retention and/ or mechanical safety devices along the way, ending with the muzzle pointed in the right direction. However, in order to fully grasp the key components of this critical movement, it's important to analyze this presentation process in more detail.

The handgun presentation process can be divided into any number of steps. Depending upon the SAI these steps can be as few as two or three or as many as six or more. At the risk of carbon-dating myself, presentation of the handgun is traditionally taught in a five-count sequence. Regardless of number of steps and presentation method, these individual sequences must be deliberate and sure. This step-by-step building-block approach has been time-proven to assist shooters in getting the handgun pointed effectively at the target. To keep within the parameters of this scope of study, the traditional five-count presentation will be covered.

Count One—Grip. Count one is critical and especially so at extreme close quarters proximity to an edged weapon. If the grip is not consistent throughout the entire presentation cycle, poor accuracy may result. There are several movements that occur simultaneously. It is important that all of these movements are done correctly.

In order to maximize physical position and range to your advantage, the body must be postured in such a manner as to lend itself to optimal performance. Such a position must enable the body to shoot, punch, grab, fall, roll and otherwise shift to positions or movements of advantage. All of this can only come from a Stable Fighting Platform which will be analyzed in greater depth later on the DT side of the house. Regardless of DTI or SAI categorization, being able to shoot accurately and effectively is a requirement of any stable fighting platform.

A common thread between both SAI and DTI is the important matter of hand positions prior to or during an actual threat engagement *prior* to the presentation of the handgun. There are only three general hand positions which will be addressed.

Each has been selected as they have been referenced in a majority of law enforcement incidents. Hands below the waist posture, represents training against the surprise attack—which is predominantly what we're trying to prepare the reader for. Hands above the waist, similar to a law enforcement field interview posture, are used to train against sudden attacks—it is a natural human reaction when physically threatened to raise the hands. Hands Away (extended) posture corresponds to the body's response as you are caught in the middle of an altercation with your fighting hands out (extended away from your body).

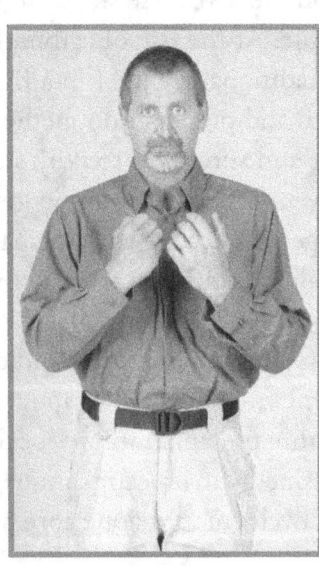
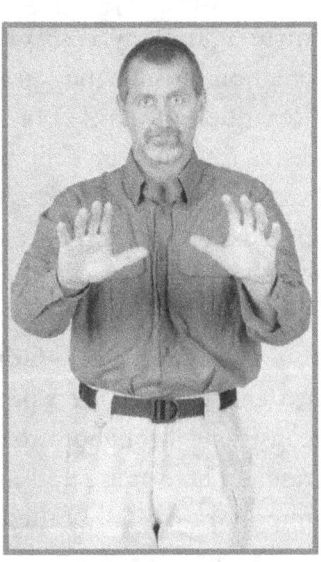

Hands Below (waist line)   *Hands Above (waist line)*   *Hands Away (extended)*

A full handgun presentation may be executed equally as effective starting from any one of these three hand positions. However, for practical purposes of a surprise knife attack, the "Hands Below" position will be utilized as it is assumed that the shooter is caught by surprise with his hands down when confronted by an attacker wielding a knife at close proximity.

Beginning from the "Hands Below" position, this "Grip Count" includes movement of the strong hand to a final firing grip on the handgun and release of any retaining devices on the holster.

Part II: Building Blocks—SAI

Since this first step is such a critical movement it warrants a closer look at all the moving parts. Let's say you walk into a room and there is a light switch on the wall. Let's also say the light switch activates three lights. You flip the switch to the "on" position and three lights instantly illuminate. One switch—three lights. The same applies to this very first movement of presenting the firearm—one movement includes three *simultaneous* component movements.

One of the three simultaneous component motions is to move the support hand to a position at Center Line/ Center Mass (CL / CM) of the body, the palm drawn in and away from the attack with the fingers of the support hand pointing slightly angled downward (about forty-five degrees down and away from CL / CM) toward the weapon side and prepared to merge with the weapon hand and form an optimal "strong hand supported" firing position.

The reason behind this particular position of the support hand fingers is to prepare the support hand not only for an extended (sighted fire) strong-hand-supported firing position, but equally as prepared to support a retracted (unsighted fire) strong-hand-supported firing position commonly referred to as "Weapon Retention Position" which will be covered in greater detail later.

To really get down to the brass tacks of this "fingers of the support-hand angled about forty-five degrees down and away from CL / CM toward the weapon side" recommendation, it's necessary to take a closer look.

The situation we are preparing the shooter for is not of a "competitive-shooting" nature, it is of a "combative-shooting" nature. Although I am personally a strong proponent of taking what really works from both worlds (the world of competition shooting and the world of combative shooting)—here we go again with my wild-ass "common threads" theory—there are certain times when application lays on one side of the fence or the other. In this particular case (bringing and *using* a gun in a "knife fight") presentation of the handgun is intended for purely combative application. Based on this combative application, a different set of requirements is forced upon presentation of the handgun:

1. That any body parts of the shooter remain out of range of contact with any hand-held weapons being wielded by an attacker against the shooter at extreme close quarters and in confined areas of operation.

2. That under extreme combative duress, the shooter is trained to position the support hand (and fingers) as far from the path of the muzzle as possible yet remain effectively positioned throughout this particular step of the presentation.

3. That under attack, at this step of the presentation process, the shooter does not yet know if the firearm will be eventually presented in an extended firing position (sighted fire) or a retracted

firing position (retention), but must be equally prepared to support either.

4. That in the heat of combat a fight won't end with a beep or a whistle, but with nothing less than effectively stopping the threat by whatever means possible. Some combative situations may not even allow for a gun to be used as the first move (see 28 Real World Reasons) and the hands must be effectively positioned for both hand-to-hand (which will be covered in greater depth later) and firearm response.

Movement of the support hand toward CL / CM with fingers pointed in the direction of the weapon is recommended as opposed to fingers pointing outward or hand away from the body as there are numerous reasons why the support hand should be drawn in as close as possible to the center of the body (as well as the fingers)—especially when an edged weapon is involved:

1. He can cut you.

2. Under duress you may cover your own hand with your own gun

3. He can pull you into a higher Scale of Injury.

4. Any of the above will compromise the chances of your winning.

5. Position of the support hand fingers is proactive in preparation to provide optimal supported for either extended (sighted fire) or retracted (Weapon Retention Position) unsighted fire based squarely upon operational conditions.

Bringing a Gun to a Knife Fight

He can cut you.

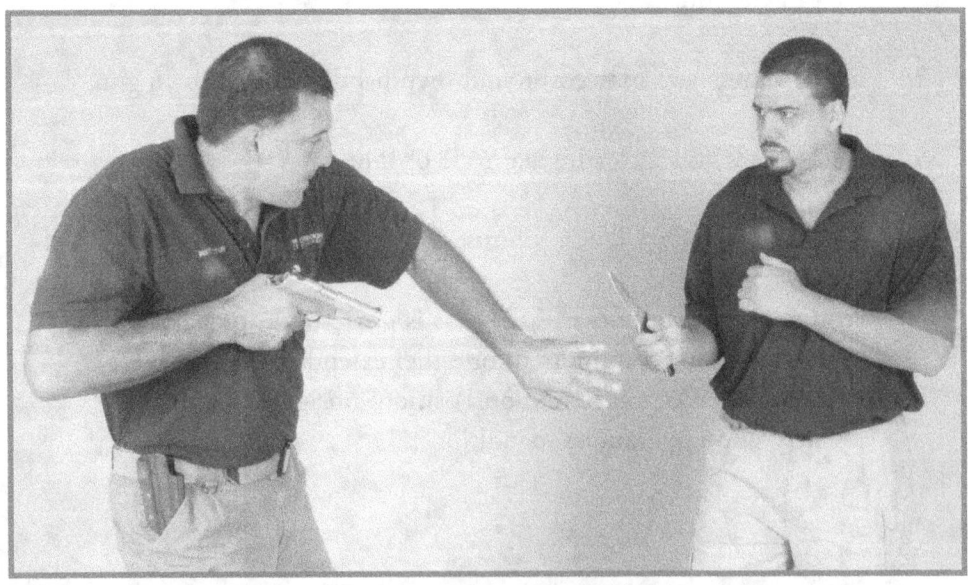

You may cover your own hand with your own gun.

Part II: Building Blocks—SAI

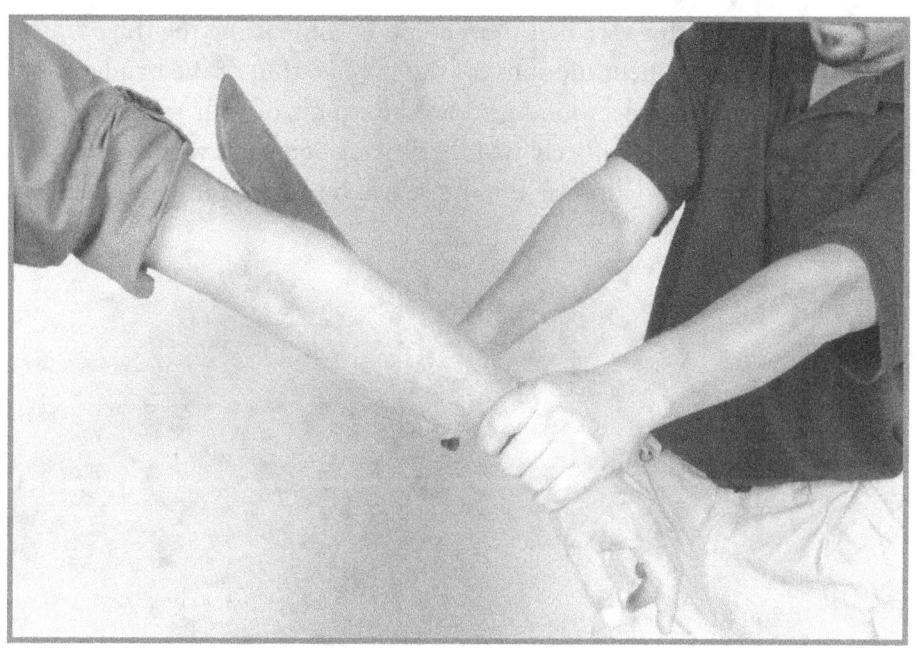

He can pull you into a higher Scale of Injury.

Proactive support-hand position—moving the support hand to a multi-use proactive combative shooting position is a good training habit.

As part of this very first movement, encompassing the three simultaneous component motions, of the presentation of the handgun it is critical to purchase a sound grip on the handle of your weapon while facing the threat squarely with both your body and with your eyes. (Moving the body to face the threat will be covered in more detail in later DTI chapters.)

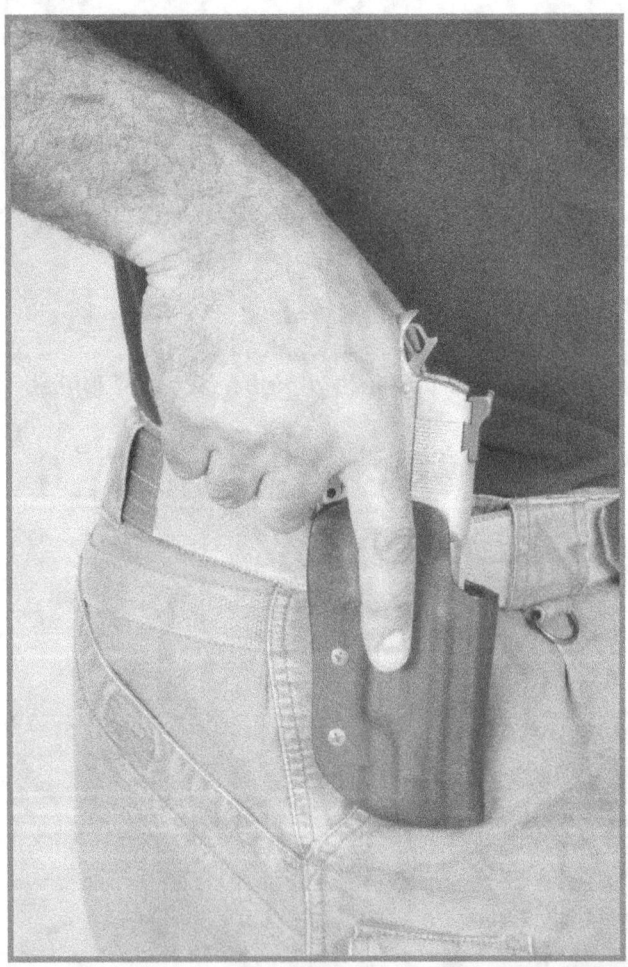

Weapon hand acquires a firm and positive grip on the handgun with the web of the hand up high to the bore line while keeping the trigger finger straight and outside of the holster.

Part II: Building Blocks—SAI

As part of this very first movement (another of the three simultaneous component motions) of the presentation of the handgun, keep your weapon arm elbow pointing straight to the rear and not bowed out again while facing the threat both squarely with your body as well as with your eyes. The superior form of keeping your elbow pointed back provides additional stabilization of the path of the muzzle on its way out of the holster and directly on target. If the elbow was pointed in any other direction this would adversely affect the path of the muzzle.

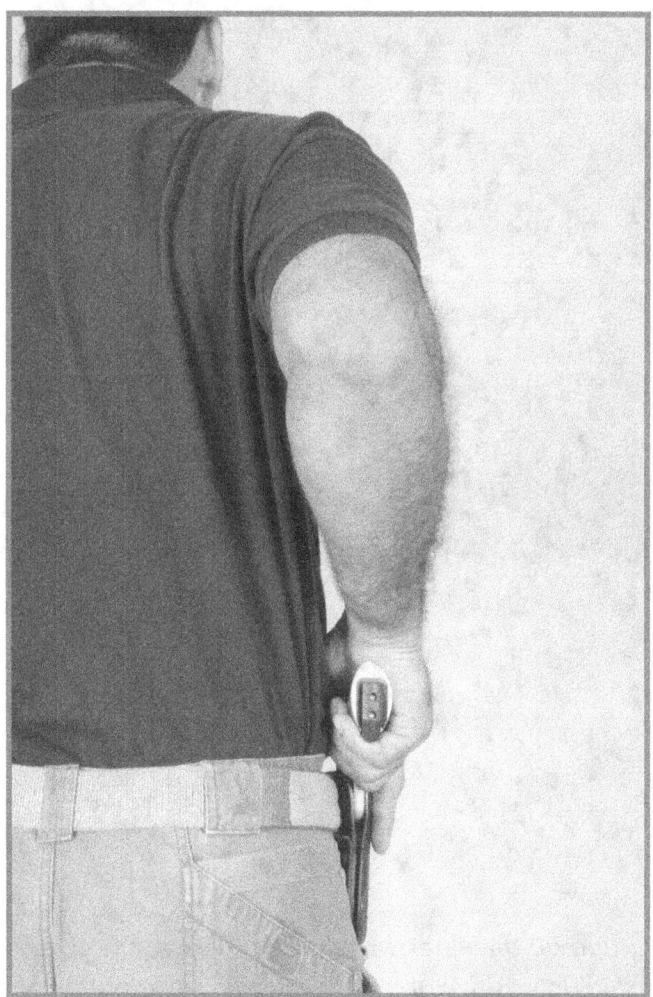

Point the strong elbow straight to the rear.

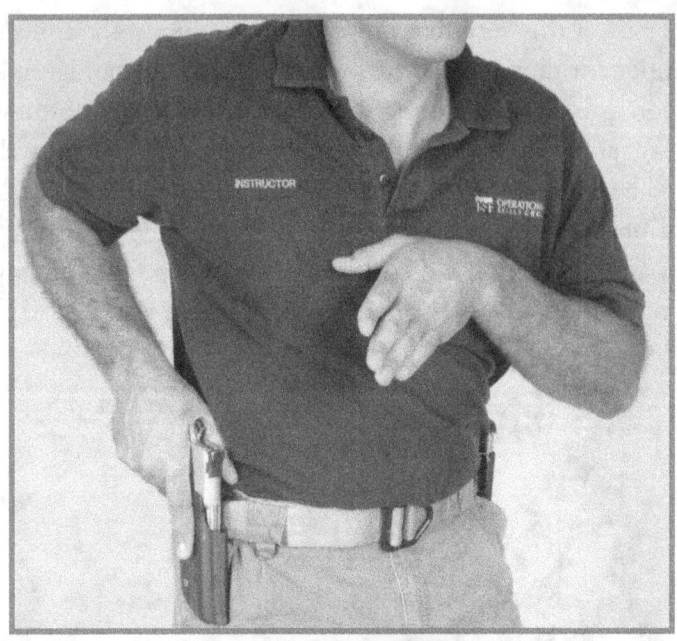

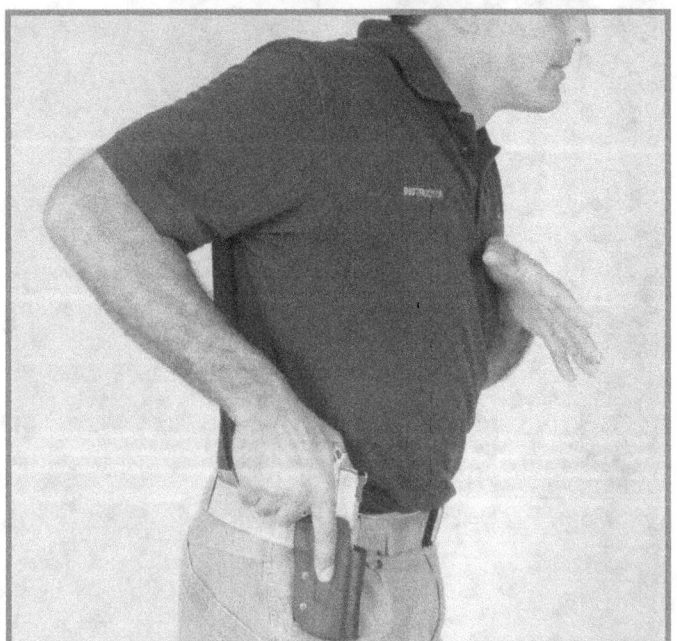

Putting all three parts of the "Grip Count" together including positive grip up high and prepared to control the bore line (with finger straight), retracted support hand (angled down and away from the attack) and elbow pointed back.

Count Two—Clear and Cant to Retention Position. This count (referred to as the "Clear Count") places the handgun in appropriate position for movement toward the target and is a two-part process. It is accomplished by first removing the handgun from its carry location. This can be lifting the gun out of a conventional holster (gun-belt or thigh holster) or pulling it from an alternate or concealed carry location.

Maintaining that same straight elbow as illustrated in "Count One" allows proactive alignment of the muzzle. The second half of this step is to turn the muzzle in the direction of the intended target (lethal threat) and raising it up pressing the shooter's wrist along side the weapon-side pectoral area ending up with the slide canted outboard at the same time defeating any mechanical safeties or locking mechanisms preparing the gun to fire.

An added benefit to "Count Two" is that it is the same position used for shooting from the Weapon Retention Position which will be covered in greater detail later. However, if it were necessary to deliver rounds downrange from this position, could it be accomplished? Even if there wasn't enough time to use both hands?

Note: It is important to cant the weapon outboard at the Retention Position in such a manner as to clear the slide from any clothing or gear that may potentially interfere with the cycling of the slide.

Based on particular SAI, at various training academies (and civilian shooting schools) this single step is sometimes divided into two separate steps—one; clear the holster and the other turn and point the muzzle toward the threat. Given the wide spectrum of reader skills and the urgency requirements of this scope of study, "Count Two" is presented to the reader as a one-step process.

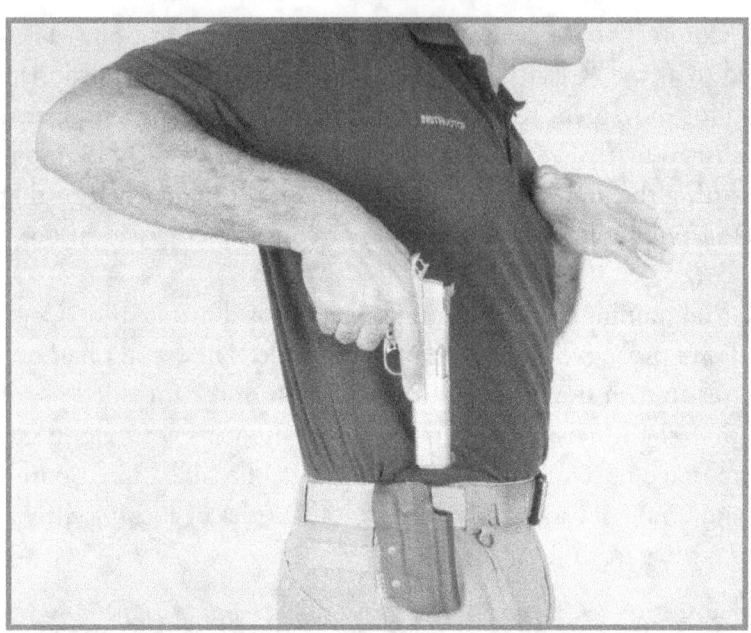

Part "A"—retrieve the handgun from the holster and pull until the muzzle clears the holster completely.

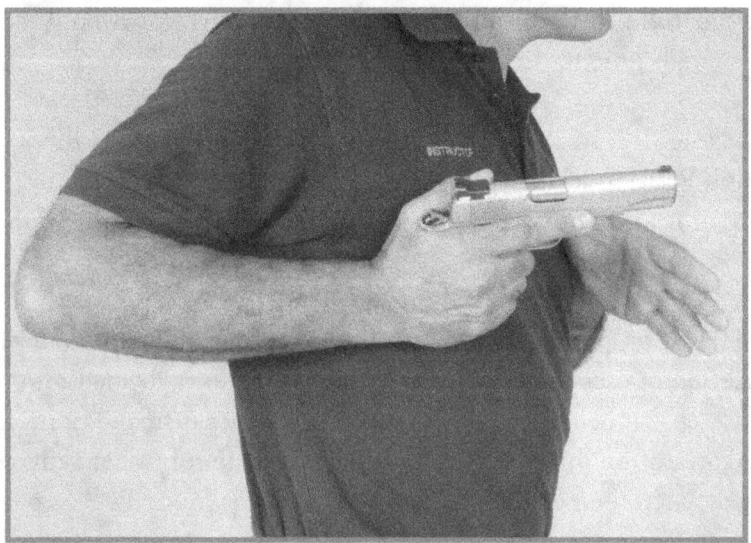

Rotate the muzzle towards the target disengaging any mechanical safeties or locking mechanisms until the strong wrist is locked and indexed along the pectoral muscle of the strong side. Keep the handgun and the forearm parallel to the ground. Cant the weapon slightly to keep any loose clothing from catching in the slide action.

Part II: Building Blocks—SAI

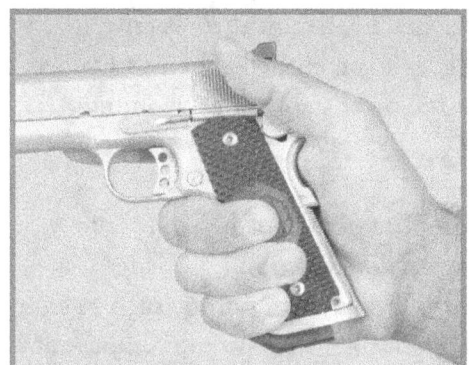

Example of disengaging the safety on a 1911 during "Count Two."

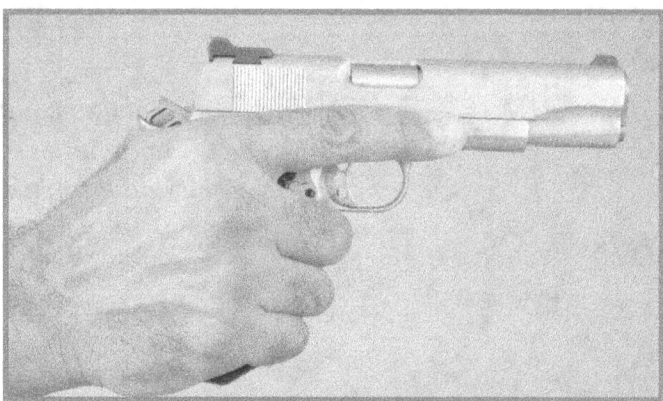

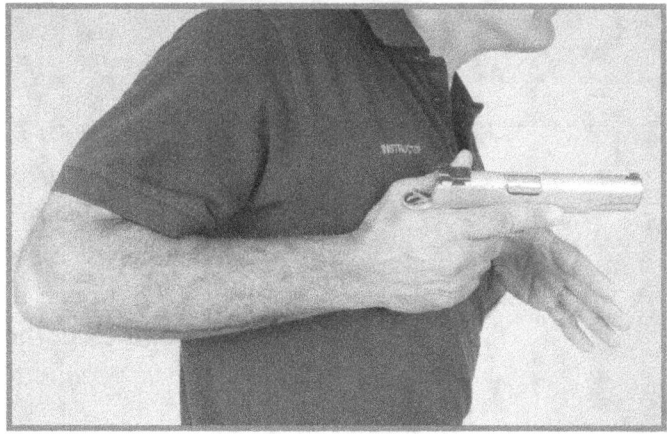

The trigger finger remains straight alongside the receiver, off of the trigger, and outside of the trigger guard. The shooting forearm remains parallel to the deck and the shooting elbow remains straight while the support-hand remains in a proactive close quarter combat support position.

Count Three—Hands come together. Count three is critical because this is when the two-handed grip is established. The two handed firing grip (strong hand supported) is the most stable of all shooting grips.

The fastest way to get the handgun pointed at the target is to thrust the muzzle straight towards the target. Common knowledge teaches us that the shortest distance between any two points (such as a muzzle and its intended target) is a straight line. Keep in mind, however, that the combative situation may not *allow* you to get this far in the presentation and that it may be necessary to deliver rounds downrange from the Retention Position.

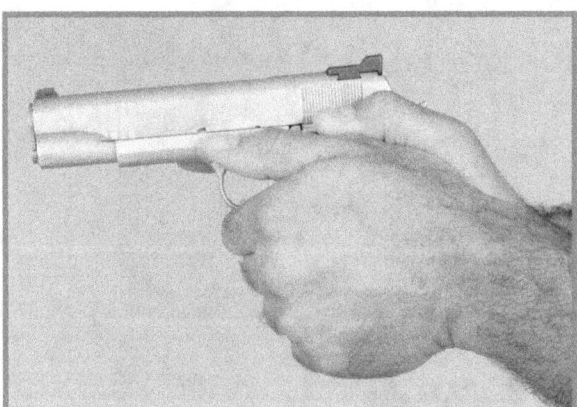

Simultaneously move both hands forward and establish a two-hand grip.

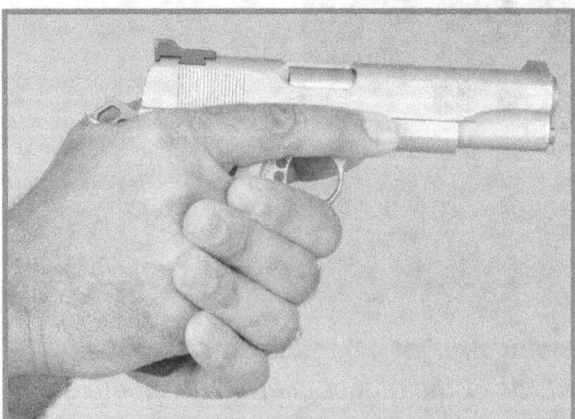

The trigger finger remains straight alongside the receiver, off of the trigger, and outside of the trigger guard.

Part II: Building Blocks—SAI

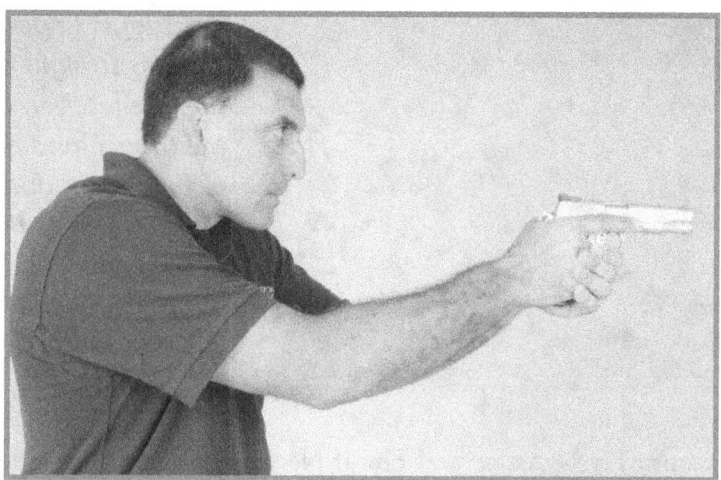

Count three should end up with the handgun starting to move toward the shooters line of sight. The intention here is to bring the weapon up to your line of sight and not lower your head to the weapon.

Count Four—Punch and Look. Count four begins with the handgun moving up to the shooters line of sight. Bring the weapon to your line of sight. Do not lower your head to the weapon. Count four gives the shooter the opportunity to confirm that the handgun has in fact been properly brought up onto the target into the Sighted Fire shooting configuration. The following is executed simultaneously:

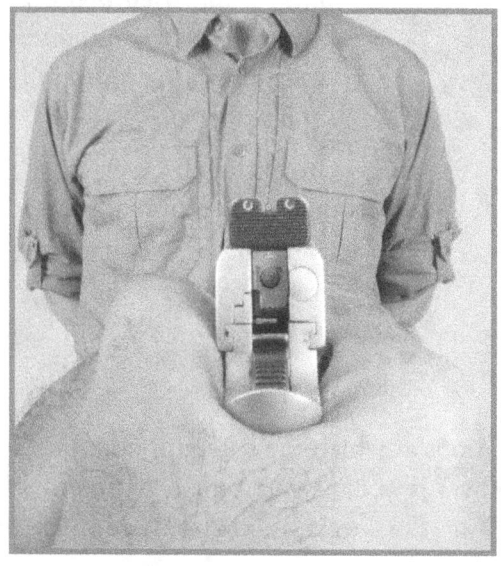

Shift your visual focus from the target to the sights using a flash sight picture to visually confirm the sight alignment and the sight picture.

Bringing a Gun to a Knife Fight

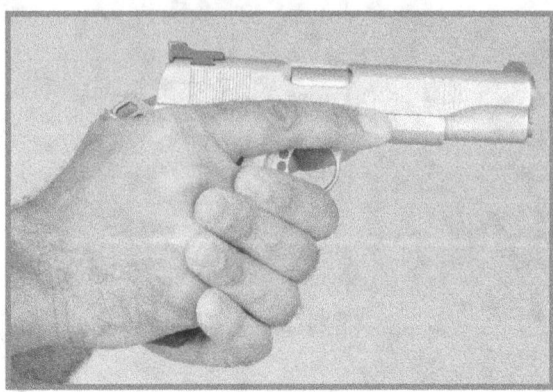

The trigger finger remains straight alongside the receiver, off of the trigger, and outside of the trigger guard. Move the index finger to the trigger and take out the slack only if you intend to fire.

Count Five—Assess and Fire if Necessary. Depending upon the condition of your environment, the condition of your threat and the condition of your weapon it may be necessary to apply lethal force to stop the threat. It must be stressed that on the count (five), the shooter may continue only when the use of deadly force is justified.

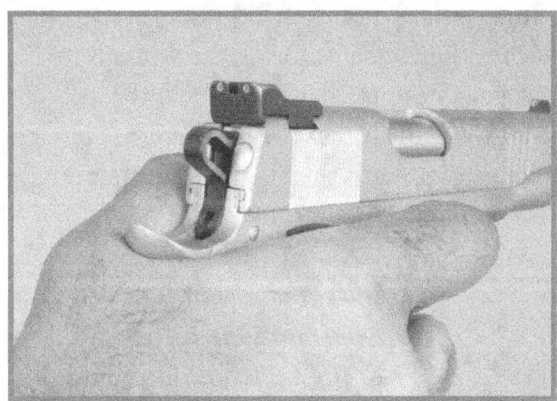

Focus on the front sight and press the trigger in a steady and controlled manner to the rear of the trigger guard running parallel to the slide until a surprised break is achieved (the hammer falls, firing the handgun "unexpectedly").

Immediately follow through with the fundamentals of marksmanship which will be covered in greater detail forthcoming.

Ready Positions

There are a number of positions at which the handgun (after it is presented) can be held. One of them is of course up on target—commonly referred to as "up on target" or "On Target." Another position is referred to as "Contact Ready" in reference to this as a specific ready position of the handgun. The third and also common is the "Low Ready" position.

The *"On Target"* position allows the operator immediate and optimal response to a potential threat or multiple threats by way of muzzle proximity to target as well as preparation to shoot. In the "On Target" position, the decision to shoot has been made, the operator's finger moves to the trigger, begins to take up trigger slack and mechanical safeties (if any) are disengaged.

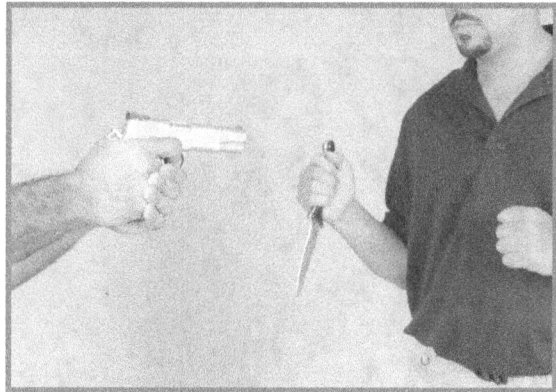

In the "On Target" position, the decision to shoot has been made, the operator's finger moves to the trigger, begins to take up trigger slack and the mechanical safety (if any) is disengaged.

The *"Contact Ready"* position allows the operator immediate and optimal response to a potential threat or multiple threats by way of muzzle proximity to target. In the "Contact Ready" position, the decision to shoot has not yet been made, the operator's finger remains off the trigger and any mechanical safeties remain engaged.

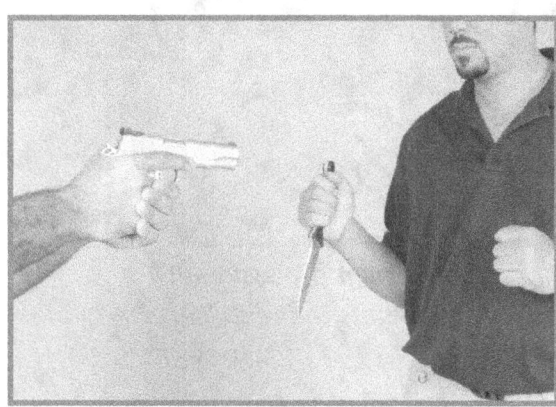

In the "Contact Ready" position, the decision to shoot has not yet been made, the operator's finger remains off the trigger and any mechanical safeties remain engaged.

Bringing a Gun to a Knife Fight

Another common ready position is what is called the "Low Ready" position or sometimes referred to as the "Low Guard" position. The low ready is a position used by the operator to allow an unobstructed line of sight to the hands of the threat while simultaneously providing a position of readiness to react to the threat should the conditions of the threat warrant.

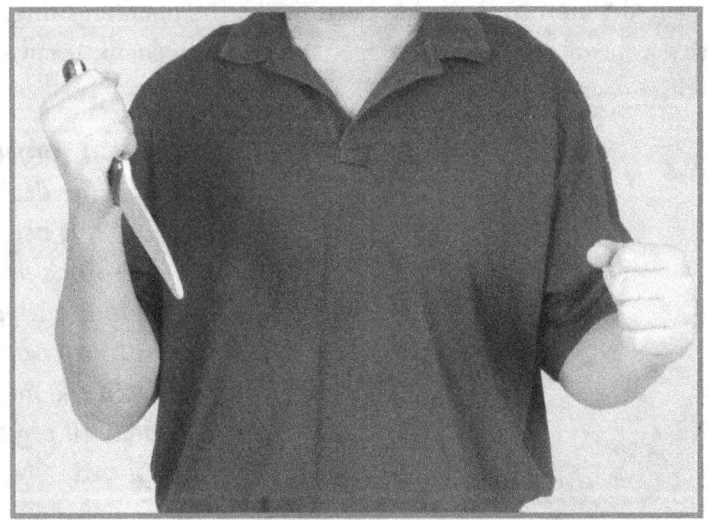

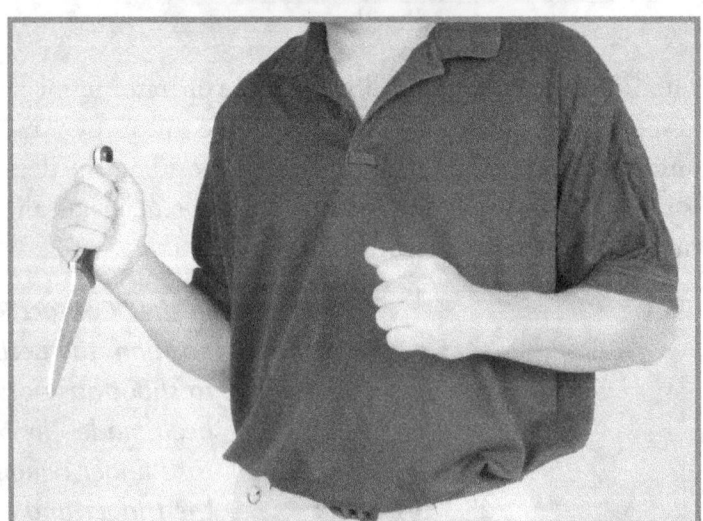

Most seasoned law enforcement professionals understand that it is the hands that can kill.

Part II: Building Blocks—SAI

Any officer who can't clearly see both hands remains at risk. The exact purpose of the low ready position is to get a clear visual confirmation that the hands are cleared and made safe.

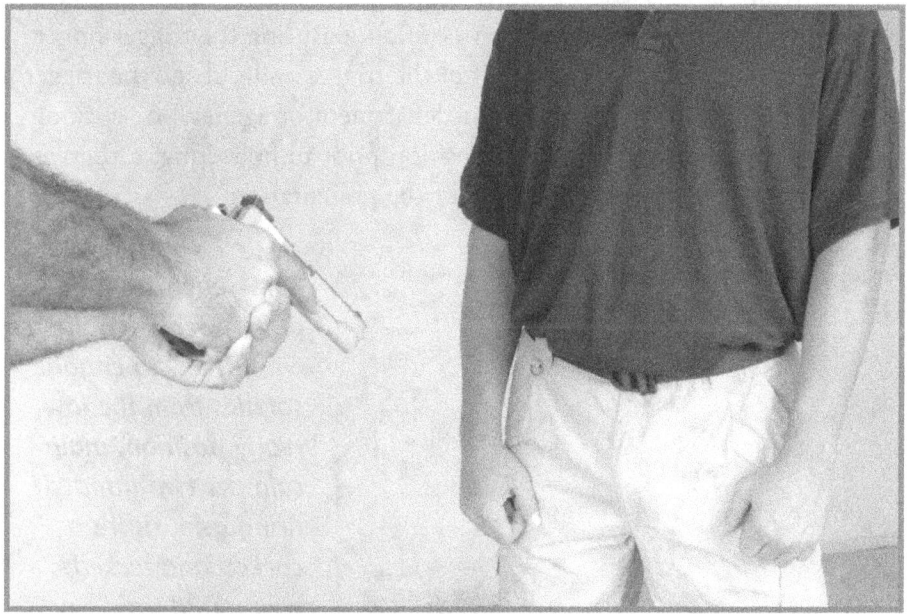

When utilizing the "Low Ready" position, the operator brings the handgun and arms to an approximately 45-degree downward angle, keeping the elbows tight against the body. The downward angle will change with proximity to allow visual identification of threats and danger areas such as the hands and possibly multiple opponents. The "Low Ready" position can also be used to assess a broader area when contact with a threat is not imminent.

Each agency policy or doctrine clearly outlines the parameters of each of the above positions. However, for purposes of this particular training, a general description of these positions is provided. If you are a peace officer, please refer to your agency's particular policy and exact training doctrine regarding these positions and their related operational application.

Holstering the Handgun

When you decide to re-holster (also considered a manipulation of the handgun), always assess the area looking for possible threats. Always holster from the Weapon Retention Position, ensuring the trigger finger is straight alongside the receiver, off of the trigger and outside the trigger guard. If necessary (required by your department or agency), de-cock or engage the safety in the low ready position prior to holstering. Otherwise, holster by exactly reversing the steps of the presentation.

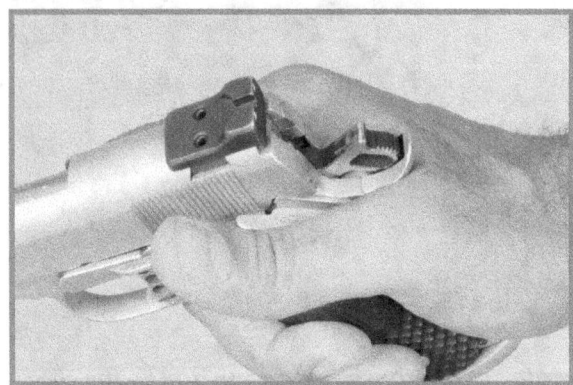

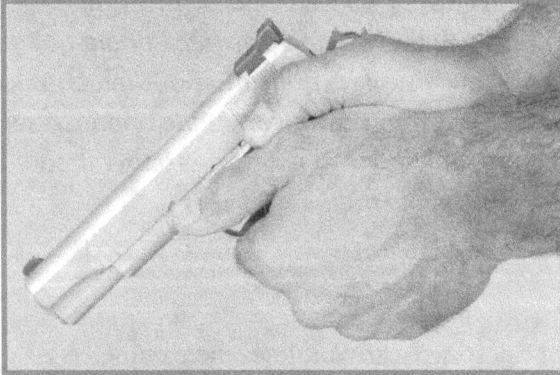

Some agencies / departments require employees, to engage safeties from the low ready position, maintain the two-handed firing grip, (if it's a cocked and locked weapon, de-cock; or if it's got a mechanical safety, then here is where you would engage the safety) and then bring the handgun back to the count two position. If not, then simply reverse the steps of the presentation and engage any external safety and or de-cocking devices while the muzzle is still pointed downrange and just prior to reversing the second step (Clear Count) and returning to the holster.

Part II: Building Blocks—SAI

It is strongly recommended (and a requirement for most high-profile operators) to NOT look at your holster when replacing the handgun back into the holster. Your eyes should remain on the subject at hand (threat area, suspect, etc.). As a matter of practical application as well as safety, law enforcement professionals are required to holster prior to moving into and handling a subject in any manner. By holstering the handgun, this eliminates any chance of a negligent discharge in any direction while the officer may be cuffing or otherwise working hands-on with a subject. The same rule applies to all Protective Services personnel. The handgun must remain in the safest position possible (optimally in the holster) especially when primary protective personnel are in proximity during movement and with the direct handling of a principal (departures, arrivals, cover and evac, etc.).

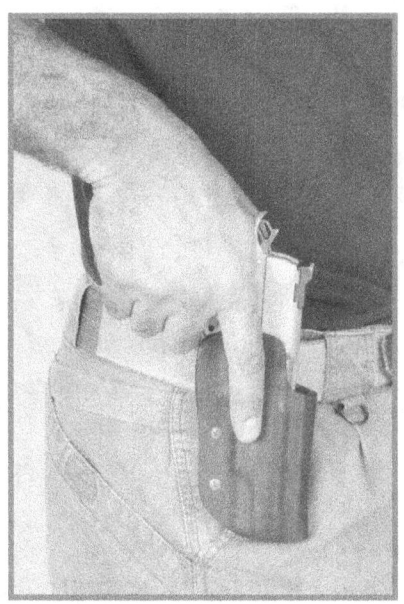

From the count two position, rotate the muzzle down and return the handgun into the holster (without looking at the holster—eyes should be constantly monitoring potential threat environment) then fasten any retaining devices. Do not place your support hand in the path of the muzzle for any reason (those of you may have retention snaps across the path of the muzzle simply move the muzzle behind the strap first and then continue to re-holster.)

MARKSMANSHIP

The third and final (last but certainly not least) of the critical components that are necessary to win a lethal confrontation involving guns against knives is marksmanship.

Marksmanship is simply the ability to hit what you're aiming at—it sounds a lot easier than it really is. There are several factors involved with handgun marksmanship. They can be simplified by breaking them into three elements aiming, holding, and gripping.

Aiming the Handgun

One of the three important elements is aiming. During the aiming process, the shooter is concerned with correctly pointing the handgun in a stable and controlled manner so the bullet will hit the target. Aiming, also known as "sighted fire," requires two additionally important components: Sight Alignment and Sight Picture.

Sight Alignment is the relationship of the front sight to the rear sight notch. Correct sight alignment consists of the front sight being centered in the rear sight notch with equal light on both sides and the top of the front sight being even with the top of the rear sight. While shooting, the shooter must keep the eyes focused on the front sight, NOT on the target.

Example of sight alignment. Notice that sights are aligned with equal light on both sides of the front sight and along one straight line on the top. Notice that the focus is placed on the front sight. Focus squarely on the front fight (sometimes called a "hard focus") will in fact blur both the rear site and the target.

As a side note there are some professional shooters out there who espouse the concept of a "soft-focus" somewhere between the front sight and the target. However, for purposes of this scope of study we'll stick to the mainstream basics.

Sight Picture consists of placing the properly aligned sights in the center of the available target. This centering is referred to as the target's center-of-mass.

A Flash-Sight Picture is a very rapid visual snapshot of the sight picture. It is how one uses the sights and is fundamental to the Modern Technique of the Pistol (as founded by Col. Jeff Cooper API click on www.gunsite.com for more info).

Flash-sight picture begins during the presentation. As the handgun intersects the line of sight to the target, the shooter changes focus from the target to the front sight of the handgun and verifies that the sights are aligned on the target.

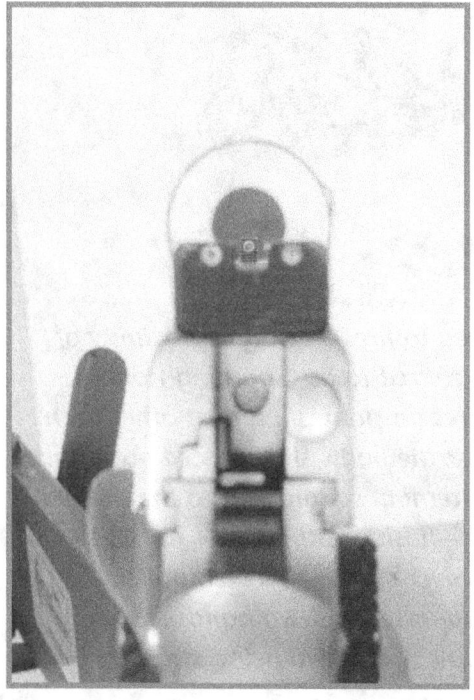

Example of flash sight picture. Notice "hard focus" on front sight with target area and rear sights falling out of focus.

In the example of firing from Weapon Retention Position (unsighted fire), there is no sight alignment and no sight picture required. The method of aiming from this retracted firing position is not visual but tactile. By squarely facing the threat, the alignment of your retention firing position hand ("pulse to vest," slide canted outboard, elbow in, etc.) with your sternum squarely facing the threat will place the muzzle in such a position as to accurately deliver rounds down range at arms length from your body. More detail on this method of fire will be covered in later chapters.

Due to the emergency nature of need to fire in extreme proximity of threat, Unsighted Fire (commonly referred to as "shooting from the Weapon Retention Position") requires no sight alignment other than shooting hand placed firmly against the body, slide canted outboard, elbow pointing straight back and sternum squared off to the threat. There is no need for a sight picture—flash or otherwise—from this retracted firing position. This maneuver can be executed utilizing either one hand (strong hand unsupported) or two hands (strong hand supported) with the most stable of the two being strong hand supported.

Holding the Handgun

Holding is the physical act of keeping the firearm stable and with a controlled muzzle aimed at the desired point of impact when firing the shot. The total length of time required includes the shooter's acquisition of a good sight alignment and sight picture as well as good trigger control.

Aligning the sights and establishing a good sight picture eats up the majority of the time (in the case of shooters who are not accustomed to firearms training) whereas trigger manipulation is a much faster process. In the case of Unsighted Fire (utilized against targets at about arms length distance), due to proximity there is no requirement for sight alignment and sight picture and therefore significantly reduces delivery time of rounds down range. Every technique comes with a price tag, however, and both methods—Sighted Fire and Unsighted Fire—have pluses and minuses. The significant advantage of Sighted Fire is that it is measurably a far more accurate shot and will allow the shooter tremendous range and accuracy. But, it comes with the price tag of eating up a lot of valuable response time.

The upside of Unsighted Fire is that it is extremely rapid, but only effective at relatively close quarters (about arms length range or closer all the way in to a contact body shot). The downside is that the sights are not being used at all which significantly decreases the accuracy of the shot.

Regardless of Sighted or Unsighted Fire, there's additionally quite a bit of *mechanical* activity that occurs when a trigger is pressed.

The depressing of the trigger past reset position (and straight toward the back of the trigger guard) disengages the trigger safety which allows full and open movement of trigger in rotation at the trigger pin which in turn directs the trigger bar to the rear of the receiver which in turn disengages the firing pin catch which in turn releases the firing pin which moves in a forward motion building momentum based on the strength of the firing pin spring and strikes the face of the primer compressing primer compound against the anvil (located inside the primer) which sparks and builds internal pressure thus blasting through the hole igniting the cartridge powder which in turn builds tremendous internal pressure which decompresses the crimp (fixing bullet to casing) causing bullet to be released in a forward direction expanding to fill (and is guided by) the lands and groves (rifling) of the barrel along the path of least resistance on out from the muzzle of the firearm heading downrange. The above description applies to the Glock ® pistol—other models may have mechanical safety and / or de-cocking devices which may add additional steps to the cyclical process.

The bottom line with regards to holding the muzzle steady (good muzzle discipline) is that it's important to hold the handgun at the right place and at the right time long enough and steady enough for all of this internal mechanical activity to take place.

Handgun Stances

Stance, or how you stand with a gun, is a fundamental of shooting. The purpose of any stance with regards to handling of a firearm is to establish a solid shooting platform by which the firearm can be held in a stable enough position with good recoil management and good muzzle control to allow the shooter to complete accurate shot placement. Historically, there are numerous shooting stances including Chapman, Weaver, Isosceles, Modern Isosceles, Modified Isosceles, etc.

However, the "Weaver Stance" and the "Modern Isosceles" are the two most common and recommended handgun stances utilized today. These two stances are also the same basic full body positions used in intermediate force defensive tactics. This means that the operator only has one basic position to learn as opposed to "this one" for SAI and "that one" for DTI.

Part II: Building Blocks—SAI

Weaver Stance.

Modern Isosceles Stance.

Which of these two most commonly utilized stances is "better" than the other is, and has been, a matter of great debate for many years. Some say one is "better" for competition shooting while the other is "better" for combative shooting. Again, the debate rages on throughout the shooting community and remains part and parcel of SAI.

Regardless of a specific shooting stance, there are three essential parts to any shooting stance. Starting from the bottom up is position of the feet position of both arms, and head position. Let's take a look at each of these in order of the traditional SAI instructional method—feet, arms / hands, and head.

Referencing lower body position and as with any shooting stance, is the foundation of the shooting platform and therefore must remain strong as both a stationary and mobile platform from which to accurately deliver rounds downrange. Position of the legs and feet provide critical structural support in bracing the shooter.

Two of the most common (and also part of the same heated debate) are the "bladed angle to the target" (part and parcel of the "Weaver" stance) where feet should be approximately shoulder width apart on a line that is somewhere between a 30 to 45 degree angle to the target with the strong side foot placed to the rear versus the "squaring off" to the target (part and parcel of the "Modern Isosceles" stance) where both feet are equidistant and remain square to the target facing downrange on a line that is 90 degrees angle to the target.

The "bladed angle" versus "squaring off" of the feet debate continues ad nauseum since there are pros and cons to both as is the case with any long-running argument. However, it all boils down to either agency / departmental training and policy requirements, or (in the case of civilian application) personal decision based squarely upon your own personal combat philosophy, what feels comfortable for your body type (what works for you) and practical application.

Leg and foot position of the Weaver Stance.

Leg and foot position of Modern Isosceles Stance.

Referencing arm position in a shooting stance, there are basically two opposing schools. One is the utilization of *isometric tension absorbing recoil* with the weapon arm fully locked out and support elbow bent and pointing downward. The other is *equidistant extended arms absorbing recoil* with both elbows slightly bent, arms slightly relaxed but fixed in position.

Shock-absorption of recoil, which of course helps control recoil, is the essence of arm position in any good shooting stance. However, the debate rages on about which of the two is superior in the operational environment. Regardless, a quality shooting stance allows the shooter good recoil management, overall balance and stability of the weapon. Later on in our study we will further analyze the shooting stances from the DTI perspective.

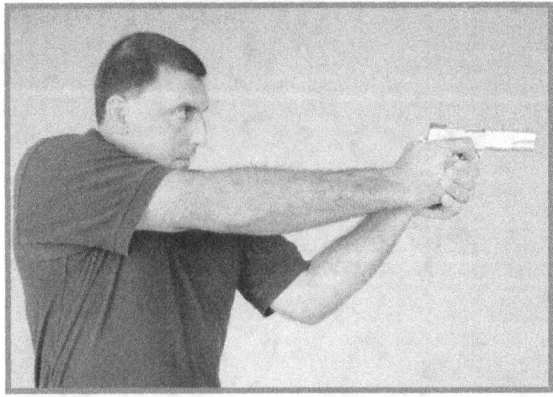

Arm position of Weaver Stance. Note characteristic position of support elbow pointing straight downward and hand pulling inward with strong arm extended and hand pushing outward to create isometric tension utilized to control recoil.

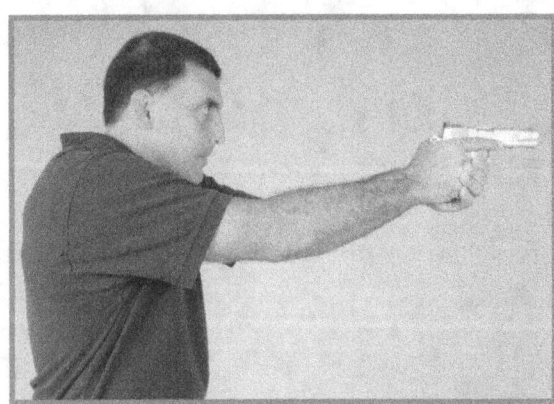

Arm position of Modern Isosceles Stance. Note characteristic position of both arms equidistant and both elbows slightly bent to create equal distribution of recoil absorption utilized to control recoil.

Finally, Head Position is very important as you want to keep the handgun as close to the optical center of your eye as possible. The head is erect and your general focus is on the threat area (aligning the sights and threat) and keeping your specific focus on the front sight of the handgun. Again, bring the gun up to your eyes and not your head down to the gun. Keeping your head up helps you maintain balance, optimal visual acuity, and breathe easier. Regardless of stance or method of holding the gun, the head position does not change.

Part II: Building Blocks—SAI

Example of less-than-optimal head position.

Example of optimal head position.

Overall body position (again from the bottom up) requires that the feet not be too far apart, but also not too close together. The knees are not too straight but not too bent either. Regardless of the choice of *specific* shooting stance, the shoulders and hips are predominantly on the same angle as the feet. The exact choice of specific shooting stance in itself (although important to form) is not as critical as the component parts of a *stable fighting platform* which will be covered later in the DTI chapters.

Gripping the Handgun

The grip is the most essential element to holding a handgun and management of recoil. Proper grip consists of the strong hand placed as high as possible on the frame of the handgun, with the bore in a straight line with the wrist and arm. The strong hand thumb should be placed as high as possible, pointing towards the target to allow room for full contact of the handgun stocks with the support hand. The thumb should be as high as comfortably possible without interfering with the function of the handgun. The purpose of this high placement of the firing hand is to maintain positive control of the weapon by effectively managing muzzle flip during recoil.

The support hand knuckles are placed over the strong hand knuckles. The support hand thumb should NEVER be placed across the back strap of a semiautomatic pistol because the slide may injure the hand when moving out of battery. The secret to a sound positive grip is to make and keep as much contact as possible with the receiver. Maximum contact with the surface of your hand and fingers with as much contact surface of the firearm as physically possible ensures a stable and functional grip. The masters of antiquity, with regard to handling of weapons, remind us that "in contact there is control and with space (loose grip) there is escape." Therefore a simple rule of thumb to remember about gripping your handgun is: "more contact equals more control." This applies to the gripping of any gun. The amount of space (escape) or the amount of contact (control) between the surface area of your hand and the surface area of the weapon determines the control of recoil and ultimately the stability of the shot.

Part II: Building Blocks—SAI

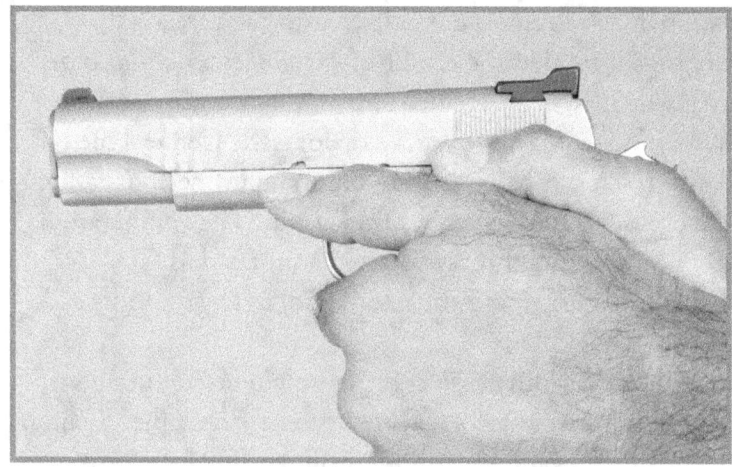

Example of optimal grip with the handgun allowing for maximum contact which enables maximum control of recoil and increased stability of the muzzle throughout the shooting cycle.

THREAT ENGAGEMENT

In the world of SAI there are literally hundreds of techniques and tactics. The majority of these focus on the combination of sight alignment, sight picture, trigger manipulation, target acquisition and engagement of the threat. It is assumed that as a responsible handgun owner that a clear and working understanding of sight alignment, sight picture and trigger manipulation is already part and parcel of the reader's tool kit. Again, as this is not specifically a firearms training program, focus will remain on our scope of study (application of a handgun in a knife attack) which is target acquisition and threat engagement with regards to Standard Defensive Response (SDR), Failure of SDR, Non-Standard Response (NSR) and Multiple Threat Engagement.

Standard Defensive Response

In training for any close-quarters combat there is necessity for a plan of action. The Standard Defensive Response (SDR) is a proven and reliable plan of action implemented as a response to a deadly force situation. The standard defensive response is delivered to the threat with two presses of the trigger fired at the center-of-mass. Center-of-mass or center mass (CM) is defined as the center of the available target usually the body. The exact position of CM is located along the Center Line (CL) of the human body which can be measured in a straight line connecting from between the eyebrows to the center of the groin. The combination of the two (center line and center mass) is often annotated as CL / CM as a reference to placement of rounds in a Standard Defensive Response.

With semi-automatic duty pistols firing only one shot per press, two presses of the trigger are two shots. Of course there are other weapon systems available, however, again, we will limit our scope of study to mainstream small-arms (semi-automatic) as well as focus predominantly on close quarter combat with reference to an edged weapon attack.

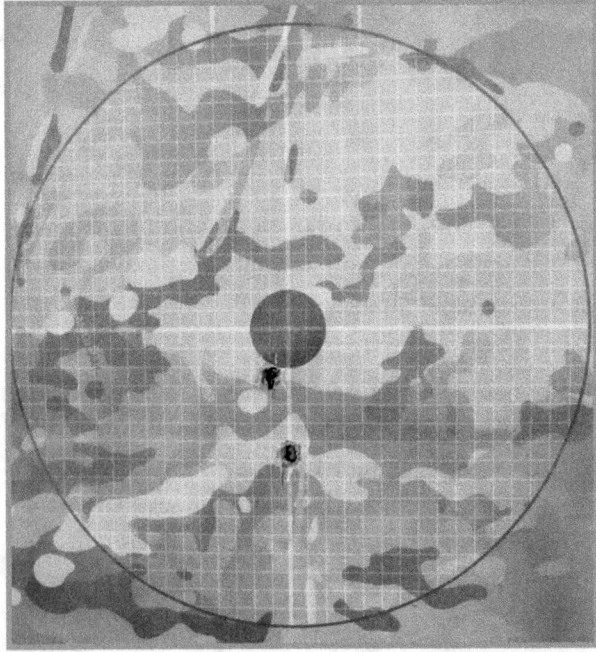

Example of a Standard Defensive Response (SDR). Notice placement of rounds at or around CL / CM.

Part II: Building Blocks—SAI

SDR Failure Response

In the event a Standard Defensive Response (SDR) ultimately fails to stop the threat, a shot to the head (brain) may be required. A center headshot (often referred to as a "failure response") will most likely stop an aggressor if the central nervous system is disrupted. The center of the head (brain) is small and can be a difficult target to hit under stress and in motion. A competent shooter who maintains good control of the handgun can accomplish this shot, as evidenced by the fact that this shot has been successfully made in numerous justified field shootings.

Failure Response Technique: If the center-of-mass torso shots fail to stop the threat, immediately adjust the sight picture to the head and fire a third shot at the center of the head as close to between the eyebrows as possible.

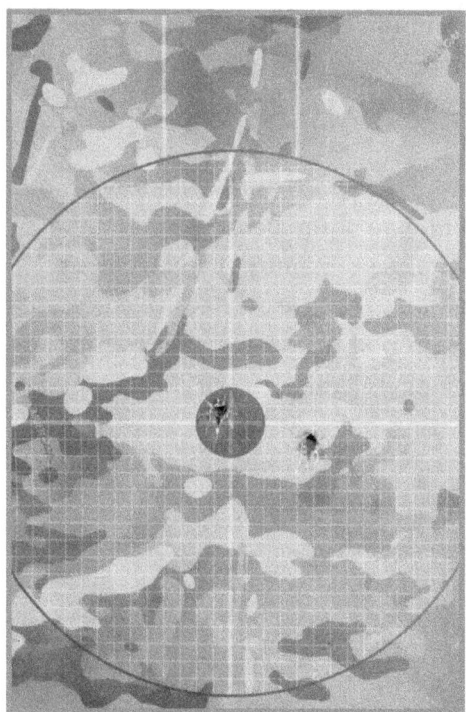

Example of two well-placed SDR rounds however, these may have failed on impact (see 28 Real-world Reasons).

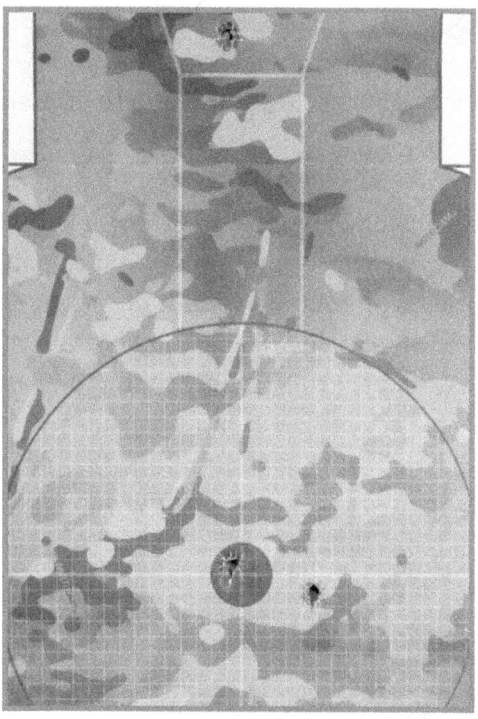

Example of response to a failed SDR.

Non-Standard Response (NSR)

Visualize yourself caught in a narrow dimly lit hallway. A tall athletic male between the ages of 18 and 34 is moving toward you with a clearly visible blade, intent, capability and speed. You nonetheless have plenty of time to present your firearm and as a matter of fact are able to apply an SDR at say about 10 yards. Well, for whatever reason (hard shirt, you missed, he doesn't realize that he's hit, etc. See 28 Real-world Reasons) he's not slowed down even a little bit.

You don't have anywhere to move to get out of the way, but you're holding a problem solving tool in your sweating hands and with an accelerated heartbeat you're faced with a definite problem. Of course you may want to try and apply an additional SDR or even try for the above failed SDR response—keep in mind that such a small target as the human head can be *very* difficult to hit in motion and under duress. What may be another optimal response to solve this problem? The answer is a Non-Standard Response or what is most commonly known as an NSR.

An NSR is any number of rounds greater than two and up to as many as is needed to stop the threat. Loosely translated this can be three or more rounds in rapid succession. At close proximity the NSR along with multiple rounds downrange additionally delivers explosive gases and fouling particles at bodily contact or near bodily contact ranges which may further influence stopping an incoming lethal threat.

Part II: Building Blocks—SAI

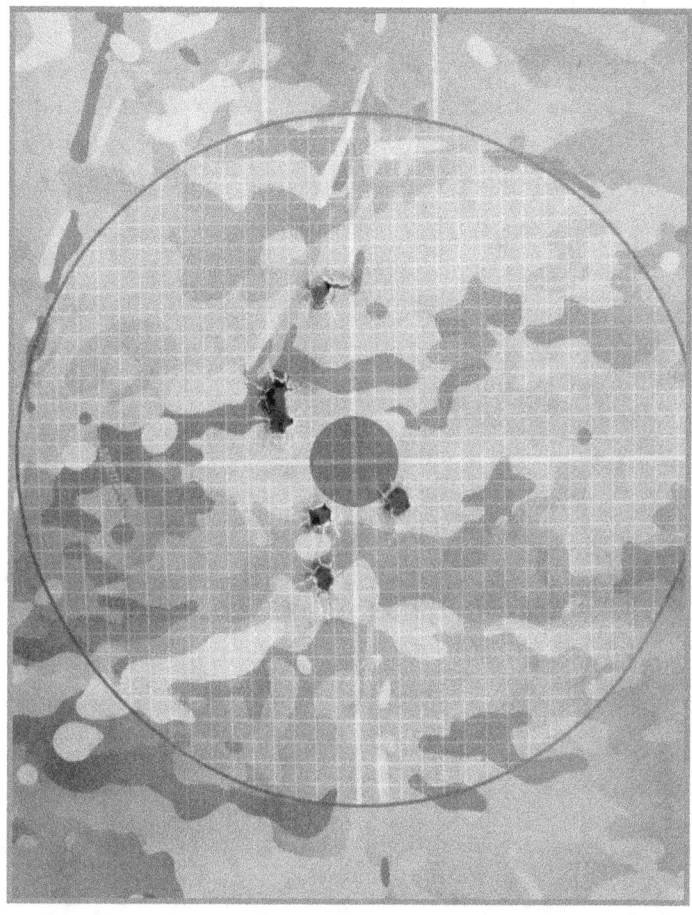

Example of a Non-Standard Response (NSR)

Multiple Threat Engagement

According to recent data on law enforcement shootings, there are multiple suspects about 45% of the time. When dealing with more than one suspect at a time, the shooter must make a critical decision: which threat should be handled first? During a situation in which only one suspect is making an overt assault, the decision to shoot is relatively easy. General rule of thumb is if you have at least two threats, engage the threat that poses the greatest threat first.

Consider these factors when evaluating relative threat: In the event of multiple attackers, determining the greatest threat is a matter of subjective interpretation. Weaponry—What type of weapon is the threat wielding? Proximity—What are the distances between you and each threat? Can an adversary that is further away pose a greater threat than one that is close? Posture or intent—What are the adversary's actions or threats against you? One of the most respected and experienced Senior Rangemasters out there today offers advice in this area "shoot the threat that scares you the most first."

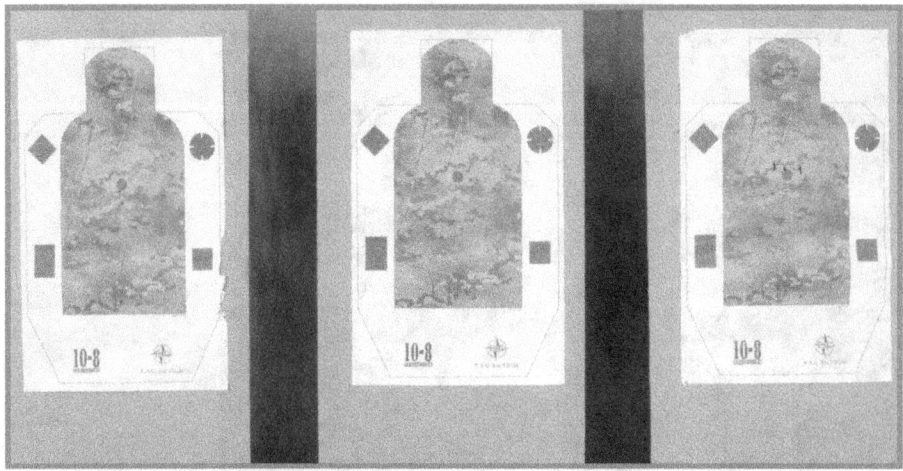

Example of multiple threat engagement.

Sighted and Unsighted Fire

In summary of Marksmanship, the bottom line is that there are two methods of firing the gun—Sighted Fire and Unsighted Fire. The decision for which to use rests squarely upon target distance. As previously covered, Sighted Fire is required at greater distances and is wholly reliant upon utilizing the front sight with good sight alignment and good sight picture. Unsighted Fire is applicable at contact range where it is not possible (nor probable) that you will be able to or even need to acquire a sight picture given the proximity of the threat and the speed at which the attack occurs. Of course, regardless of what type of fire, the need for good trigger control and muzzle discipline remains critical.

Example of Sighted Fire—an example where time and space allow usage of the sights.

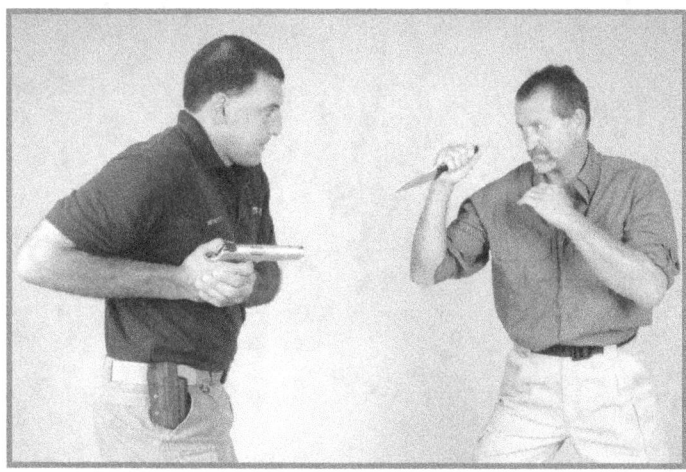

Example of Unsighted Fire—an example where time and space do not allow usage of the sights.

THE TWO-SECOND RULE

Since we're on the topic of speed, it has been documented that the average close quarter attack occurs in about two seconds. In fact the time-tested "21-foot Rule" (which will be covered in greater detail later) states that an athletic male between the ages of 18 and 34 can close the distance of 21 feet in less than 2.5 seconds—closer to the 2 second mark. Now that's pretty quick and, of course, puts you way behind the action-reaction power curve. In order to be successful in reaction to something that occurs at those speeds and close reactive distances it's critical that your techniques and tactics be sound, rapid and easy to utilize—all the basics in under two seconds.

PART III
BUILDING BLOCKS: DTI

SECRETS OF DEFENSIVE TACTICS

Since this is not specifically a defensive tactics instruction (DTI) course our scope of study will be limited to the application of DTI in close-quarter battle (CQB) as it pertains to defense against an attack with edged weapons (including a knife).

Taking this to the practical application level (and running parallel to SAI) if you are planning on taking a gun to a "knife fight," then by the nature of such a lethal engagement (due to proximity, speed, surprise, etc.) it is critical that you bring not only firearm skills to the fight (as these skills are specific to only the weapon itself—such as manipulation and marksmanship, etc.) but also *defensive tactics* skills.

DT skills differ from handgun skills in that handgun skills apply to a specific weapon system. Although handgun skills may of course be "translated" to other similar weapons systems (for example trigger control, sight alignment, etc.), they are nonetheless relegated to the world of SAI. DT skills on the flip side of the coin are modular and adaptable in nature and can be applied to any range of weapons (personal weapons, edged weapons, impact weapons, flexible weapons, etc.) *including* small arms. In other words even with *nothing* in your hands, DT combative concepts and physical skills may be effectively utilized.

The first step toward winning any fight (knife or otherwise) with a gun is of course to *bring* and also *know how to use* a gun—the weapon is equally as important as the training to use that weapon. Professional operators will tell you that training is more important than the weapon. In fact when I was teaching at the USMC base in Quantico, Virginia (USMC TBS—The Basic School) back in the old training building (circa 1999) one had to climb a set of stairs to get up to the old MACE (Martial Arts Center of Excellence). In that stairwell there was a huge mural painted in blood-red that filled the entire wall halfway up the stairwell. You couldn't go up that flight of stairs without it jumping out at you. It read "One Mind—Any Weapon."

In four words or less, that pretty much sums up the core capability of defensive tactics. The combative concepts and skills of personal defense by far exceed any specific weapon. Some of you old-timers reading this may well-remember the old adage: "the mind is the most powerful weapon."

HARDWARE AND SOFTWARE

Since we're on the topic of combative concepts and physical skills, overall proficiency with DT starts with familiarity of a technique and with the direct application of that technique. The body of knowledge regarding the usage of DT is quite vast and could (and does) fill volumes. However, again, for purposes of our scope of study we will focus predominantly on that aspect of training dealing with winning a fight utilizing a gun against an attacker with a knife.

Again running parallel to SAI, the training materials in this study block are divided into two parts—combative concepts (software) and combative application (hardware). The same computer analogy applies to DT as well—one cannot work without the other.

Step one—turn on the computer (that's your brain), get your head in the game. In a fight for your life you will need every fiber of awareness that you can muster. The key point here being awareness (software).

Two of the best kept secrets with regards to the development of DT skills are *Mindset* and *Control of Position, Range and Mobility*. Each one of these key training areas is a complete study on its own.

However, the training material contained herein is limited in volume to fit the scope of our study as it pertains to small arms defense against an edged weapon attack. Regardless, these are the *critical components* that are necessary to survive a lethal confrontation involving firearms. The most important of the three being mindset (software).

DEFENSIVE MINDSET

The defensive mindset of SAI is identical to that of DTI in terms of being proactively prepared for a lethal encounter. In fact the Conditions of Awareness also directly apply in the DTI world—yet another commonality between the worlds of SAI and DTI that often goes unnoticed.

The Conditions of Awareness are augmented by the world of DTI in that it offers reciprocal combative concepts which are equally as applicable in the SAI setting. The combative concepts that are regularly presented as part of the DTI litany often accompany any standardized program of instruction. However, due to the filters of political correctness (which have unfortunately metastasized like a cancer throughout all layers of our bureaucracy), they are not often permitted to share the same spotlight as SAI—due to their political "incorrectness"—even though they are directly applicable.

Violence of Action

Regardless of how politically incorrect it may seem; knives, guns and lethal engagements involving one or the other or both are just that—lethal engagements.

Let's face it most human beings are peaceful critters. We get up in the morning, scratch our nuts, empty the contents of our colon, brush our teeth and go to work with little or no issues other than maybe a traffic jam or some inclement weather. Violence of action is not part of the majority of our way of life. However, it needs to be both recognized and fully embraced. Having a knife at your throat is also not an everyday occurrence for most of us. The need for violence of action is paramount and very much a part of the defensive mindset.

What we're talking about here is a fight to the death. To clarify, that is one person (predatory human assailant—aka "the threat") armed with a dangerous weapon, willfully attempting to inflict severe bodily injury and or death on another individual (the victim) for whatever reason. There's no other way around it, this activity is considered a violent, aggressive action and as such is commonly referred to as "Violence of Action."

If you happen to be an individual who is assaulted or otherwise attacked by another individual in a violent physical action at close quarters and you choose to reach for your cell phone and dial 911—then you qualify as a "victim." If you happen to be an individual who is assaulted or otherwise attacked by another individual in a violent physical action at close quarters and you choose to ignore it—then you qualify as a "victim." If you happen to be an individual who is assaulted or otherwise attacked by another individual in a violent physical action at close quarters and you are from California and choose to send loving and caring thoughts to reach out and help your attacker as he himself is merely a victim of our society—then you most *certainly* qualify as a "victim."

Violence of action can only be met by violence of action. We have all heard the old phrase "fight fire with fire" well the same exact principle applies here—violence of action at such proximity and lethality can only be met with violence of action. Any response less than violence of action will result in victimization, severe bodily injury and / or death.

With application of violence of action your attacker's not thinking offensively any more. Watch any boxer when he's under a barrage of punches. When he's not on the offensive he's barely hanging in there and all he can do to remain standing while the other guy continues slamming away at his head—violence of action. Take the example of the military providing cover fire. While those rounds are flying down range at a cyclical rate *nobody* wants to pop their head up and go on the offensive—you take cover and stay down until the rain is over—violence of action. It's been proven time and time again—added to your defensive mindset, violence of action when needed, will work like a charm.

Forward–Aggressive–Effective

One of the most important aspects of maintaining a Defensive Mindset is the development of a personal mantra with regards to any attack on your person. Most of us already know that the best defenses is a good offense, but how this is applied as a defensive mindset in the world of DTI is what makes it work.

For example, you are faced with a violent threat and he's so close you can smell urine on his pants, by the time you turn to run it's too late now you've given your back to the threat, making a very bad situation even worse. Sure, if there's time and space to exit out of there then yes, best option is to not be there—but that's not what we're talking about here—you don't have that option—you're only viable option is to stay and fight. The very first and foremost is to face forward—face the threat—stay in his face as he is in yours. Another old adage that the Masters pass down to us is as applicable today as it was millennia ago, "lose sight—lose the fight."

Another important aspect is aggressiveness. When have you ever seen two professional boxers not be aggressive? When one of them is about to get knocked out. Which of the two teams in any professional sports walks away the winner? The more aggressive of the two.

Aggressiveness is a critical component of Violence of Action. By attacking the attacker you force his defense and turn the tables of fate in your favor. Remaining aggressive is your only option if you're forced to stay and face the threat head on.

Lastly, but certainly not least is *effectiveness*. If you're going to use your gun and you've checked of all 28 boxes then you'd best place that round effectively. What would be the consequences of shooting over his head or into the dirt next to him as opposed to shutting down his brain box? Even if all you have is a golf club or a baseball bat or even your bare hands—you need to be effective. Tapping the guy lightly on the shoulder with your index finger will do you no good whatsoever.

You can be forward and aggressive but *not* effective. As an example you can be yelling, pointing your finger right into his grill and moving toward him, but where is the effectiveness? You have not made any *effective* physical contact. If you're into a lethal confrontation that deep and you fail to be effective, then you're in the same exact situation as any other victim. The magical formula is the power of all three—Forward–Aggressive–Effective.

Fightin' Ain't Easy

Nowhere in the brochure of life does it say that fighting is easy. If it were so easy then we would all be boxers.

Boxers are some of the best-trained and most-conditioned athletes of our modern era as a result of how much discipline and hard physical work it takes to stay in fighting shape.

Speaking of boxing, there's a very good friend and training partner of mine, his name is Bill Hall (former US Army, USBP and FAM), who was ranked 3rd in the world in kickboxing. As a professional boxer Bill fought more than sixty-eight professional bouts and I don't even *know* how many amateur fights. Following his professional career he became a law enforcement officer and eventually went to work for the government (and at the time of this writing just finished his Masters Degree). Throughout his career, he is also a DTI and an SAI instructor, we've had the chance to work together professionally many times and one of his time-proven patented Bill-isms always stuck in my head because of its veracity. It is applicable to boxing, kickboxing, gun fighting, knife fighting or any other fighting (and I quote) "Fightin' ain't easy, fightin' ain't pretty and size does matter."

In fact, Bill Hall is founder of OSBD Inc. a professional contract services provider of personal weapons striking skills including boxing and kick-boxing. Personal weapons such as hands, feet, knees, elbows, etc. can be applied in an aggressive and effective manner to deliver strikes (or distractions). If you close your hands and make a fist for example, this personal weapon is made readily available for any close quarter contact range engagement. How to use your hands, feet, elbows, knees, etc. and other personal weapons in self-defense, for sport or personal safety is an entire subject unto itself.

Personal weapons are unique to any other weapon (ballistic, edged, impact, etc.) in that you are born with them, carry them around with you your entire life and eventually expire with them still attached.

You carry them wherever you go and they are legal personal-defense assets regardless of city, county, state or country. In order to remain focused on our primary scope of study, suffice it to say that a good solid punch, crushing elbow or driving knee applied to the right part of the human body can generate tremendous destructive force. It is the opinion of this author that the development of hard skills in the area of personal weapons is a critical component in the repertoire of any defense-minded citizen carrying a gun.

ACTION–REACTION

Anyone who has been involved in individual sports or team sports or was a cop or in the military or any other profession which utilizes hard skills as part of their career, knows full-well from first hand personal experience that reaction is slower than action.

A burglar breaks into a home in the middle of the night and sets off the alarm (takes a matter of seconds). The family who lives in that home runs downstairs to find the screwdriver and a broken window and dial 911 (takes about 3 minutes). After being dispatched the boys roll up anywhere between maybe 15 to 45 minutes after the call. Action—

burglar breaks the window (matter of seconds), reaction—cops rolling up to the scene (matter of minutes).

On a more personal combative level, let's say you end up in a situation where some guy punches you straight in the snot-locker. This may take about a half-second (time of action) and as a direct result your eyes start to water, you may be seeing little white glowing dots (depending on how hard you were hit) and while recoiling backward you make the decision to retaliate with a strike of your own to his face. By the time you accomplish this task the reaction time is nearly quadruple the time of action. Moral of the story: Reaction is slower than action.

The Power Curve

This principle of reaction being slower than action is common knowledge amongst first responders, and is often referred to as the "Action-Reaction Power Curve." By the very nature of their profession they are *always* behind the power curve as an action has occurred (could be a traffic accident, fire, natural disaster, shooting, bank robbery, etc.) and they are called upon as a reaction to that action

Applied to a DTI scenario the Action-Reaction Power Curve (sometimes abbreviated as "the Power Curve") can be used as a tool and actually reversed on an opponent at close quarters. As an example let's say one boxer is dominant through the first two rounds and he's obviously in control of the fight. Well, the other boxer is doing nothing but reacting to his opponent—this other boxer is considered "behind the Action-Reaction Power Curve" or "behind the Power Curve." Luckily for this guy he is in better condition than the other guy who was dominating the fight in the first two rounds. When the bell rings and both boxers walk away from their respective corners, the guy with better physical conditioning starts to dominate and as a direct result of his better conditioning has reversed the Power Curve.

The same thing happens to cops all the time. In a typical encounter where a LEO is confronting a suspect face to face, the suspect starts to get froggy and begins to dominate the scenario (the cop is behind the power curve here), the cop will immediately move to the next level of acceptable use of force to gain control of the situation thus reversing the curve and gaining the upper hand placing the suspect on the reaction side of the action-reaction power curve.

Action always is faster than reaction—this is just a plain law of physics. The converse is also true that reaction is slower than action. The winner in any fight is always in control of the curve. While his opponent is busily trying to react to his actions, the fighter in control of the action-reaction power curve is who ultimately wins.

Gross and Fine Motor Skills

In the world of DTI (which also, incidentally, applies to SAI) there are two methods by which humans may work body mechanics or "motor skills": Fine Motor Skills and Gross Motor Skills.

Fine Motor Skills are those skills requiring the usage of the smaller muscles and bones in particular those of the hand and more specifically the fingers. Examples of fine motor skills would be a dentist working on your teeth or a heart surgeon performing open heart surgery on a patient. More common examples would be using your fingers to play an instrument like guitar or a piano, or typing on your computer or even tying your shoes. These are all examples of application of fine motor skills.

Gross motor skills are those skills that require a minimal number of complex movements. These are skills requiring little or no thought and little or no movement with little or no training and can be executed more readily under pressure. A good example of a gross motor skill would be two boxers smashing each other with 8oz gloves, wraps and tape wrapped around their fingers and wrist locking them into place. A baseball player reaching up with his glove arm to catch a baseball is also considered a gross motor skill. More common examples would include reaching for a coffee cup or turning a door knob.

According to physicians, under stress (and with an adrenaline dump) blood tends to leave the extremities and pool near the larger muscle groups—enabling gross motor movements but detracting from fine motor movements. What this tells us is that the usage of gross motor skills is more reliable than the usage of fine motor skills under duress—like being attacked with a knife at close quarters. The concept here is the least amount of movement (least number of steps) and simplicity of movement (easy-to-execute gross motor skills).

Little movement and simple movement are the magic formula to economy of motion in any DTI scenario.

Pain Compliance versus Mechanical Compliance

In the world of DTI there are two methods of compliance which may be utilized to influence the physical position of an adversary. These are traditionally known as Pain Compliance and Mechanical Compliance. An example of pain compliance would be say a pressure point located on the face or certain positions on the body. An example of Mechanical Compliance would be an arm-bar or a choke out.

In the world of SAI if you ended up in an altercation where in the heat of battle instead of striking the intended target you may have hit a non-vital areas and due to the pain the attacker may possibly submit after a while. Whereas if you hit the brain box dead-center at the "T" intersection (bridge of the nose), that would shut down his electrical system and illustrate a clear example of mechanical compliance.

It is a fact of nature that certain individuals have a pain tolerance so high that you would swear they are brain dead. No doubt if you're an alpha male reading this, you have been in an altercation with just such a person. He's the kind of guy you can crack square in the jaw with an aluminum baseball bat and he spits out a tooth and just smiles at you. Whereas other people yelp out loud, become disoriented and start projectile vomiting from a paper cut. Especially in a close quarters and in a life- or death struggle with guns and knives you can't afford to take a gamble on which end of the spectrum your opponent may be—aluminum baseball bat or paper cut. Moral of the story: err on the side of mechanical compliance.

Any effective DTI technique must be executed with quickness (2.5 seconds or less) so as to regain control of that space / time / action / reaction power curve, be adaptable (modular to both SAI and DTI), utilize gross motor skills and affect mechanical compliance. Incidentally the same requirements apply to any SAI technique.

Cycles and Gaps

Regardless of point of origin (from SAI or DTI), both schools share the combative concept of cycles. A cycle can be defined as a course or series of events or operations that recur regularly and usually lead back to the starting point. An example of a reliable cycle in nature would be each day starting with a sunrise and ending with a sunset only to begin the same exact cycle again the next day. Referencing combative application, every aspect of personal combat regardless of weapon is subject to these cycles of action. As an example, in the world of SAI there is the eight-step mechanical cycle of action of a semiautomatic pistol:

1. Feed—round from magazine is moved up feed ramp

2. Chamber—round is mounted in chamber

3. Lock—chamber is locked

4. Fire—pin strikes primer igniting cartridge powder launching round

5. Unlock—gas pressure moves slide back unlocking spent casing

6. Extract—spent casing is extracted from chamber

7. Eject—spent casing us ejected from slide assembly

8. Re-cock—pin and hammer (if any) is re-cocked

As well as the 8-Step cycle of handgun presentation:

1. Grip.

2. Clear and Cant to Retention Position.

3. Hands come together.

4. Punch and Look.

5. Assess and fire if necessary

6. Drop firearm down to Low Ready

7. Look and Assess

8. Holster

At the end of each cycle the loop returns to step one and the cycle begins all over again. The core concept of any cycle of action with regards to combative application is that there is a start of some activity, a change in that activity and an end of that particular activity leading to the option of that same cycle fully capable of being run again and in the exact same order.

The key point here is that it's the same order, same steps, and exact same series of actions with no changes. What this allows is consistency of repetition (cycling of the slide, presentation of the firearm, etc.) which is a solid step in the direction of reliability with both your weapons and your tactics.

OODA Cycle

Perhaps the most well-known (and widely disseminated) cycle of action shared by both SAI and DTI is the OODA Cycle. Also known as the "OODA Loop," it is a decision making cycle defining the procedural steps by which an operator reacts to a threat. Working knowledge of the OODA Loop enables the manipulation of situations where an operator can make definitive and appropriate decisions quicker than his adversary.

Founded by military strategist and US Air Force Fighter Pilot Colonel John R. Boyd (USAF Ret.—Deceased), the OODA Cycle has been proven as a cornerstone of operational interaction.

Col. Boyd served in the Army Air Corps from 1945 to 1947 and subsequently served as a U.S. Air Force officer from July 1951 to August 1975. Known as "Forty-Second Boyd" for his ability to beat any opposing pilot in aerial combat in less than forty seconds, Colonel Boyd was considered an icon by his students and a master-level instructor fighter pilot. When asked about the secrets of his success in aerial combat the Colonel responded with his "hypothesis" that fighter pilots, (this also applies to ground operators and is equally applicable to law enforcement personnel) "undergo a continuous cycle of interaction with their environment." This particular "Cycle of Interaction"—fully adopted by both SAI and DTI became thereafter known as the OODA Cycle. Boyd emphasized that this decision cycle is the central mechanism enabling adaptation and is therefore critical to survival.

The OODA cycle is divided into four interrelated and overlapping processes through which an operator cycles continuously:

1. Observation—Observe the threat.

2. Orientation—Orient to the threat—at what range, what are his capabilities.

3. Decision—Decide, determination of a course of action based on one's current mental perspective, that is make the decision to engage or disengage the threat—the decision to shoot or not to shoot.

4. Action—Take action based on your decision (physically presenting the handgun and actually taking the shot or not based on your decision).

As with any violent physical confrontation, the three critical elements that continually change are:

1. Condition of the environment

2. Condition of the threat

3. Condition of your weapon system(s).

The OODA cycle continues to run from the beginning each time one of these three changes—which can be as rapidly as thousandths of a second.

Observe, Orient, Decide, Act—the OODA cycle is utilized by military and law enforcement professionals alike in every imaginable operational environment.

As an example of the practical application of this cycle of action, let's take the example of a law enforcement scenario. Cop OBSERVES that a pedestrian shouldn't be snooping around the back door of a closed bank at 3:00 AM wearing a long trench coat. Officer ORIENTS to this observation—how many of them, are there any observable weapons, how far away are they, etc. He then DECIDES to call this one in and finally ACTS by reaching for his radio and physically calling it in. As he's calling it in the *condition of the threat* changes as the suspect moves forward and the entire OODA Cycle starts all over again—the officer OBSERVES the approaching suspect open his coat apparently reaching for something inside, the cop ORIENTS to the new set of circumstances (changes in condition of his environment, threat and weapon system(s), DECIDES that this is not a good scenario and that it's time to go to guns and ACTS by presenting his firearm and handling the situation accordingly.

Reactionary Gap

A baseball player way out there in center field observes that the batter hit the ball and watches its trajectory from point of impact all the way up and over to near his location. He has plenty of time to react an even must wait for the ball to come down before capturing it in his glove. The next play, however, the pitcher barely ducks out of the way in time to save his life as the batter, in merely tenths of a second, drills the ball straight towards his head.

These are examples of Reactionary Gap. The outfielder has plenty of *space* in which to react to the ball and because of that vast amount of space has plenty of *time* to react. Whereas the pitcher, due to the speed of the incoming projectile, has very little space to react permitting him equally as little time to react. There is a relationship between space and time. The more space available the more time you have to react. The less space available—the less time you have to react—in both SAI and DTI this is known as the Reactionary Gap.

Liability Gap (Injury-Distance Relationship)

Revisiting the Scale of Injury (SOI) there is a direct correlation between scale of injury and distance from threat. Distance can be measured in potential personal damage based on weapon system, specific bodily target (hard or soft) and scale of injury. The closer your opponent gets to you the higher your potential for injury.

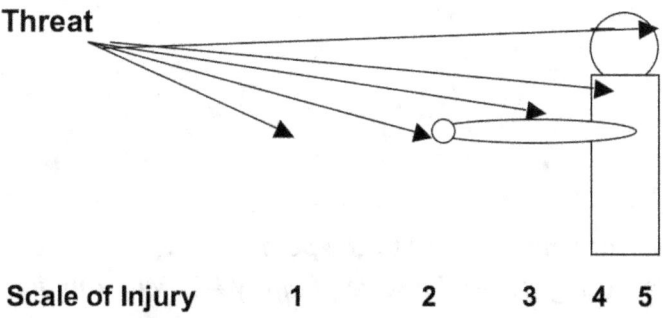

Bringing a Gun to a Knife Fight

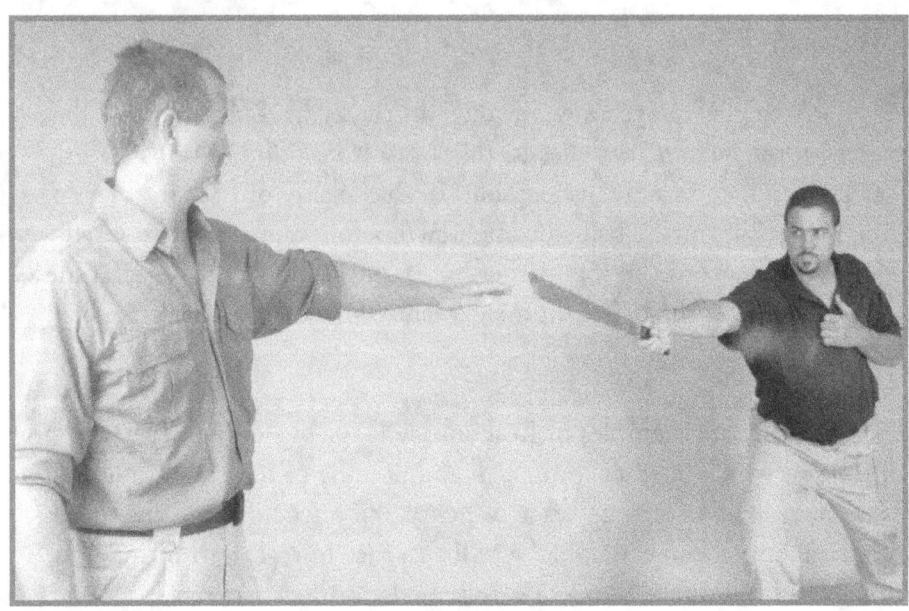

With no contact between yourself and the threat you are at the lowest level on the scale of injury—1. No Injury.

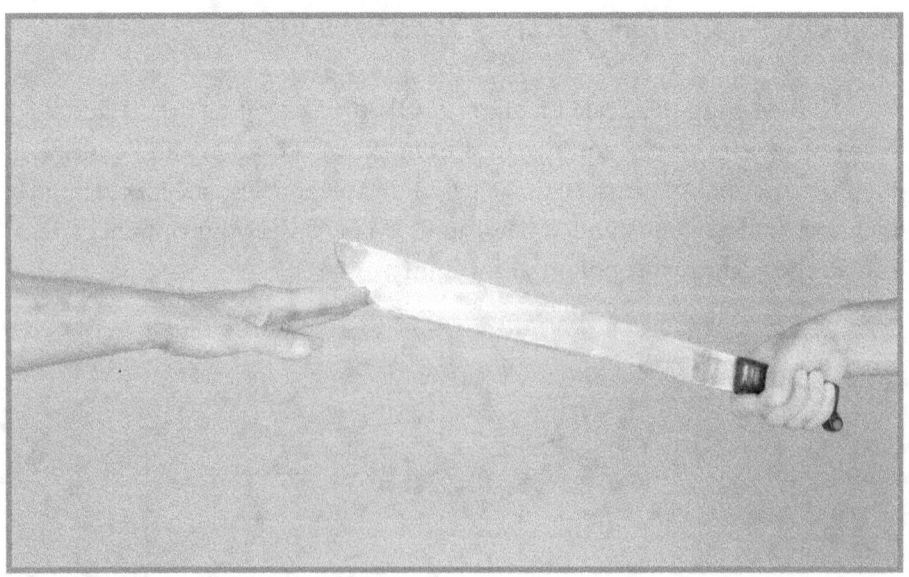

As your adversary moves closer to the point of physical contact this places you one rung up on the scale of injury—2. Minor Injury.

Part III: Building Blocks—DTI

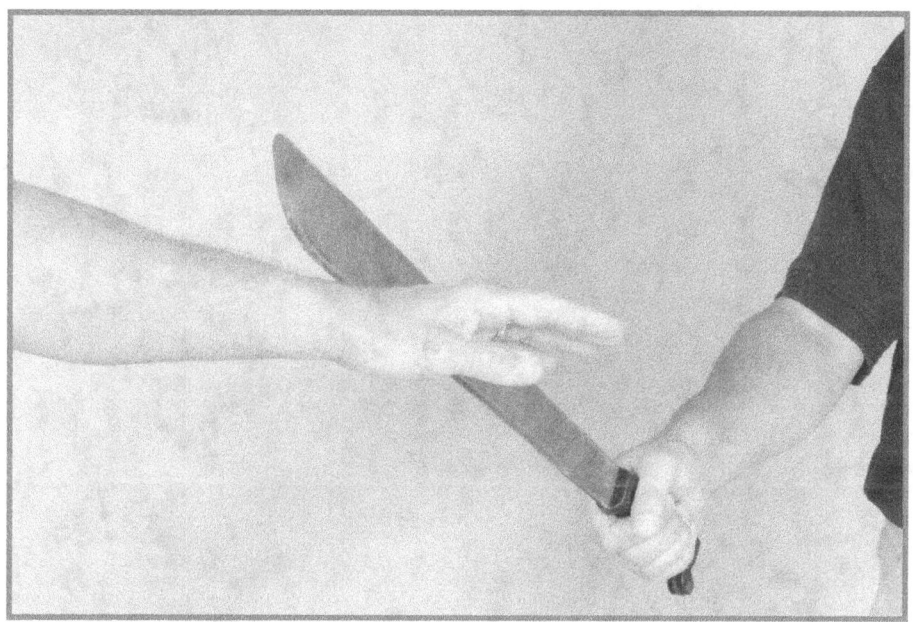

As your adversary moves even closer this places you at a higher level on the scale of injury—3. Recoverable Injury.

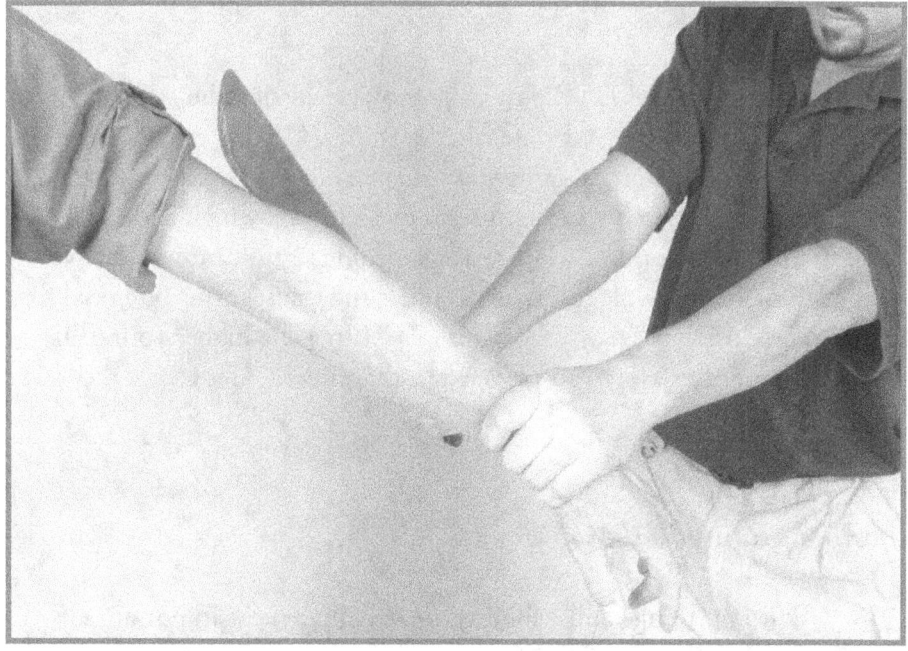

As your adversary moves yet closer this places you higher on the scale of injury—4. Unrecoverable injury.

Bringing a Gun to a Knife Fight

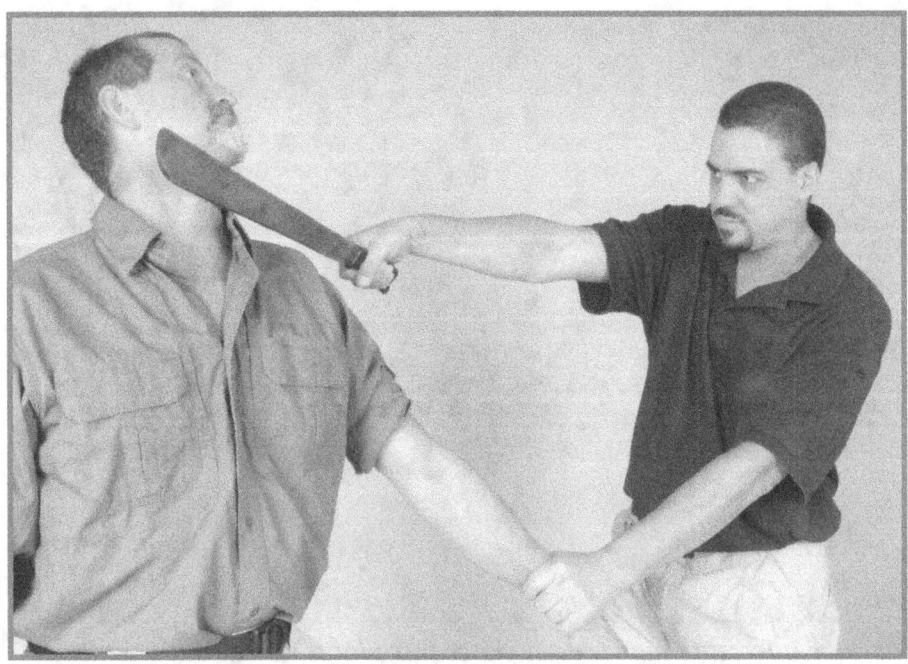

As your adversary moves directly in contact with your vital organs this places you at the highest level on the scale of injury—5. Death.

In the world of DTI, physically moving outside the range of SOI mechanically decreased your potential for injury. Getting outside of that dangerous range of contact gains you valuable operating space. As previously covered, increased space ensures increased time which allows more time to formulate options. More space and time significantly lowers your potential for injury while less space and less time raises your potential for injury. The closer you get to the threat ("Get In") the higher your SOI, whereas the further away you move from the threat ("Get Out") the lower your SOI.

Position, Range and Mobility

Position, Range and Mobility are the three most important elements of controlling any fight. Control of these three is critical to your control of the fight. Either you control the fight or the fight controls you.

You want to be able to utilize control of these three elements to your advantage to turn the tables of the action-reaction power curve. Keep in mind that in any surprise physical altercation you are automatically behind the power curve. Due to the speed and proximity of such an engagement and close quarters, decreased space, decreased time and increased potential for injury places you directly behind the power curve and therefore out of control of the fight. Your only chance to take back control of the fight is to take back these three critical components.

Control of these elements in the heat of battle is similar to control of the gas pedal, brakes and steering wheel of a moving vehicle. Should you lose control of the steering wheel then at least you still have two-thirds control of the vehicle with at least both pedals under your control—you still control the vehicle and only one-third of the vehicle controls you. If you lose all three (steering wheel, both pedals) now the vehicle controls you and you no longer control the vehicle and are at the mercy of the actions of the vehicle. The same applies to Position, Range and Mobility. If you are in control of your position (assume an advantageous position), in control of your Range (how far away you are form your opponent) and in control of Mobility (moving targets are more difficult to hit than stationary targets) then you are in control of the fight and of your opponent. The degree to which you lose any of these three components is the degree to which you lose control of the fight.

Control of Position

The first and foremost of the three critical components of controlling any fight is Control of Position. Another common thread between SAI and DTI is gaining an advantageous position in the fight, whether it is a gunfight or a fistfight or a knife fight. You want the upper hand and in the case of physical position, the very best place to be in any altercation is in a relatively safe position.

It's best to remember close quarters combat is generally where contact can be made with your body by a dangerous weapon (such as a knife for example) so there are both safe and unsafe physical positions based on proximity. Again, these are all relative to the ever-changing dynamics of a deadly physical altercation. A safe position is also referred to (by several DTI academies) as a "Green Zone" and an unsafe position is often referred to as a "Red Zone." We have two positions with reference to control and these are Safe and Unsafe (aka Green and Red) zones.

At a range where you can reach out and touch him with a bullet yet he cannot touch you with a knife is considered a Safe Range (aka Green Zone).

At a range where you can reach out and touch him with a bullet yet he cannot readily make contact with a knife (his weapon is initially pointed AWAY from you) is also considered a relatively Safe Range (aka Green Zone). Even though this is at close range it's still considered relatively safe as compared to the Red Zone.

Part III: Building Blocks—DTI

You want to be able to utilize control of these three elements to your advantage to turn the tables of the action-reaction power curve. Keep in mind that in any surprise physical altercation you are automatically behind the power curve. Due to the speed and proximity of such an engagement and close quarters, decreased space, decreased time and increased potential for injury places you directly behind the power curve and therefore out of control of the fight. Your only chance to take back control of the fight is to take back these three critical components.

Control of these elements in the heat of battle is similar to control of the gas pedal, brakes and steering wheel of a moving vehicle. Should you lose control of the steering wheel then at least you still have two-thirds control of the vehicle with at least both pedals under your control—you still control the vehicle and only one-third of the vehicle controls you. If you lose all three (steering wheel, both pedals) now the vehicle controls you and you no longer control the vehicle and are at the mercy of the actions of the vehicle. The same applies to Position, Range and Mobility. If you are in control of your position (assume an advantageous position), in control of your Range (how far away you are form your opponent) and in control of Mobility (moving targets are more difficult to hit than stationary targets) then you are in control of the fight and of your opponent. The degree to which you lose any of these three components is the degree to which you lose control of the fight.

Control of Position

The first and foremost of the three critical components of controlling any fight is Control of Position. Another common thread between SAI and DTI is gaining an advantageous position in the fight, whether it is a gunfight or a fistfight or a knife fight. You want the upper hand and in the case of physical position, the very best place to be in any altercation is in a relatively safe position.

It's best to remember close quarters combat is generally where contact can be made with your body by a dangerous weapon (such as a knife for example) so there are both safe and unsafe physical positions

Bringing a Gun to a Knife Fight

based on proximity. Again, these are all relative to the ever-changing dynamics of a deadly physical altercation. A safe position is also referred to (by several DTI academies) as a "Green Zone" and an unsafe position is often referred to as a "Red Zone." We have two positions with reference to control and these are Safe and Unsafe (aka Green and Red) zones.

At a range where you can reach out and touch him with a bullet yet he cannot touch you with a knife is considered a Safe Range (aka Green Zone).

At a range where you can reach out and touch him with a bullet yet he cannot readily make contact with a knife (his weapon is initially pointed AWAY from you) is also considered a relatively Safe Range (aka Green Zone). Even though this is at close range it's still considered relatively safe as compared to the Red Zone.

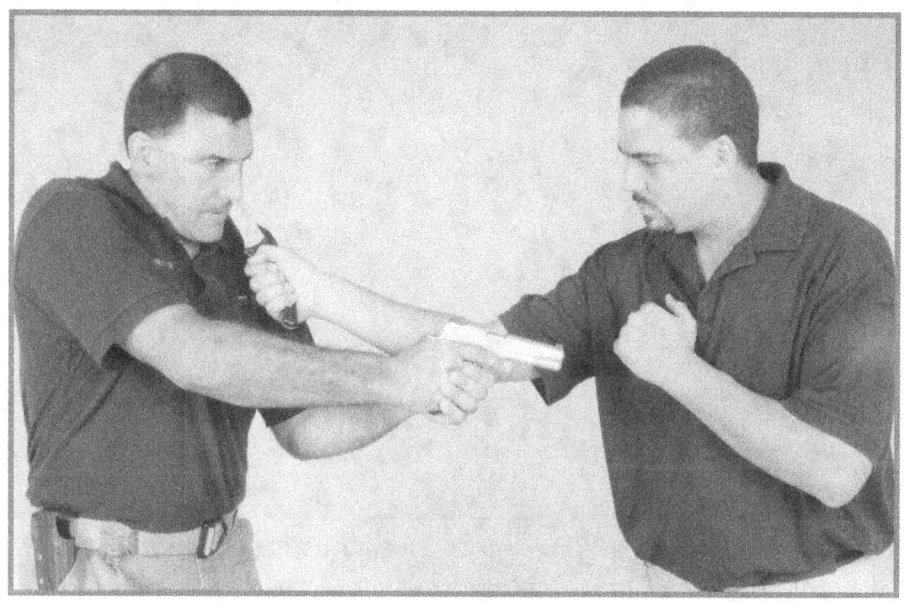

At a range where you can reach out and hit him with rounds and he can reach out at closer ranges and dramatically increase your bodily injury (at least a level 5 [death] on the Scale of Injury [SOI]) is considered Unsafe (aka Red Zone).

Control of Range

Equal to Control of Position, the next of the three critical components of controlling any fight is Control of Range. In the world of DTI there are only two ranges of lethal combat—Contact Range (CR) and Non-contact Range (NCR). The safer of these two is NCR due to its placing of your body out of physical range of the attack and thus placing you at the lowest possible level on the SOI and additionally creating valuable time and space. The problem as with any CQB is of course effectively managing the fight at Contact Range which will be addressed in extreme detail in Part IV.

Bringing a Gun to a Knife Fight

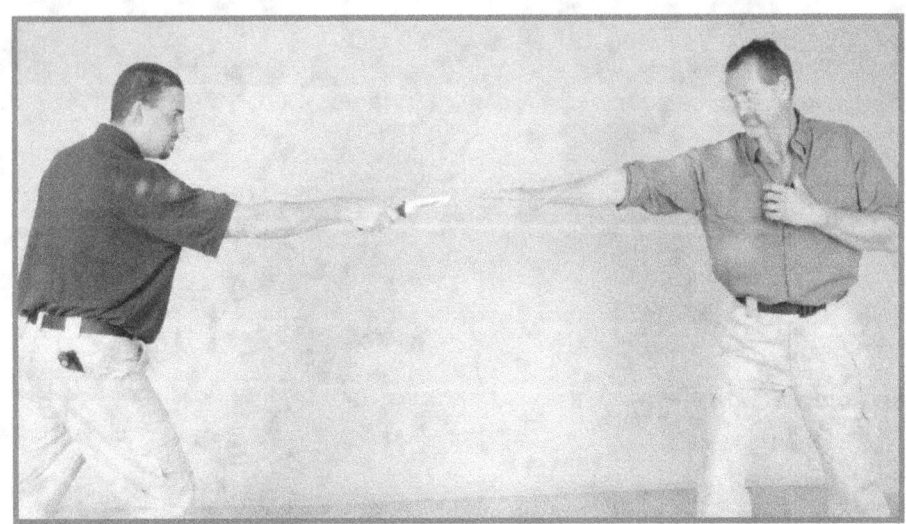

Non Contact Range (NCR) is also considered a Safe or Green Zone.

The very dangerous Contact Range—where Scale of Injury begins.

Control of Mobility

Equal to Control of Range, the last but certainly not the least of the three critical components of controlling any fight is Control of Mobility. Yet another common thread between SAI and DTI is the fact that a moving target is more difficult to hit than a stationary target. The optimal goal in any CQB scenario is to continually make yourself a hard target. The only way to do this is to gain full control of your mobility.

Again in SAI and DTI there are a number of ways to move the human body ranging from a bunny-hop (not recommended as a result of loss of stability and loss of muzzle discipline) to the "groucho" (a form of tactical movement utilized by operators when "shooting on the move").

Movement of the body straight back and away from the threat as appealing as it may seem is not optimal. Moving straight back has a number of drawbacks:

1. It places you in an unstable position and moving in a less-than-optimal direction.

2. At some point the forward moving attacker will eventually over-run your backward movement and place you in the Red Zone.

3. You are moving toward an unknown and cannot see the terrain into which you are precariously stepping. This can be especially hazardous to your health in the case of gas/oil platforms, docks, elevators, stairwells, cliffs, etc.

4. He can see where you are going and you cannot—this gives him the advantage by moving you to a position of *his* advantage.

5. Placing rounds down range accurately while moving backwards is a less than optimal tactical maneuver.

Bringing a Gun to a Knife Fight

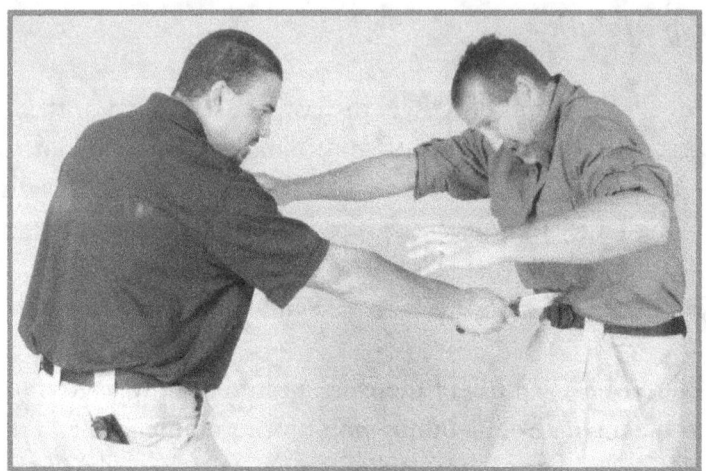

Backward movement away from a knife attack using your legs only is not recommended.

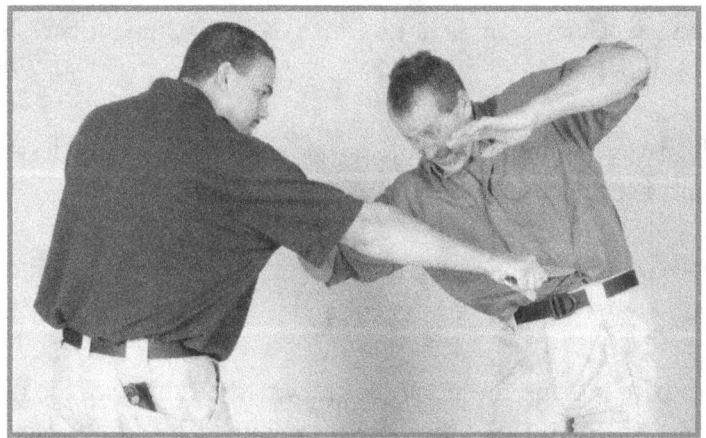

Lateral movement away from a knife attack again using only your legs is also not recommended.

If you must move backward it's better to step off to a 45 degree angle as this allows mechanical advantage over your opponent's reach and consequently lowers your potential for injury on the SOI. Additionally by stepping off 45 degrees this flips the action/reaction table and puts you in control of the curve as your opponent now has to react to you. In this situation you have full control of your *Position, Range, Mobility* and the action-reaction power curve. In one single movement, you have effectively placed him on the defensive.

Angular (45 degree) movement back away from a knife attack is strongly recommended.

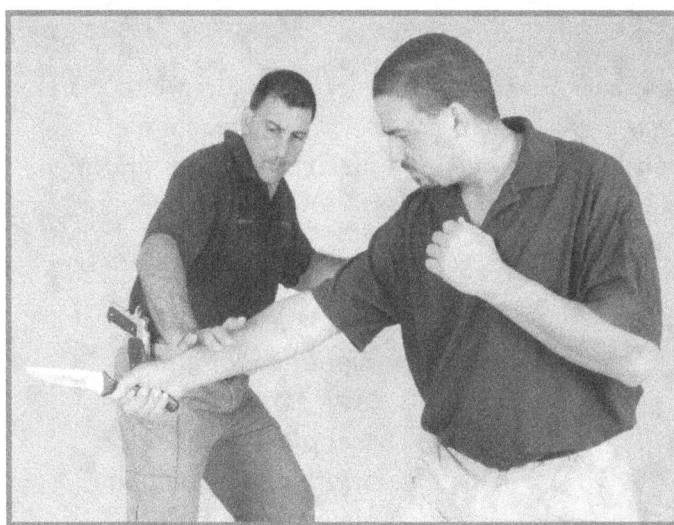

Additionally angular (45 degree) movement forward utilizing the hands to immediately deflect away the incoming knife attack is strongly recommended.

STABLE FIGHTING PLATFORM

In order to maximize physical position and range to your advantage, the body must be postured in such a manner as to lend itself to optimal performance. Such a position must enable the body to shoot, punch, grab, fall, roll and otherwise move to positions or movements of advantage. This variety of choices can only come from a Stable Fighting Platform (SFP).

Hands and Feet

In review of hand positions (see Presenting the Handgun, Count One—Grip) there are three that have been covered: Hands Above, Hands Below and Hands Away.

To reiterate, it is imperative that we gain the ability to fight from any one and all three positions regardless of what may by going on around us. From just below the belt-line and upward, utilizing one of these three hand positions is of course extremely important but only half the equation. The remaining half of the body necessary to deliver accurate placement of rounds from a stable fighting platform includes the legs and position of the feet.

Maintaining a stable base with feet at least shoulder width apart so that if someone was to push against your body you would remain stable and be additionally able to operate a firearm, move quickly, or go to hands on. Combining the hands and the feet together as per above forms a Stable Fighting Platform.

Example of a Stable Fighting Platform with Hands Above feet planted shoulder width apart pointing down range facing the threat.

Moving the Stable Fighting Platform

As was previously covered—moving targets are more difficult to hit than stationary targets. Although a Stable Fighting Platform (SFP) is very desirable and an optimal body posture in a fight for your life, it becomes vulnerable if it remains stationary. The idea is to continually move the SFP to positions of advantage and away from those of disadvantage. There are a number of methods to accomplish this task. The most stable of these is to move the SFP from position A to position B while keeping the SFP in tact. The shortest distance between two points is a straight line.

A _____ B

**The shortest distance between two points is a straight line.
Less space equals less time.**

One of the ways to move the SFP is to simply walk forward or backward or left or right (placing one foot in front of the other aka "Cross Stepping"). If you're going to do this, referred to in the industry as "Shooting on the Move," then the "Groucho" method of moving the Stable Fighting Platform is recommended.

Another method of moving the Stable Fighting Platform is the "Step and Slide" aka "Slide Step" (some firearm academies refer to this method as "Big Step followed by Little Step) in which case a large step (heel first followed by toe) is followed by a smaller replacement step.

As with all methods, there is a price tag for everything—that is a plus and a minus. The upside for the Grouch method is that it is ambulation with a quickness as moving targets are much more difficult to hit than stationary ones. However, the price tag for moving at speed is accuracy. The upside of the Step and Slide method is stability of footing and greater accuracy in shot placement. However, the downside is of course not moving the Stable Fighting Platform very quickly—slow moving targets are easier to hit.

The determining factors on choice of movement is condition of your environment, the control factors of relative position and range (distance from your threat at initial engagement). General rule of thumb on all movement regardless of speed, method or direction is to stay with the basics on the move maintaining good muzzle discipline and accurate shot placement. Don't let all the fundamentals of shooting fall apart just because you're moving the Stable Fighting Platform.

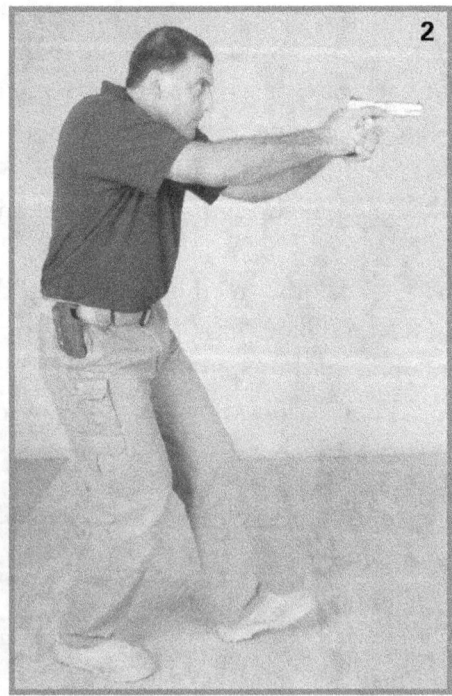

Part III: Building Blocks—DTI

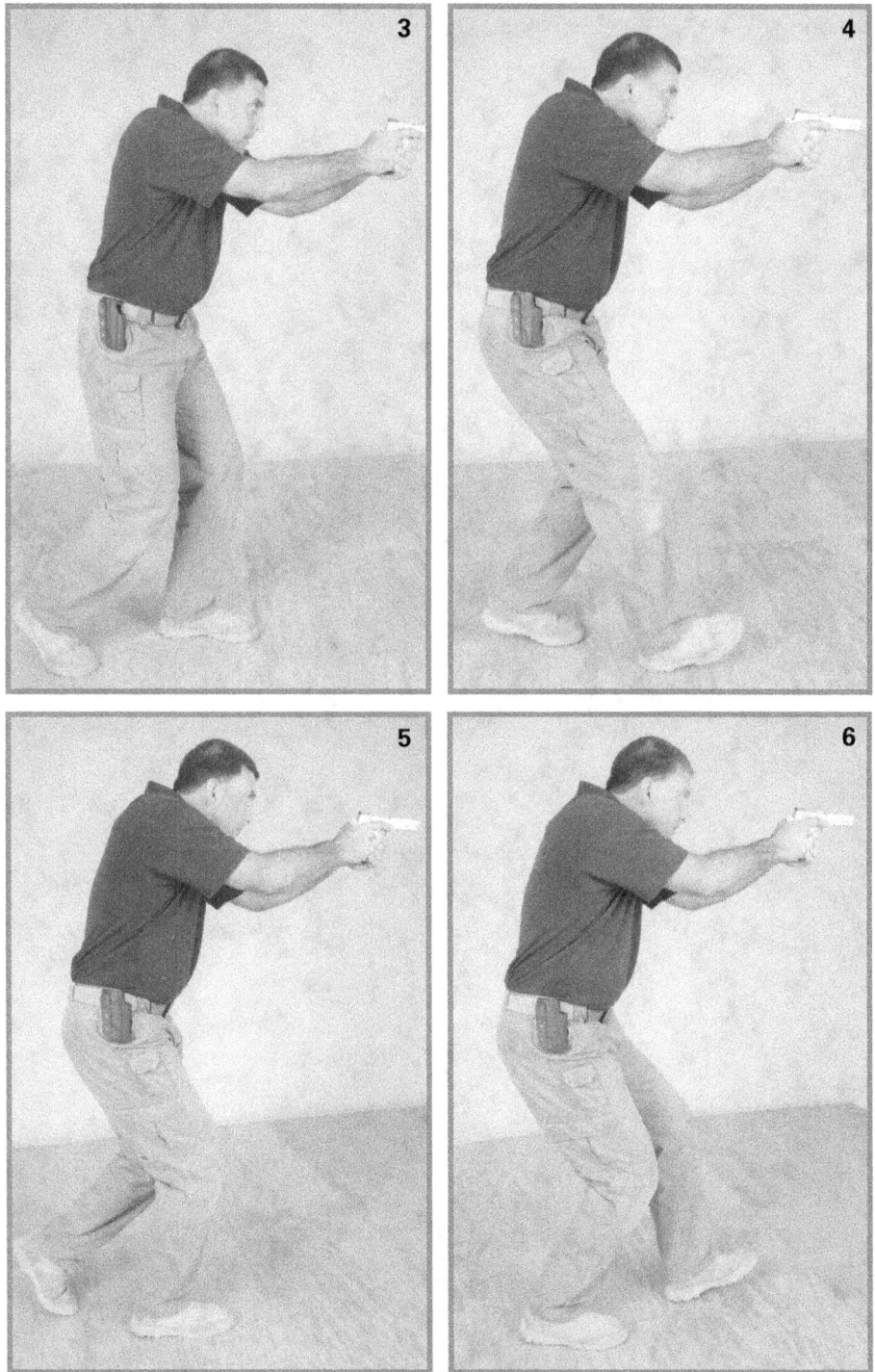

The cross-step or "Groucho" mobility sequence utilizing good muzzle discipline.

Bringing a Gun to a Knife Fight

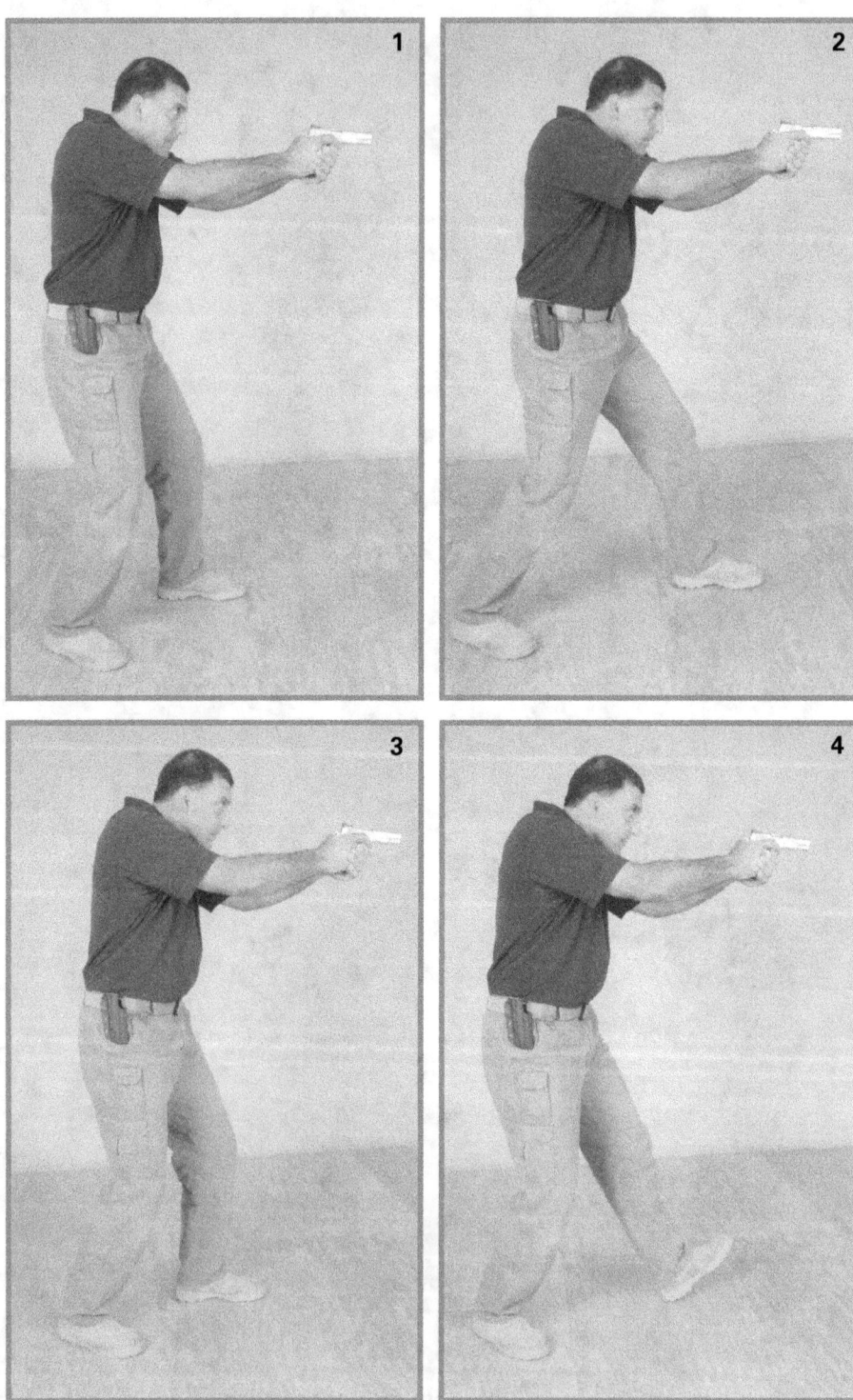

Part III: Building Blocks—DTI

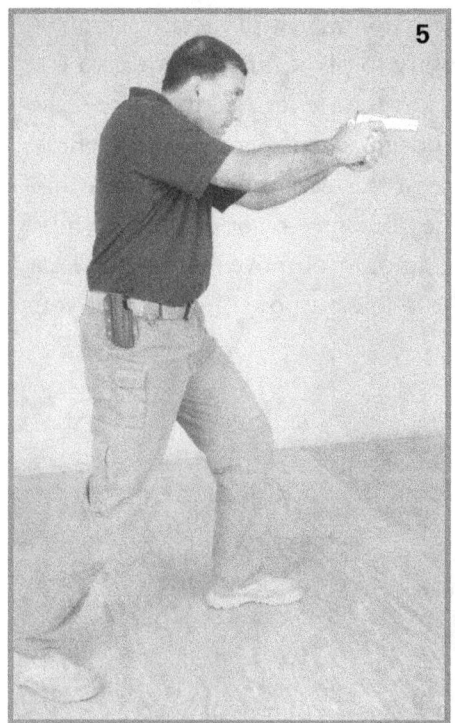 

The Step-slide method of moving the Stable Fighting Platform from position "A" to position "B" utilizing good muzzle discipline.

As with any tactical movement including the usage of a handgun, muzzle discipline is critical to accuracy of shot placement (and of course safety).

Pivots

In addition to moving the SFP forward, backward and with lateral movement, it may be necessary in the heat of physical CQB to turn your body in such a way as to bear your weapon on target to one side or the other to face the threat directly—also known as pivoting. Common to both SAI and DTI it is critical to engage the threat by facing the threat.

Combative circumstances and environment will dictate actual requirements; however it may be necessary to pivot *into* the threat to face it directly or to pivot *away* from the threat to face it directly. These movements of the SFP are approximately 90 degrees to the target. As applicable to moving the SFP in a straight line in the least amount of space and corresponding least amount of time, the 90 degree pivot of the SFP must be executed in a similar manner—least amount of movement in the least amount of time. Keep in mind that the whole purpose of control of your mobility is to regain the Power Curve.

Turn your head and immediately face the threat If you loose sight you could lose the fight.

Once the decision has been made to step toward the threat a helpful hint to pivoting is to turn the near foot pointing the toes toward the threat in anticipation of pivoting in that direction. Similar to moving the SFP with cross steps or shuffle steps, the foot that's in the direction you want to move is the one that moves first.

Stepping forward with the far leg initiates movement of the SFP pivot toward the threat—facing to engage threat.

Although stepping back is not recommended (stepping backward into the unknown, you can't see where you are going, etc.) the condition of your environment and especially the condition of your threat may dictate the necessity to pivot back and away from a threat. Keep in mind that CQB is a thinking-man's game and one must remain diligently solution-oriented millisecond by millisecond throughout the fight. Pivoting away from the threat may not be optimal, but may truly end up being your only option to gain those valuable commodities of space and time.

Bringing a Gun to a Knife Fight

Turn your head and look. Face the threat. If you lose sight you could lose the fight.

Once the decision has been made to step away from the threat a helpful hint to pivoting is to turn the far foot pointing the toes toward the threat in anticipation of pivoting away from that direction. Similar to moving the SFP with cross steps or shuffle steps, the foot that's in the direction you want to move is the one that moves first.

Stepping back with the near leg initiates movement of the SFP pivoting away from the threat—facing to engage threat.

Soft and Hard Targets

Effective use of targeting is one of the keys to proper weapon manipulation (sight alignment, good trigger control, and accurate round placement). It is essential that the operator understands both lethal and less-than-lethal capabilities of the selected weapon of opportunity—that is your bare hands or your handgun as both are applicable at such close contact ranges (very little space) and at such speeds (very little time to react) especially with relationship to SOI (Liability Gap).

Targets on the human body are classified into two categories, hard targets and soft targets. Hard targets include bone, tendon, muscle and other elements of the skeletal system. Soft targets include eyes, throat, and major blood channels. The primary targets for lethal weapons are the soft targets.

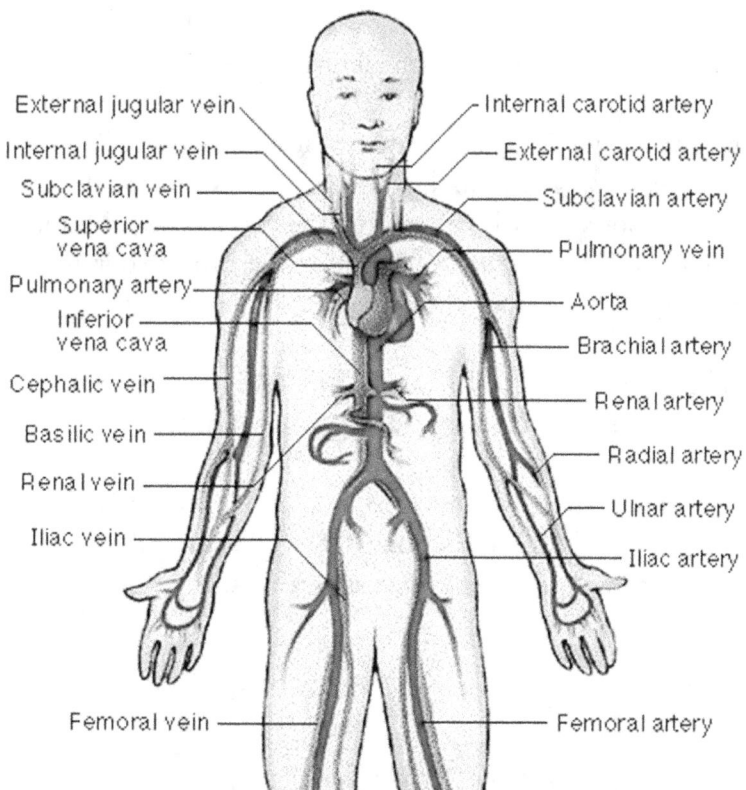

Soft Targets of the human Body

COMMITTED AND UNCOMMITTED ATTACKS

In any engagement with an enemy whether it be military, law enforcement or knife versus gun; regardless of the attack scenario there are only two types of an attack—these are known as a committed attack and an uncommitted attack. There exist no other types of attack.

An uncommitted attack is when your opponent is just standing there holding capability and intent [waving a knife at you and yelling from a distance] but not in any way physically changing distance—at this point you are still at NCR and have not yet engaged the SOI. In this scenario—with plenty of witnesses around—and you are fortunate enough to have already gone through all the cycles of action (including checking off the 28 boxes)—you stand at the ready with your blaster pointed in the right direction at NCR. From the legal perspective may you press off a round here?

A committed attack is given all of the above PLUS he takes that first step toward you which decreases the space, thus decreasing your reaction time physically raising your potential for injury and of course he's now in control of range and mobility which places you at a disadvantage as you have (if not already lost) given up the curve. Now with capability, means and clear demonstration of intent on the part of your attacker, from the legal perspective may you press off a round here?

Regardless of school (SAI or DTI), these two types of attack are considered to be either "Committed" or "Uncommitted."

If you remember watching that one Indiana Jones movie scene where Harrison Ford (as Indiana Jones) is faced with a sword wielding threat—was his opponent committed or uncommitted?

Part IV
Bringing a Gun to a Knife Fight

Combining Both Worlds

Now armed with the essential building blocks of both SAI and DTI firmly in place, presentation of the meat and potatoes materials of "How To" defeat a knife attack utilizing a handgun can begin in earnest.

The modular building blocks of SAI (Defensive Mindset, Conditions of Awareness, SOI, Handgun Presentation Cycle, Ready Positions, SDR, NSR, Multiple Target engagement, etc.) and DTI (Violence of Action, Action-Reaction Power Curve, Gross Motor Skills, Mechanical Compliance, OODA Cycle, Reactionary Gap, Liability Gap, Control of Position, Range and Mobility, Moving the SFP, etc.) can be combined in such a manner as to form our proverbial "bridge across both worlds" aka "seamless progression of training technology." As previously mentioned, it is the intention of this training material to facilitate the *commonalities* between DTI and SAI. The final step in this reconciliation is streamlined integration of the SAI / DTI modular blocks.

Building this bridge of commonalities includes both sides of the totality of defensive shooting—the combative concepts (software) as well as the physical techniques (hardware). Defensive Mindset, Conditions of Awareness, Scale of Injury, Action-Reaction, Cycles and Gaps, Control of Position, Range and Mobility are equally as important as Handgun Manipulation, Marksmanship, and mobility of the Stable Fighting Platform.

VIEW FROM ABOVE

Stepping back a little bit, let's take a 30,000 foot satellite photo at the problem we're really trying to solve here. There you are walking along minding your own business (hopefully not in Condition White) and all of a sudden out of the clear blue pops out a bad guy wielding what appears to be a sharp and pointed metallic object—identified by you as a knife—capable of delivering severe bodily injury and of course death (as per SOI). How do you respond?

Given the development of tools in the toolbox as presented in the previous sections of this manuscript obviously there are some questions that need answers. Let's start with safety first. Are you in a crowded parking lot with many innocent bystanders; are you located in your own home? What or who is your backstop—your own family members (wife, kids, etc.) team members, partner?

Now let's look at specific SAI / DTI considerations: Where are you in the OODA Cycle? Have you made the decision to utilize the handgun? If so have you checked off all 28 boxes? At what range is your opponent? Are you in a position of advantage or disadvantage (Red Zone or Green Zone)? Are you mobile or stationary? Where are you in the Liability Gap? Where are you in the Reactionary Gap? Where are you on the SOI? Do you have sufficient time to execute the Presentation Cycle? Are there single or multiple opponents? Are you in control of Range? Are you in control of Position? Are you in control of Mobility? Is your opponent in control of the fight? Are you in control of the fight? Have you assumed a Stable Fighting Platform? Can you move the SFP? Is this a committed or uncommitted attack? Do you have the space to move? Do you have the time to move? Which plan of action have you decided based on your OODA loop? By the way—did you in fact, bring a gun to this knife fight?

Now that's only the first couple of dozen questions or so that need answers and pretty darn quickly (PDQ). While nanoseconds burn away rapidly, the complexion of the game changes immediately as you fight to continue monitoring the condition of your threat, the condition of your

Part IV: Bringing a Gun to a Knife Fight

Danger can and does appear at the most inopportune and unexpected moments.

environment and the condition of your weapon system(s) moment by moment.

Where do we even start? How can we possibly answer all these questions, collect and analyze all this information, make a split-second decision based on processing and analysis of all that information and act upon that decision in a timely manner? The answer is the same answer to the question "How do you eat a roasted Elephant?" One piece at a time. We will analyze the above problem in a logical and progressive manner—one piece at a time.

An optimal approach to the solution of these many questions is to organize the training data into specific divisions. One can then analyze challenging a lethal threat (aka bringing a gun to a knife fight) from two combative ranges NCR and CR, further divided by area of operational engagement—open areas of engagement (parking lots, sidewalks, city parks, etc.) and confined areas of engagement (narrow hallways, staircases, airplane aisle, elevators, small rooms, etc.) and yet again divided into scenarios resulting in lower-end SOI and working toward the highest—that is from best case scenario to worst case scenario—from no injury to higher-level injury. In summary and for training purposes these divisions will be by range (NCR / CR), areas of engagement (open and confined) and SOI (from 1–5).

A fight needs to start from somewhere, you just don't sit in front of your television set and blink and then bam there you are standing in front of two gang-bangers armed with switchblades. "What if" scenarios can be without limit, so for sake of getting right to the point (no pun intended) a purposely selected and instructional-controlled set of scenarios will be utilized. Scope of study will focus on common-example scenarios as based on a combination of student input and actual incident reports over the past decade.

In an attempt to connect with the full range of readers, the following study will utilize civilian scenarios only (besides, all of us eventually go off duty at some point.) Any professional operator can easily read

Part IV: Bringing a Gun to a Knife Fight

between the lines here and superimpose these critical training components onto job-specific scenarios.

(If you happen to be a professional operator, have checked off all the boxes and have all the t-shirts, then please keep in mind that the pace of this training material needs to remain tenable to the full range of reader—from the greenest SAI / DTI student to the most seasoned retired professional.)

In addition to the scenarios, "Play-by-plays" and "Close-up Replays" will be utilized for deeper analysis. New instruction blocks as well as specialized drills are included as part of the training scenarios. Reference to technical SAI and DTI building blocks *will be italicized* for convenience of study reference.

SCENARIO 1—OAE AT NCR AND N/S

Beginning with the conditions of the environment, we'll start with an *open area of engagement (OAE)*, outdoors, late at night (low-light), little or no innocent bystanders (witnesses), in a concrete parking structure, you are on foot on your way from the elevator to your vehicle and yes carrying a concealed and loaded firearm (handgun) accessible to your weapon hand and on your person. You are additionally in *Condition Yellow* (as we should be at this time of night and in this environment) and have your keys in one hand and your cell phone in the other. However, this is one of the very rare times that you're not flapping lips on the phone.

You notice some movement up ahead in the periphery. You have *observed* something out of the corner of your eye at which point you have entered into the *OODA Cycle* (Observe) and have switched from *Condition Yellow* to *Condition Orange*. Your senses heighten and you move quickly to the next step on the *OODA cycle* (Orient). Utilizing your knowledge of *Control of Position, Range and Mobility* you determine your time and distance from the vehicle. You then decide to move toward a *position of advantage (POA)* in such a manner as to prepare for engagement of threat in a SFP and then finally *act* out your plan physically, all the while monitoring the *condition of your threat, the condition of the environment and the condition of your weapon system(s)*.

Suddenly and without warning, out pops a menacing-looking large athletic male wielding what appears to be a sharp and pointed metallic object, identified by you as a knife, capable of delivering severe bodily injury and, of course, death. This change in the *condition of threat* causes you to switch to *Condition Red* and run another *OODA loop*. You have *observed* that this threat although currently at NCR is heading straight toward you swinging a shining blade back and forth now engaging in conversation with you.

Now *oriented* to this new set of circumstances you register and process some important data: Threat is at NCR, in motion, closing quickly, armed with a dangerous weapon, I'm literally a few footsteps away from my vehicle, I remember that my gun is loaded and I'm pretty

Part IV: Bringing a Gun to a Knife Fight

Scenario 1—Out of nowhere an assailant appears at non-contact range in an open area of engagement, with time and distance on your side this likely altercation results in sufficient response time.

sure there's one in the tube, and I think I can get to it in time because of the NCR distance, but instead of taking time for the gun I think I can make it to the car in time. Next you make an important *decision*: Man, I'm close enough to the car. Have the keys in my hand, but I may have to go to guns—don't have enough time for both, gonna have to make the call here—OK car—safe bet. You finally *act* upon that decision. You work the keys into the car door fling it open slam it shut lock it and slam the same key into the ignition turn and zip out of that parking space. The threat remains at NCR sees that you're no longer a viable target, secures the blade and slips back into the darkness. Your SOI is at 1 his SOI is at 1. Tied at a score of 1 to 1, you drive away without a scratch. You drive away the victor.

Play by play: You had plenty of time and plenty of space—huge *Reactionary Gap* and with room to spare. He was at *NCR* the entire time and you were operating in an *open area of engagement* with plenty of space to move around. He used his legs to initiate a forward and aggressive approach you used your legs to counter that approach by moving your body to a *POA*. You were operating in the *green zone* and remained fully aware of the *condition of the threat*, the *condition of the environment* and the *condition of your weapon systems*. You made the best decision possible here to exit and extract from the engagement (*get out*) without a scratch. The *Liability Gap* put you at an *SOI* score of 1 and without incurring any criminal or civil liabilities.

Part IV: Bringing a Gun to a Knife Fight

SCENARIO 2—OAE AT NCR

Beginning with the conditions of the environment, we'll start with an *open area of engagement*, outdoors, late at night (low-light), a few innocent bystanders (witnesses) shuffling back and forth to and from their cars, in a concrete parking structure, you are on foot on your way from the elevator to your vehicle across an open area and yes carrying a loaded and concealed firearm (handgun) accessible to your weapon hand and on your person. You are additionally in *Condition Yellow* and have your keys in one hand and your cell phone in the other. However, this time you are talking on the phone and alternating your *Condition of Awareness* from *Condition White* to *Condition Yellow* and back to *Condition White* again as you try and place part of your attention into the conversation and part of your attention on to your environment.

While jabbering and looking forward you notice some movement of to the side. You have observed something out of the corner of your eye at which point you have entered into the *OODA Cycle* (Observe) and have switch from *Condition White/ Yellow* immediately to *Condition Orange* (awareness of a specific threat).

Your senses heighten, tell your wife that you'll call her back in a little bit and you move quickly to then next step on the *OODA cycle* (Orient). Utilizing your knowledge of *Control of Position, Range and Mobility* determine your time and distance from the vehicle. You then decide to move toward a POA in such a manner as to prepare for engagement of the threat in an SFP and then finally *act* out your plan physically, all the while monitoring the *condition of your threat*, the *condition of the environment* and the *condition of your weapon system(s)*.

Suddenly and without warning, out pops a menacing-looking large athletic male wielding what appears to be a sharp and pointed metallic object, identified by you as a knife, capable of delivering severe bodily injury and, of course, death. This change in the *condition of the threat* causes you to switch to *Condition Red* and run another *OODA loop*. You have *observed* that this threat although currently at NCR is heading straight toward you with his blade and his gaze fixed. Gaining speed and

Scenario 2—A concealed assailant waits for a victim of opportunity below exterior stairs in an open area of engagement.

Part IV: Bringing a Gun to a Knife Fight

closing the *Reactionary Gap* rapidly and as a result significantly raising your potential for severe bodily injury or death he is now trying to engage in pointed conversation with you.

Now *oriented* to this new set of circumstances you register and process some important data: Threat is at NCR but rapidly approaching *Contact Range*, in motion, closing extremely quickly, armed with a dangerous weapon, I'm literally a few footsteps away from my vehicle, I remember that my gun is loaded and I'm pretty sure there's one in the tube, and I think I can get to it in time because of the NCR distance, but he's moving PDQ and I don't really think I can make it to the car in time. Next you make an important *decision*: Man, I'm getting close to the car and have the keys in my hand, but I may have to go to guns—don't have enough time for both, gonna have to make the call here—really like to make the car but oh [expletive] he's on me. He moves to the very edge of NCR and you realize that the car is not an option—time to go to guns. You then *act* upon that decision.

Training Note: In the world of defensive shooting there is a price tag for everything. If you're moving you compromise shot placement; however, if you remain stationary then you are a stationary target but the up side is that this allows better shot placement. Accurate shots cost time.

The thought "the price tag for speed is shot placement" rips through your noodle as you are in the process of dropping everything in your hands and although in the middle of the OODA Cycle you check off all 28 boxes *(Real World Reasons)*, move to an SFP and commence the 8-Step cycle of *handgun presentation*: 1. Clear away your concealment garment(s) and simultaneously grip the firearm while defeating any retention devices on the holster system. 2. Clear from your carry position and Cant to Retention Position. 3. Hands come together. 4. Punch and Look. 5. Assess the situation.

You stop mid-cycle here and as a direct result of change of *condition of threat*, start a new OODA Loop *observing* that the bad guy stopped in his tracks and switched gears from a *committed attack* to an *uncommitted attack*.

Bringing a Gun to a Knife Fight

Barely at the edge of NCR you attempt issuing verbal commands but nothing understandable makes its way from your lips. Regardless, bad guy gets the full story loud and clear from both the intent he reads in your eyes and the *forward–aggressive–effective* placement of your *front sight* at *contact ready* about three meters from his face.

He freezes, as a direct result, for a spilt second and your *OODA cycle* kicks down to *orient* to this new *condition of the threat, condition of your environment* and *condition of your weapon system*. He backs off to full NCR while you maintain control of the firearm with *good sight alignment, sight picture, muzzle discipline* and hang tough at the "and fire if necessary" part of the presentation cycle Step 5. Other folks start screaming "He's got a gun! He's got a gun!" (by the way they are referring to *you*) and by now the bad guy's already in another zip code.

What is the condition of your threat? No longer present, so you complete your Presentation Cycle *without firing a single round* from Step 5 to Step 6. Drop down to *Low Ready*, 7. Look and Assess, and finally 8. Holster. Reattaching all safe-carry / retention devices, you keep your eyes downrange in the last-seen area of threat, reach for and recover your grounded gear.

You work the keys into the car door fling it open slam it shut, lock it and slam the same key into the ignition turn and zip out of that parking space. The threat remains nowhere to be seen. Your SOI is at 1 his SOI is at 1. Tied at a score of 1 to 1, you drive away without a scratch. No "knife fight" here—you are the victor.

Play by play: You really didn't have that much time or space—small *Reactionary Gap* and with not a lot of room to spare. He was at NCR for a while but moved dangerously close to the dreaded *Contact Range*. You were operating in an *open area of engagement* with plenty of space to move around but also a lot of friendly bodies in the background and you weren't really so sure about taking that shot if it was needed. You were operating in the *Green Zone* most of the time but knocking at the door of the *Red Zone* as he closed that *Reactionary Gap* so quickly. Man it was shocking how fast it went down. You were fully aware of the ever-changing *conditions of the threat, the condition of the environment and the condition of your weapon system.* You made the best decision possible to go to guns, not fire a shot, and exit without anyone getting your license plate (hopefully). But you got out without a scratch. Liability Gap (even as narrow as it was) puts you at SOI score of 1—No Injury and without incurring any criminal or civil liabilities (you hope). You walked away the winner.

The 21-Foot Rule

While we're on the subject of a bad guy closing the gap very quickly with an edged weapon, there's a certain retired Salt Lake City, Utah, police lieutenant named Dennis Tueller who in the early 1980's developed a seminal (and now universally accepted) training principle regarding reactive-response to an attack with an edged weapon from a distance of approximately twenty-one feet.

Police Lieutenant and Field Commander Dennis B. Tueller (Ret.) is a 25-year veteran of the Salt Lake City Police Department. For his many years of service as his department's primary Firearms & Tactics Instructor and Range Master, he received the "Chief's Award" for*:* *"Outstanding performance in developing firearms policy and providing firearms training."* An Assistant Chief also recognized Dennis for his supervision of the Field Training Officer Program, writing: *"Due to your leadership our FTO Program is one of the best in the country."*

A former Practical Shooting Champion, Dennis has become an internationally recognized instructor in firearms, officer safety, winning mind-set, survival tactics, and related subjects. He is a member of the International Law Enforcement Educators and Trainers Association, The Glock Shooting Sports Foundation and is a Life Member of the National Rifle Association. He Served On The Board Of Directors Of The International Association Of Law Enforcement Firearms Instructors (1989-92), is still an active member, and frequently presents training as a guest instructor at their U.S. and International Training Conferences.

An author, speaker, consultant, and court-recognized expert witness on police firearms training and the judicious use of lethal force, Lt. Tueller is respected as one of the top officers in his field. He researched and developed a training protocol and published the seminal article, *"How Close is Too Close"* (S.W.A.T. Magazine, March 1983) identifying critical concepts which influenced a revolution in tactical training doctrine (the *"Tueller Principle"*). He is also the writer, co-producer, and host of an award-winning educational video tape entitled *"Choose Your Weapon... a Guide to Selecting the Self-Defense Handgun."* Dennis has been a featured presenter on the Law Enforcement Television Network, has hosted the *"Action Law Enforcement Video Magazine,"* and has testified before the Judiciary Committee of the U.S. House of Representatives regarding firearms legislation. As the former Director of Training for Action Target, Inc. (the largest manufacturer of shooting range equipment in the U.S.) he planned, organized, and conducted *Practical Shooting Range Development and Use* training seminars, and is consistently a top-rated presenter at their annual *Advanced Law Enforcement Training Camps*.

As an instructor and coach for Thunder Ranch, the American Pistol Institute, Defense Training International, The American Small Arms Academy, International Training Consultants, The Police Training Division, and the U.S. Department Of Energy National Training Center, Lt. Tueller has trained numerous firearms instructors, police officers, security agents, S.W.A.T. teams, military personnel, and responsible law-abiding civilians throughout the free world. Dennis is currently (as of this writing) a Firearms Instructor for Glock Professional, Inc., and conducts Glock Armorer Courses and Instructor Workshops for law enforcement agencies and firearms professionals throughout North America.

Lt. Teuller writes: "In March of 1983 *S.W.A.T. Magazine* published an article I had written entitled: *"How Close is Too Close?"* This article shared some recently observed concepts and tactics regarding reaction and response times during armed confrontations involving contact-weapons.

One of the first to comment on this article and elaborate on these concepts was an author and firearms instructor named Massad Ayoob. In his writings he has referred to this as the "Tueller Principle." He also conducts a training exercise for his students to demonstrate these principles which he calls the "Tueller Drill." I appreciate his acknowledgement of my contribution to our profession (though I am concerned that my name could end up on a subpoena someday because somebody got hurt running the "Tueller Drill"—be careful what gets named after you!)

Over the years, the terms "21-Foot Rule" or sometimes the "Tueller Rule" have crept into the lexicon as expressions of these concepts. And while I understand the desire to have a concise phrase to make the point, I don't care to use the word "rule" and have tried to avoid it in any of my writing or training on this subject.

Why not a "rule"? Because words have meaning. What do you think of when you hear the word "rule"? *"Follow the rules..." "Don't break the rules..." "That is a violation of the rules..."* In that context, the "21-Foot Rule" could be incorrectly interpreted to *require* you to shoot someone who is fifteen feet away brandishing a knife. Conversely, it could be erroneously inferred that "the rule" *prohibits* the shooting of this same would-be slasher if he is twenty four feet and nine inches away. This may be over-stating the case, but I don't think so, as I have heard people express both of these views when discussing the subject.

The folks at Calibre Press also referenced my original article in their second textbook on officer survival entitled: "The Tactical Edge," and further expanded on the concepts and principles in their excellent training video: "Surviving Edged Weapons." They coined the term "proximics" and refer to the "reactionary gap" when presenting scenarios depicting realistic attacks that highlight the principles of time, distance, reaction, and response. I very much prefer this terminology, as it is more open-ended and takes into consideration the countless variables that will exist in our armed confrontations. Variables in addition to proximity, such as the physical size and condition of both the aggressor and the defender, the presence of obstacles, cover, bystanders, partners, the terrain, footing, lighting, environment, etcetera, etcetera, etcetera. All of these factors combine to create the "totality of circumstances" which will drive our use-of-force decisions.

Understanding, training with, and correctly applying these principles can help you preempt an assault, prevail against your attacker, and successfully survive the legal aftermath."

Accepted as training standard throughout the professional training community, the Tueller Principle continues to be utilized in the development of action-reaction awareness and shooting skills. This important training principle states that an average male between the ages of 18 and 32 can close a gap of approximately 21 feet in about 2.5 seconds. This gives the reader a sort of time frame for time and space relationship (Reactionary Gap) with regards to how quickly—and accurately—shots must be placed down range.

Reverse-Tueller Drill

If you're interested to see how well you would fare in Scenario Two, go ahead and try this simple live-fire square-range drill you can run to test your ability to meet or exceed the Tueller Rule requirements.

Set Up: Be sure you are at a secured range and you are cleared hot from the RM and RSOs. Following all safety and range rules, set up paper targets and stand at the seven yard line. Wearing additional garment to simulate concealed carry, face down range, make ready to a full load and holster. Remain facing downrange in the *hands below* position and ask your partner (unarmed) to face up range and place his hand on your shoulder. At visual command of the RM he will release your shoulder and begin running up range (in the direction he is facing) as quickly as possible.

Part IV: Bringing a Gun to a Knife Fight

Drill: The RM / RSO will issue commands and run shooting string first by the numbers and then all as one motion dry fire and then lastly using live rounds. Instead of audio or visual command, simply wait until your partner releases your shoulder. Once you feel the release of your shoulder draw your weapon from concealed carry and deliver two round center mass on the target as rapidly and as accurately as you can. After delivering two rounds to the body, come to the low ready, look, assess and recover to your holster. Upon hearing the rapport of the second shot your partner will stop running and mark his place. Once you are safely in the holster and the RM / RSO has called the line safe you may wait for the command to turn and face up range. On the command of turn, you may now see how far your partner made it before you got your second round into the target—providing you got your hits. This drill will provide a shooter in training some degree of reality-check on his / her ability to handle a threat at seven yards based on the Tueller Principle.

Stand holstered with hands above and in a stable fighting platform at the seven yard line facing safely down range.

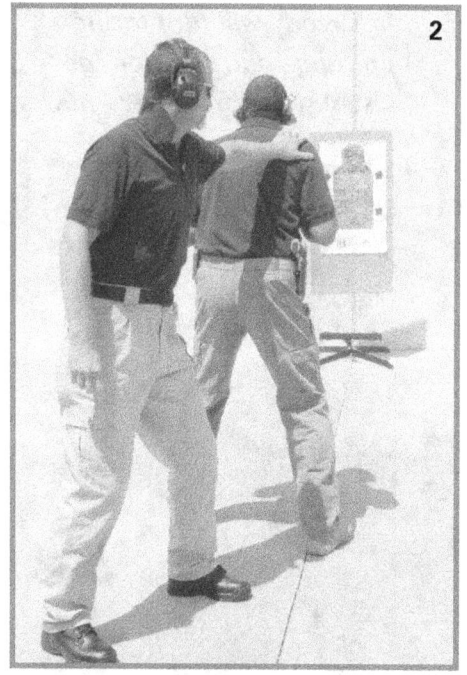

Remain facing safely down range—training partner places hand on shoulder and checks with the shooter to find if he is ready to run the drill.

Bringing a Gun to a Knife Fight

Role player, after checking with the shooter to find that he's ready will turn facing up range and wait for "go" visual signal from RM / RSO.

Observing "go" visual signal from RM / RSO role player removes his hand from your shoulder and begins to run up range. Utilizing tactile sensing of removal of role player's hand from your shoulder as your cue, you execute a full presentation followed by two rounds to the body.

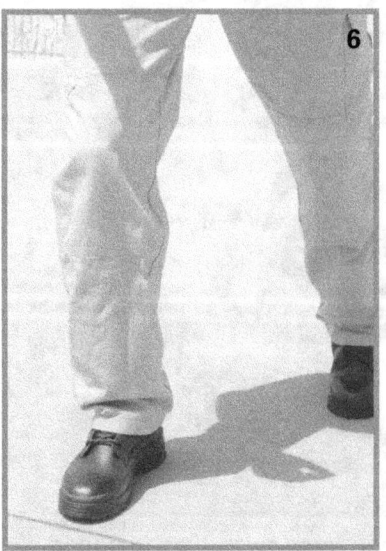

Role player waits until the sound of the second round before stopping his movement up range.

Mark the front of the role player's boot at the exact position he stopped running (at the sound of the second shot).

Scenario 3—CAE at NCR

Beginning with the conditions of the environment, we'll start with a *confined area of engagement (CAE)*, indoors (hallway), late at night (low-light), no noticeable bystanders or pedestrians (witnesses) in the hallway but some are shuffling back and forth to and from their cars. In the hallway of a concrete parking structure, you are on foot on your way from the elevator to your vehicle traveling down a long, dimly-lit corridor and, yes, carrying a concealed and loaded firearm (handgun) accessible to your weapon hand and on your person. You are additionally in *Condition Yellow* and have your keys in one hand and your cell phone in the other. You are not talking on your cell phone and remain in *Condition Yellow*.

You notice some movement up ahead on one side of the corridor—but it's too dimly lit to positively identify. Nonetheless you have *observed* something out of the corner of your eye at which point you have entered into the *OODA Cycle* (Observe) and have switch from *Condition Yellow* to *Condition Orange*. Your senses heighten, and you move quickly to the next step on the *OODA cycle* (Orient). Utilizing your knowledge of *Control of Position, Range and Mobility* determine your time and distance from the confined area of the hallway to open space. You then decide to move toward a POA on one side of the space-limiting hallway *(Condition of your Environment)* in such a manner as to prepare for engagement of threat in a SFP and then finally *act* out your plan physically, all the while monitoring the *condition of your threat, the condition of the environment* and *the condition of your weapon system(s)*.

Suddenly and without warning, the shadow appears again and coming at you from a short distance (yet still at NCR) a menacing-looking large athletic male wielding what appears to be a sharp and pointed metallic object, identified by you as a knife, capable of delivering severe bodily injury and, of course, death. This change in the *condition of the threat* causes you to switch to *Condition Red* and run another *OODA loop*. You have *observed* that this threat although currently at NCR is heading straight toward you with his blade and his gaze fixed. Gaining speed and closing the *Reactionary Gap* rapidly he is now preparing to thrust into your abdomen.

Bringing a Gun to a Knife Fight

Scenario 3—An attacker waits concealed indoors in a confined area of engagement.

Part IV: Bringing a Gun to a Knife Fight

Now *oriented* to this new set of circumstances your heart starts pounding faster as you register and process important data: Threat is at NCR but rapidly approaching *Contact Range*, in motion, closing extremely quickly, armed with a dangerous weapon, I'm too far to reach the end of the hall way and no time or space to turn back without getting skewered, I remember that my gun is loaded and I'm pretty sure there's one in the tube, and I think I can get to it in time because of the NCR distance, but he's moving PDQ and I don't really think I can make it to the end of the hall especially past him and that giant knife.

With palms sweating, you make an important *decision*: Man, he's right on me, one more step and he'll be at *Contact Range*, I may have time to step out of the way, but I may need to go to guns—don't have enough time for both, gonna have to make the call here—I'd really like to step out of the way but oh [expletive] he's on me. He moves even closer to Contact Range. He's just about to place you from Green Zone to Red Zone. Your mind is processing at light speed—movement forward no longer an option—time to go to guns. You recall that accurate shots cost time, but you also need to move out of the way of the incoming blade. You finally *act* upon that decision.

The thought "price tag for speed is shot placement" enters into your mind for a split second as you are in the process of dropping everything in your hands and although in the middle of the OODA Cycle you check of all 28 boxes (*Real World Reasons*), change your physical posture from unstable to an SFP, you immediately move off the line of attack (LOA) to 45 degrees angled back to your strong side and simultaneously (while moving your SFP form point A to point B) commence the 8-Step cycle of handgun presentation.

Training Note: Stepping 45 degrees off the LOA while simultaneously presenting the firearm very effectively changes your physical position (new GPS coordinates) and the totality of the dynamics of the fight in your favor. Moving off the LOA places you in control of the *power curve* and forces your opponent to react to you. Now realizing he's behind the curve your opponent MUST react to your new physical positioning if he wants to stay in the fight. Unfortunately for him you have now gained the upper hand in both time and position.

Right smack in the middle of your *handgun presentation cycle:* 1. Clear away any concealment garment(s) and simultaneously grip the firearm while defeating any retention devices on the holster system. 2. Clear from your carry position and Cant to Retention Position. 3. Hands come together. 4. Punch and Look. 5. Assess the situation. You stop mid-cycle here and start a new OODA Loop *observing* that the bad guy is continuing to move toward you in a full *committed attack*. Barely at the edge of NCR you managed to somehow simultaneously move your center mass off the line of attack 45 degrees to the strong side (but you forgot draw in your support hand to your center in the heat of battle and left it hanging out there so he caught a little piece of your hand with his knife and that reminds you to bring it in to your center. *(Remember that light switch analogy?)* Since he's now so close *(Contact Range)* you are forced into the *Red Zone* and forced to change from a *sighted fire* position into the *retention position*. Instantly and due to proximity of threat, while he's trying to catch up (his reaction slower than your action—by your simultaneous 45 degree step plus firearm presentation you have placed him behind the *power curve*) you give yourself the green light—this is a good shoot. A new thought rips through your mind like a tornado and stops your cycle of action dead in its tracks— man, everything's riding on this next shot; my house, my car, my career, my mortgage, my family even my own personal freedoms if this is tried criminally and or civilly, all riding on the outside edge of each of these bullets and at their terminal resting place. Nonetheless, you have decided in your mind that this is a good shoot (time and the legal system will either confirm or deny that assertion in the future) so you apply *unsighted fire* from the *retention position* and hammer two rounds toward *center mass* of the assailant. He freezes for a spilt second. It appears to be the case that at least one of the rounds maybe hit, but you can't tell if you got a hit (and if it was a hit then was it a hit to a vital or not) and your *OODA cycle* kicks down to *orient* to this new *condition of the threat, condition of your environment and condition of your weapon system.*

Part IV: Bringing a Gun to a Knife Fight

He drops away rapidly and staggers backward into the darkness to full NCR holding on to his belly while you maintain control of the firearm and since the range changed you switch back to the superior *sighted fire* position with your arms now extended.

Unable to attain good sight alignment and a good sight picture as your target has changed physical position in such a manner as to impair your visual acuity, you can't really take another shot, but hang tough at the "and fire again if necessary" part of the presentation cycle Step 5. When he, apparently wounded, staggers back and away, dropping the knife and slipping back into the darkness.

Observing that your opponent has dropped his weapon, may, in fact, be mortally wounded (although you have no real confirmation he's even been hit), you observe that the threat is no longer present, complete your Presentation Cycle from Step 5. to Step 6. Drop down to Low Ready, 7. Look and Assess, and finally 8. Holster. Reattaching all safe-carry / retention devices, you keep your eyes downrange in the last-seen area of threat and reach for your grounded gear.

You finally make it to the end of the hallway—threat nowhere in sight and get to your car holding on to your cut hand. You work the keys into the car door fling it open slam it shut lock it and slam the same key into the ignition turn and zip out of that parking space. The threat remains nowhere to be seen and has become a permanent part of the darkness. Your SOI is at 2 (maybe 3) his SOI is at least 3 (perhaps 4, maybe even a 5)—you have no way of confirming hits other than observable physical reaction. You drive away toward a clinic as you can see that you need a few stitches. Bad guy scored an SOI 2 and you scored possibly a 3 or 4 (may even be a 5) on the SOI. Although sustaining a level 2 injury, you remain the victor.

Play by play: You really didn't have that much time or space to operate—small *Reactionary Gap* and with not a lot of room to spare. He was at NCR for a while but moved dangerously close to the dreaded *Contact Range*—in fact at the end of his charge he did in fact change ranges from NCR to *Contact Range*. You were operating in a *confined* *area of engagement* and not much space to move around. No innocent pedestrians (to the best of your knowledge—but your focus was predominantly on the threat) so you seemed sure about taking that shot if needed. You were operating in the *Green Zone* most of the time but eventually ended up in the *Red Zone* as he closed that gap so very quickly. You forgot to draw in your support hand and the price for that mistake was a level 2 on the SOI. Could be much worse—but could also have been better. Man it was shocking how fast it went down.

You were fully aware of the ever-changing *conditions of the threat, the condition of the environment* and the *condition of your weapon system*. You made the best decision possible to go to guns and were agile enough to turn the tables on your opponent by moving 45 degrees angular and back off the LOA to your strong side placing him on the reaction side of the fence, behind the curve and at a position of both time and space disadvantage. You managed to simultaneously move off LOA and complete the *Presentation Cycle* and in a timely manner. Yes, he caught a piece of your hand, but you managed to get at least one maybe two round placements. You were fortunate to have handled the threat in a *forward, aggressive and effective* manner.

You were doubly fortunate to exit without anyone getting your license plate (hopefully). But you sustained a *Recoverable Injury* and without incurring any criminal or civil liabilities (you hope). All in all it wasn't really all that bad if you look at it from the big picture of winning or losing the "knife fight"—you won.

Close-up Replay 1: Legs versus Legs. In order to move the knife from position A to position B your opponent had to move the vehicle which carried the knife (that being his body) via the use of his legs. He used his legs to move toward you and you used your legs to move 45 degrees off the line of attack angular to your strong side. Had you not used your legs and just stood there and relied solely on a clean and flawless handgun presentation with no malfunctions (mechanical or operator) to solve the problem, this immobility would have placed you at much closer range and of course dramatically increased your SOI—instead of your hand, it could have easily been your throat that got cut to the bone had you not moved off to a POD.

Although really not part of this training program, it's important to note that (in the case of a non-sworn civilian) you just presented your firearm, dispatch at least two rounds down range at another human being and most likely hit your target. If you lived in California, it would be *you* who ended up in jail in the end for defending your life using a firearm against that poor helpless victim of our capitalistic society, but what about other states? Are you familiar with your state gun laws regarding appropriate follow-up if you are involved in an actual shooting? Do you have a gun-educated attorney on retainer?

Weapon Retention Position

Let's take a closer look at this *weapon retention* position. In this scenario you were trying to operate in a very *confined area of operation* and due to proximity of the attack, trying to maintain a *sighted fire* position without moving out of the way would have ended up in disaster.

Remaining stationary along the LOA in full sighted fire position places your Center Line (C/L) and Center Mass (C/M) including both hands at risk for increased injury as well as compromising shot placement—less than optimal.

Similarly, even if you did move out of the way and kept your arms extended in a sighted fire position, although perhaps less of a disaster, this would have still significantly increased your SOI for although you may be delivering rounds downrange, your opponent is simultaneously hacking away at both your extended arms, hands and fingers and within a matter of tenths of a second—may have even reached your neck.

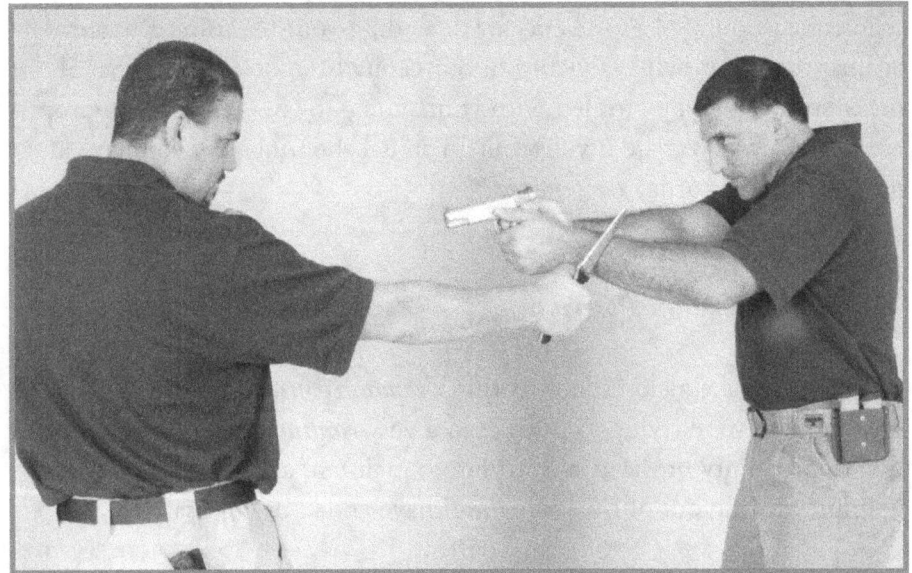

Moving off LOA, but still in full sighted fire extended position may decrease SOI to C/M, but again both hands are at risk for increased injury as well as compromise of shot placement—less than optimal.

Given the very confined area of engagement (CAE), it is critical that you utilize what valuable little space is available to deliver maximum effectiveness with minimal injury.

Part IV: Bringing a Gun to a Knife Fight

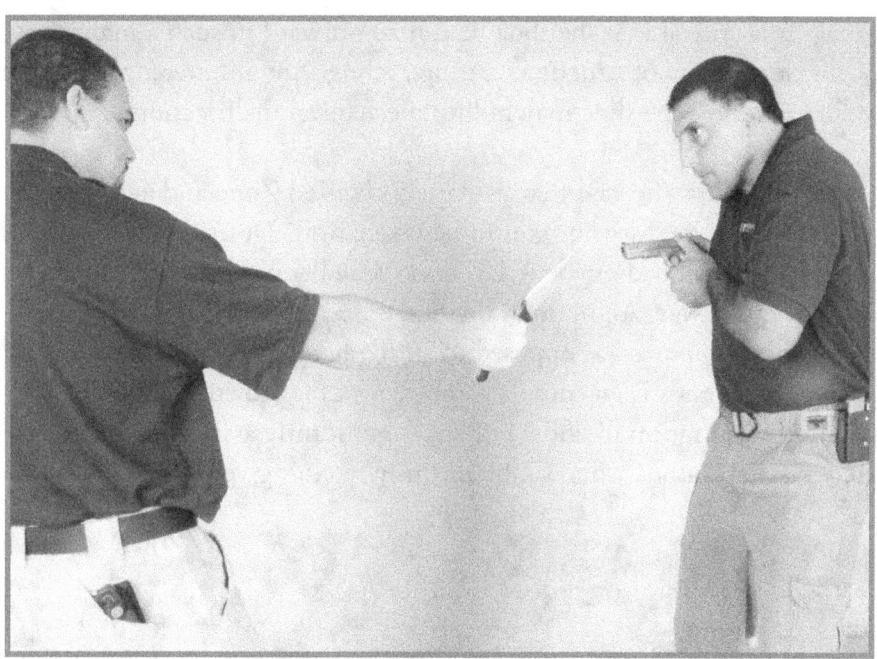

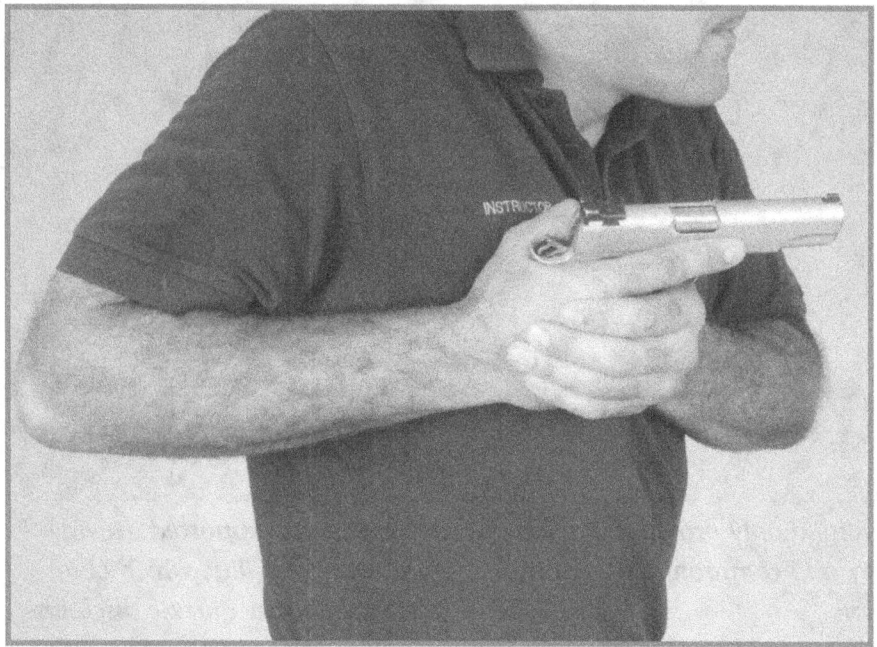

Key reference points of the Retention Position are: Pulse to vest up high, slide canted outboard and muzzle pointing in, strong side supported.

It is critical that the slide be canted outward in such a manner as to run clear of any obstructions during cycling. Any interference with the cycling action of the slide may induce mechanical malfunction.

Since it is the case that you are in the Red Zone and at CR these conditions are ripe for your gun to be taken away. Don't fool yourself into thinking that any bad guy who has done time behind bars *doesn't* train to take your gun away. An optimal method of weapon retention is to utilize strong hand supported as opposed to strong hand unsupported. The usage of two hands is far more advantageous as it provides not only stability and concentration of effort but also significantly assists in your accurately placing rounds while simultaneously retaining your weapon.

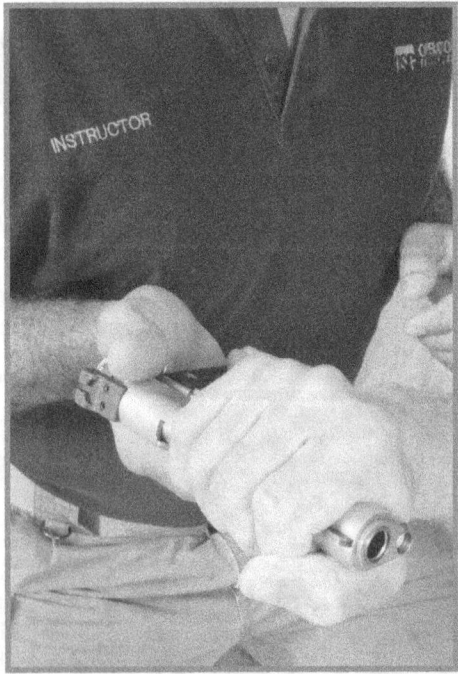

Strong hand only provides limited stability and compromises weapon retention.

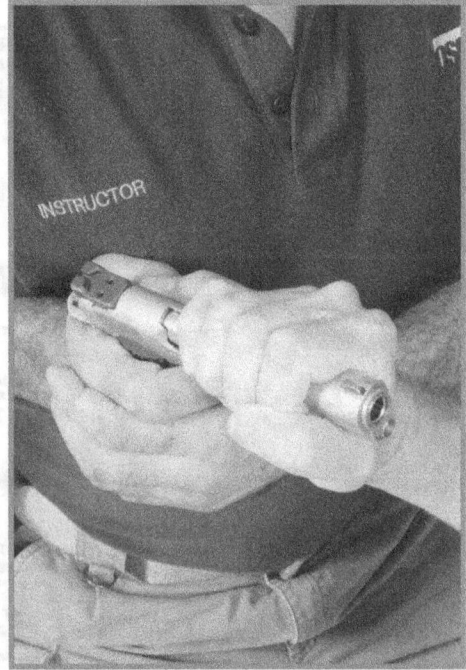

Strong hand supported provides maximum stability, which conducive to better muzzle discipline, which in turn enables more accurate shot placement and additionally supports weapon retention.

Part IV: Bringing a Gun to a Knife Fight

In the world of defensive shooting and with regards to the retention position, there are two opposing schools of thought. One says just get the weapon out of the holster as fast as you can and "rock and lock" (down low right at hip level) on your opponent—the plus is speed, the downside is measurable decrease in round placement accuracy. The opposing school of thought is to take the extra fraction of a second to bring the muzzle up higher and supported (with two hands) thus dramatically increasing placement potential—the price tag: time. The method you choose as the shooter under duress is of course a personal training preference. However, it has been proven in case history that in combative (defensive) shooting, shot placement is paramount over speed.

Weapon Retention Live Fire Drill

If you are personally interested in which retention technique would serve you best under stress, go ahead and try this simple live-fire square-range drill you can run to test your ability to respond from the weapon retention position.

Set Up: Be sure you are at a secured range and you are cleared hot from the RM and RSOs. Following all safety and range rules, set up paper targets and stand at the three yard line. Wearing additional garment to simulate concealed carry, face down range, make ready to a full load and holster. Remain facing downrange in the *hands below* position ready to follow range commands.

Drill: The RM / RSO will issue commands and run shooting string first by the numbers and then all as one motion dry fire and then lastly using live rounds. The first set, on the command of "up," you will deliver two rounds to center mass of the target from the "rock and lock" position (removing the pistol from the holster and pointing it toward the target while still at your hip level and pressing off two rounds in that same position.)

The second set, on the command of "up," you will deliver two rounds center mass of the target from the *weapon retention position* (pulse to vest up high, slide canted outboard and muzzle pointing in, strong side supported). At the end of these sets, the RM / RSO will then run you through the same exact sets but on a timer. After running several full sets, what are your best times? Which method was faster? Which method was more accurate? Which of the two would you have used if it were you actually in this scenario?

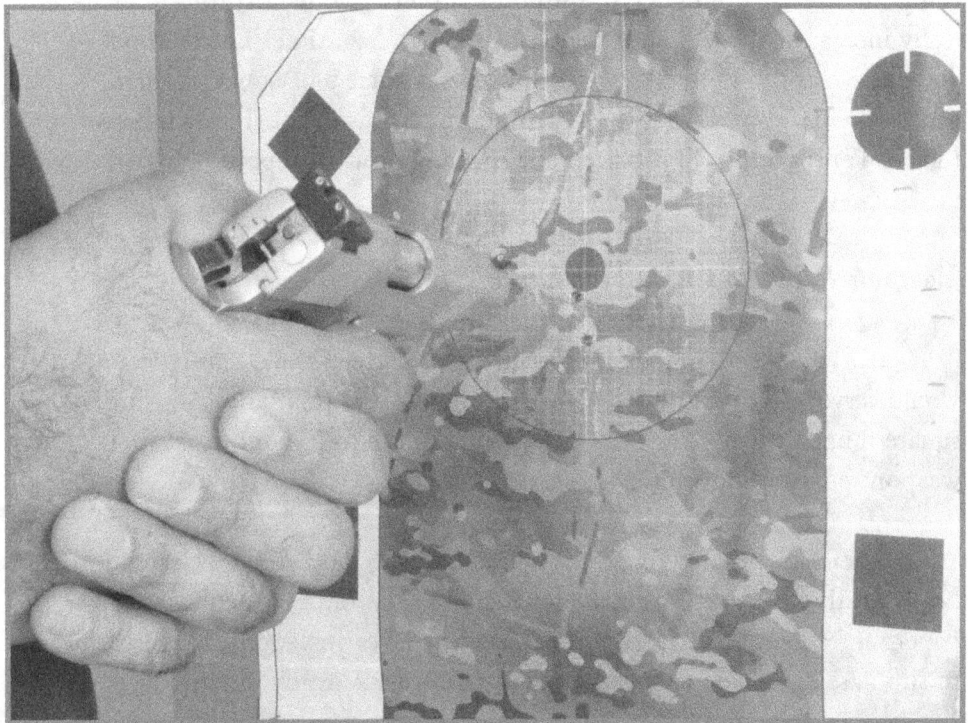

Close-up Replay 2: Shot Placement Cycle. Zooming in on exactly what happens at the exact moment the first round went off, as well as firing the second round, there was a tremendous amount of physical activity by way of cycles of action within cycles of action. The first layer was of course checking off the 28 boxes *(Real World Reasons)*—then if no problems there, we moved on to the next layer of cycles.

Although this section covers Weapon Retention *(unsighted fire)*, for comprehensive illustration purposes, the following detailed hot-wash of a *Shot Placement Cycle* additionally covers the "what if" example of *sighted fire*.

SHOT PLACEMENT CYCLE

The first cycle of action when faced with a deadly threat:

OODA Cycle

1. Observe

2. Orient

3. Decide—this threat needs to be stopped and the decision to shoot has been confirmed

4. Act—time to go to guns.

Then, the second cycle kicks in:

Gun Handling Cycle (GHC)

GHC1. **Handgun Presentation Cycle (HPC)**

HPC1. Clear away your concealment garment(s) and simultaneously grip the firearm while defeating any retention devices on the holster system.

HPC2. Clear from your carry position and Cant to Retention Position defeating any mechanical safeties.

HPC3. Hands come together.

HPC4. Punch and Look.

GHC2. Sight alignment

GHC3. **Sight Picture Cycle (SPC)**

SPC1. Optic nerves prepare eye to find the front sight at the moment it moves onto the target.[1]

SPC2. Eyes focus on vetted target.

SPC3. Eyes then re-focus from target to front sight.

SPC4. Eyes then follow the top of the muzzle through recoil cycle and

SPC5. Return to focus on the front sight.

SPC6. Eyes then move either to assess a neutralized threat or right back on the front sight based on the dynamic condition of the threat.

GHC4. **Trigger Control Cycle (TCC)**

TCC1. Decision is to shoot,

TCC2. Conscious decision is transmitted to conscious-neural receptors via bio-chemical processes which move as

TCC3. Nerve impulses traveling down nerves to axonal nerve endings where the

TCC4. Axonal ending produces neurotransmitters

TCC5. Crossing synaptic space to muscle fibers

---

[1] The human eye is able to see almost thirty pictures a second, which is why video must display at approximately thirty frames per second to avoid presenting a jerky image. Among those who haven't trained extensively to build their speed, the pause for sight alignment and sight picture is often the longest part of the draw-to-firing sequence.

TCC6. Leading to a chain of additional biochemical processes which lead to

TCC7. Contraction of the target muscles which

TCC8. Apply leverage on the bones and joints which then

TCC9. Engage trigger manipulation by way of a controlled press directly to the rear of the trigger guard with the trigger finger in such a manner as to induce a Trigger Break Cycle.

TCC10. **Trigger Break Cycle (TBC)**

TBC1. The depressing of the trigger past reset position disengages the trigger safety which allows

TBC2. Full and open movement of trigger in rotation at the trigger pin which in turn

TBC3. Directs the trigger bar to the rear of the receiver which in turn

TBC4. Disengages the firing pin catch which in turn

TBC5. Releases the firing pin which moves in a forward motion building momentum based on the strength of the firing pin spring and

TBC7. Strikes the face of the primer

TBC8. Compressing primer compound against the anvil (located inside the primer) which

TBC9. Sparks and builds internal pressure thus

TBC10. Blasting through the hole

TBC11. Igniting the cartridge powder which in turn

TBC12. Builds tremendous internal pressure which

TBC13. Decompresses the crimp (fixing bullet to casing)

TBC14. Causing bullet to be released in a forward direction expanding to fill (and is guided by) the lands and groves (rifling) of the barrel along the path of least resistance on out from the muzzle of the firearm and heading downrange.[2]

GHC5. Mechanical Cycle of Action (MCA)

MCA1. Feed—Another round from the magazine is moved up the feed ramp

MCA2. Chamber—round is mounted in chamber

MCA3. Lock—chamber is locked

MCA4. Fire—pin strikes primer igniting cartridge powder (launching second round)

MCA5. Unlock—gas pressure moves slide back unlocking spent casing

MCA6. Extract—spent casing is extracted from chamber

MCA7. Eject—spent casing is ejected from slide assembly

MCA8. Re-cock—pin and hammer (if any) is re-cocked

---

[2] The cycling process presented is applicable only to the Glock® pistol. Other handguns may have alternative processes such as mechanical safety and cocking/ de-cocking devices which add additional steps to the cyclical process. The Glock® Pistol cycle additionally involves the disengagement and reengagement of three safeties—Trigger Safety, Firing Pin Safety and Drop Safety.

HPC5. Assess the situation and if needed deliver rounds (in this case a third round)

GHC6. Follow-through

GHC7. Reacquire sight picture

HPC6. Lower the muzzle down to Low Ready,

HPC7. Look and Assess, and finally

HPC8. Holster (without looking at your holster).

In summary there are, (depending on how far you want to break it down) at least a half-dozen cycles within cycles of the Shot Placement Cycle. These include, but are not limited to: the OODA Cycle, Gun Handling Cycle (GHC), Handgun Presentation Cycle (HPC), Sight Picture Cycle (SPC), Trigger Control Cycle (TCC), Trigger Break Cycle (TBC), Mechanical Cycle of Action (MCA), etc. representing over 58 individual processes (depending upon particular firearm) all precisely timed and executed perfectly in sequence (provided there are no malfunctions ANYWHERE along the way—including holding that muzzle on target the entire time) and all within a matter of less than 1.5 seconds.

The old saying "there are no guarantees in life but for death and taxes" directly applies to CQB. All of these "cycles of action" cost valuable time. All of this perfectly timed activity looks great on paper and sounds good in practice, but there can be absolutely no mistakes in any of the 58 mechanical, biological, chemical, physical and operational steps and dynamic conditions throughout the Shot Placement Cycle including any of the cycles of action or the cycles within cycles including Operational (human) or Mechanical (firearm, ammunition, etc.) malfunctions or *any* other of the 28 Real World Reasons.

In addition to all of this, now add the stress of an attacker trying to chop your head off with a Bowie knife, adverse physical and environmental conditions such as confined areas of engagement, inclement weather and personal injury. What is the optimal solution to overcoming such obstacles? The "A" answer is consistency in training—the exact reason why special operations personnel spend so much of their time honing reactive response skills.

Presentations While Moving off LOA—Strong Side

Handling a life-threatening attack at extreme close quarters is risky business. If you don't get out of the way of that incoming attack then the fight intensifies as the SOI potential increases dramatically *(Liability Gap)*, the amount of time you have available to respond decreases *(Reactionary Gap)*, your tactical options are narrowed down to only a very few viable alternatives and your overall chances for winning (and even survival) are compromised exponentially.

The safest method of handling this type of dangerous threat, as simple as it sounds, is—just don't be in the path of the blade! You can move your body anywhere else in the known physical universe, except for those coordinates placing you at the edge or tip of that blade at the same time and the same place as your opponent. Sure sounds easy, but the trick is actually doing it.

Since he needs to use *his legs* to bring the weapon in range enough to make contact with your body then you can use *your legs* to create the time and space for you to check the 28 boxes and *forward–aggressive–effectively* go to guns. There are some basic rules that, easily followed, can increase your odds dramatically.

At NCR you still have time to move your body because at that distance he still can't reach out and strike you with the knife. Yet as he rapidly approaches *Contact Range* there remains very little time and space for you to effectively respond. If you remain stationary (no *control of mobility*), then you may as well brace for impact (recall lawnmower and

Part IV: Bringing a Gun to a Knife Fight

garbage-disposal analogy). However, if there was a tactic you could utilize to buy sufficient space and time to complete the half-dozen or so *Cycles of Action* needed to press the round off, then your odds of making it out in one piece are greatly improved.

As he moves, you move—use your legs against his legs. Since this particular scenario allows a little wiggle room you may as well use it to buy space and time. Looking at this solution even closer, the direction you move can also give you an advantage.

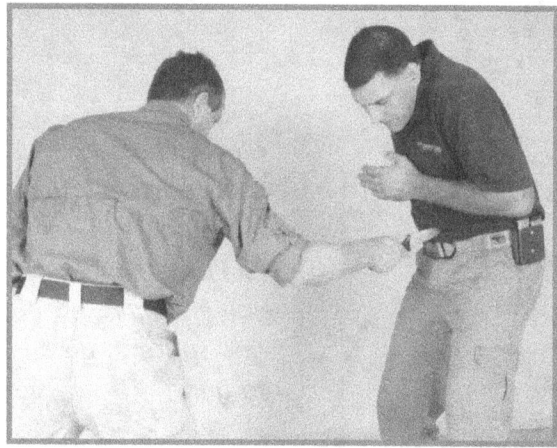

If you remain stationary, he will eventually close in from NCR and go to Contact Range forcing you from Green Zone to Red Zone, allowing you zero reactionary gap and increasing your SOI—you can take it like a man for the team.

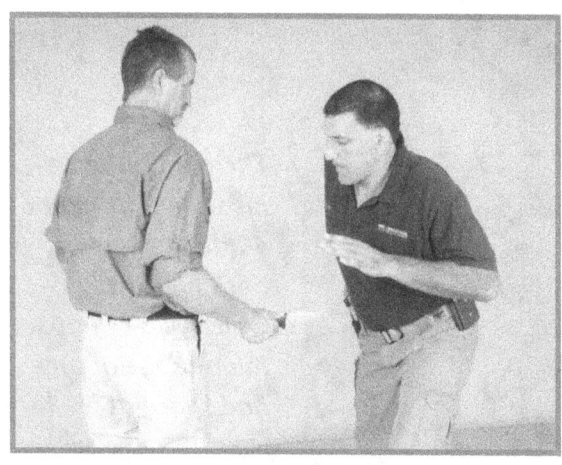

If you move forward into the blade, aside from the obvious problem of moving straight toward an incoming razor blade, you have changed from NCR to Contact Range and stepped out of the Green Zone and into the Red Zone. This would also decrease your time and space, increase your potential for injury and severely reduce your reaction time completely eliminating your option to go to guns.

Bringing a Gun to a Knife Fight

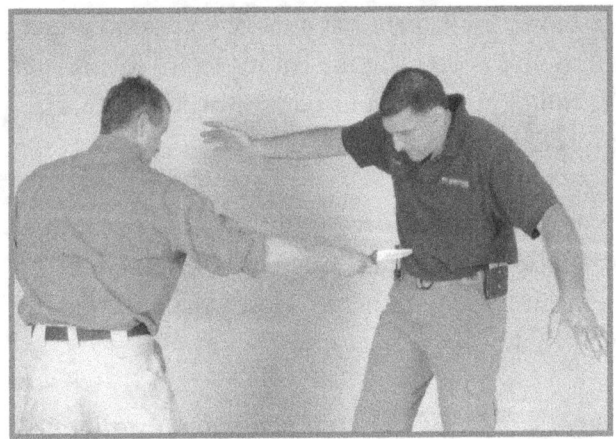

Moving straight back is of course an option but as covered in detail above (see **Control of Mobility**) *may possibly be a very short term gain but doomed to failure in the long run.*

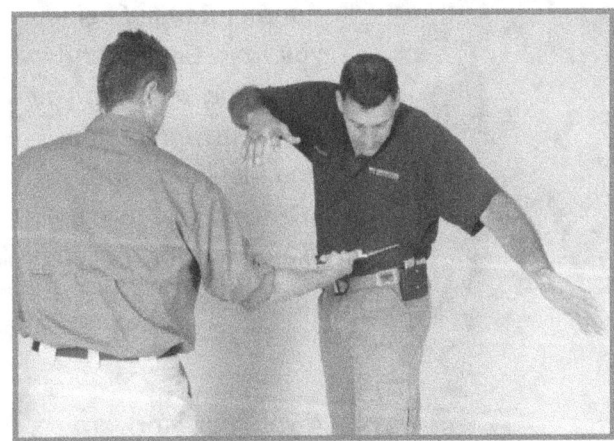

Moving laterally is of course another option but still can't quite buy you enough time and space to go to guns.

The optimal movement here would be 45 degree angled back and away, which allows maximum usage of time and space at NCR.

Part IV: Bringing a Gun to a Knife Fight

Now that we've determined an optimal direction (remember there are two more scenarios that will cover the "what ifs" going through your brain right now), what would be the most effective way to both move in that direction and go to guns? The answer is plainly—simultaneously.

If you remain stationary and *then* go to guns well you've wasted time and if you move your SFP from position A to position B and *then* go to guns you've also wasted time. Optimal usage of time and space is to execute your presentation on the move and toward an optimal direction.

How to move toward a POD in a 45 degree angular movement while executing a perfect handgun presentation:

Starting from the Hands Above position, face the threat and prepare to move 45 degrees off the LOA to the strong side.

Step One: Referring back to our light switch analogy again, we're going to hook on one more light to the circuit. Imagine that there is an imaginary string tied from your strong side foot to your weapon hand wrist. Moving your strong side foot back 45 degrees and away from your attacker (keep in mind that he's still at NCR) this is the light switch that pulls your strong hand into the "Grip" step of the **Presentation Cycle** *(step one), brings your support hand to your center mass and simultaneously places your foot in a deep step 45 degrees and back and away from the incoming attack.*

The very first step (first half of a shuffle step as per above) in this process immediately draws your center mass (location of all your vital organs) off the LOA and away from the blade in the best possible physical POA. It simultaneously creates space, which increases your response time, decreases your SOI, puts you halfway into a SFP, pulls your support hand out of the path of the blade, and places your strong hand firmly in place at Step 1 of the Presentation Cycle—total time cost: about a half second.

Step Two: Bring the support foot under your body weight into a solid SFP and while that's happening simultaneously execute the remainder of the Presentation Cycle up to the point of look and assess the situation (step 5.)—total time cost: about a half second. Notice increased distance (greater Reactionary Gap allowing more time and more space), change of direction and position of handgun facing the threat (muzzle up squarely on target, strong hand supported Weapon Retention position).

Part IV: Bringing a Gun to a Knife Fight

By completing this simple *gross-motor* two-step movement, you have effectively *Controlled Mobility*, literally stepped off the LOA, completed your *Presentation Cycle* (to the point where it needs to go), changed your physical position in time and space, which instantly gives you control of the *Power Curve* thus forcing your opponent to react to your new position and all of this in less than 1.5 seconds.

If the scenario starts out with even more space between you and the assailant, then this same movement of LOA strong side may also be executed resulting in sighted fire. The following sequence illustrates moving off the LOA to the strong side and due to increase in Reactionary Gap, ending up with the firearm in the *sighted fire* position.

Same as above begin with a Stable Fighting Platform and in the Hands Up position facing the threat.

2. Same as above simultaneously move the strong side leg 45 degrees back and away from the attack while executing first step of Handgun Presentation Cycle. Notice lower center of gravity and vital CL / CM moved off LOA.

3. Now with an increased Reactionary Gap this allows you full sighted fire position strong hand supported and in a Position of Advantage.

Part IV: Bringing a Gun to a Knife Fight

Live Fire off LOA—Strong Side Drill

If you're interested to see for yourself how this technique works, go ahead and try this simple live-fire square-range drill you can run to test your ability to respond at NCR by moving 45 degrees off the LOA to the strong side.

Set Up: Be sure you are at a secured range and you are cleared hot from the RM and RSOs. Following all safety and range rules, set up paper targets and stand at the three yard line. Wearing additional garment to simulate concealed carry (if applicable), face down range, *Make Ready* to a full load and holster. Remain facing downrange in the *Hands Above* position ready to follow range commands.

Drill 1: The RM / RSO will issue commands and run shooting string first by the numbers and then all as one motion dry fire and then lastly using live rounds. The first set, stand directly in front of your target and upon range commands, make ready and come to a full load. Upon audio command, you will step off the LOA 45 degrees to the strong side and deliver two rounds to the center mass of the target from a sighted fire position (arms extended).

Facing downrange starting out from NCR, stand greater than arms length from the target in a Stable Fighting Platform and in the Hands Up Position.

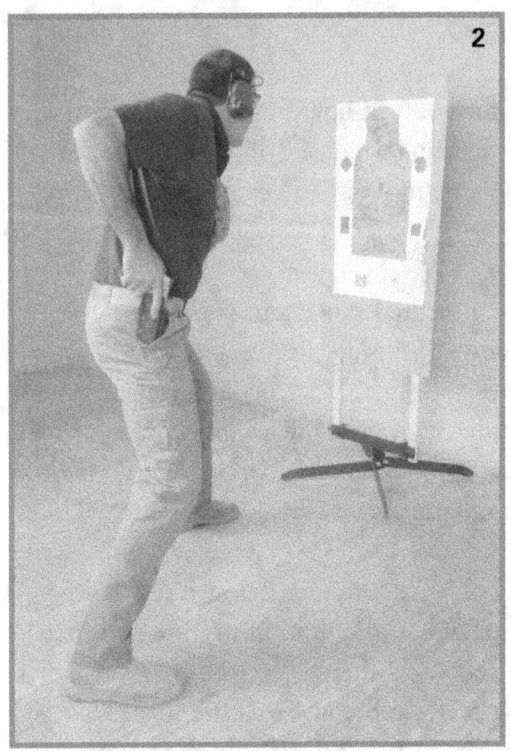

Execute first part of shuffle step plus "Grip" step of Handgun Presentation Cycle immediately followed by

Execution of second half of shuffle step including two rounds to the body from a sighted fire (hands extended) position.

Part IV: Bringing a Gun to a Knife Fight

The second set, the RM will issue the exact same commands however, this time try delivering those same two rounds from weapon retention position.

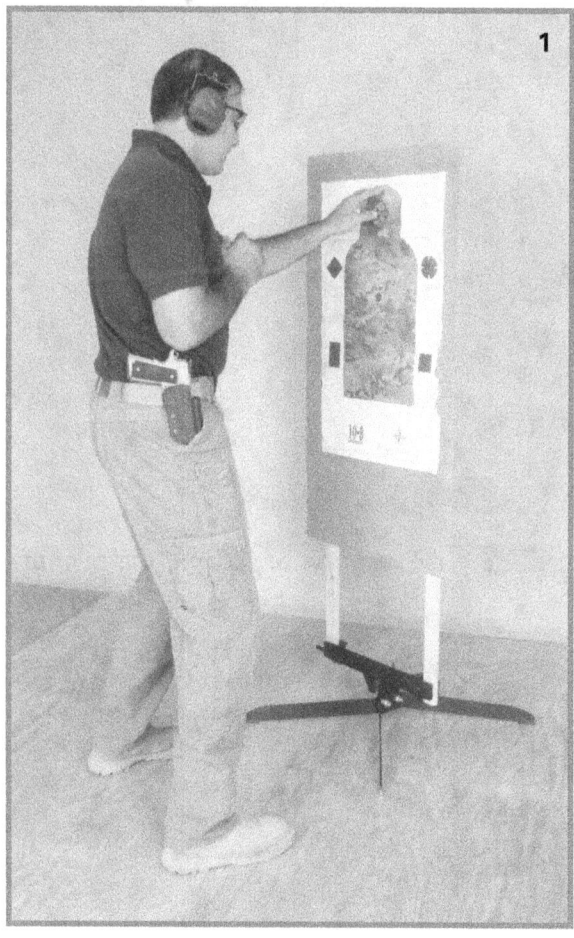

Facing downrange starting out from NCR, stand at arms length (or closer) from the target in a Stable Fighting Platform and in the Hands Up Position. If your RM / RSO will allow, begin with your support hand touching the target.

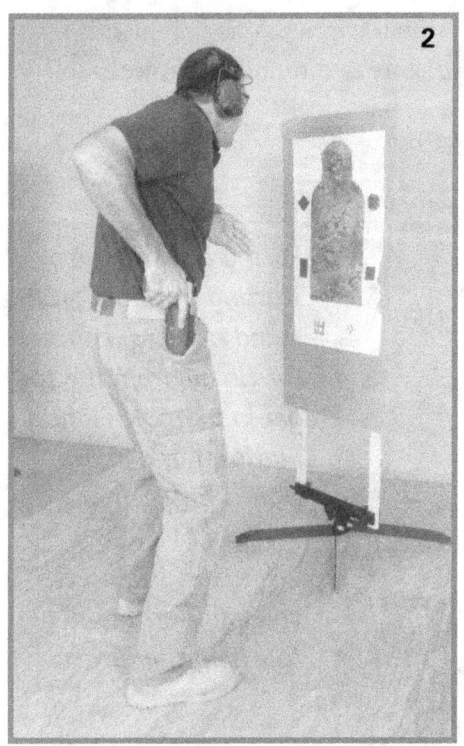

Execute first part of shuffle step (of course removing support hand away from target) plus "Grip" step of Handgun Presentation Cycle immediately followed by

Execution of second half of shuffle step including two rounds to the body from an unsighted fire (hands retracted) Weapon Retention position.

Part IV: Bringing a Gun to a Knife Fight

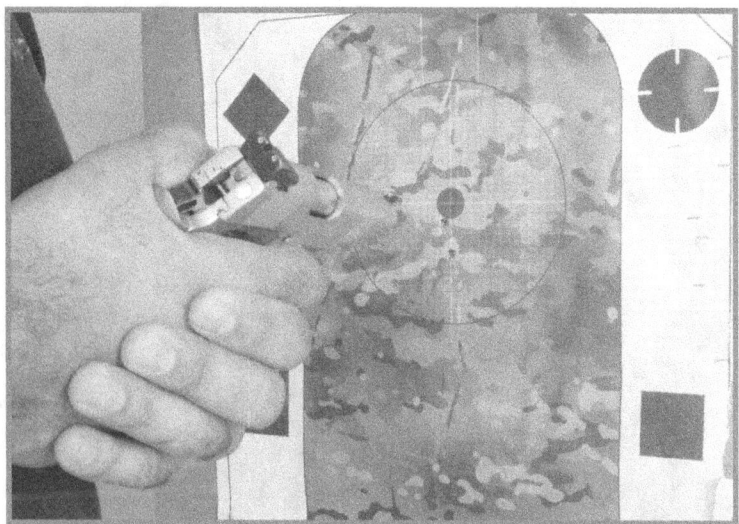

Remember to keep the basics of an optimal Weapon Retention Position—retracted hands (strong hand supported) up high and wrist pressing against vest with slide canted outboard, muzzle pointed in squarely to the target.

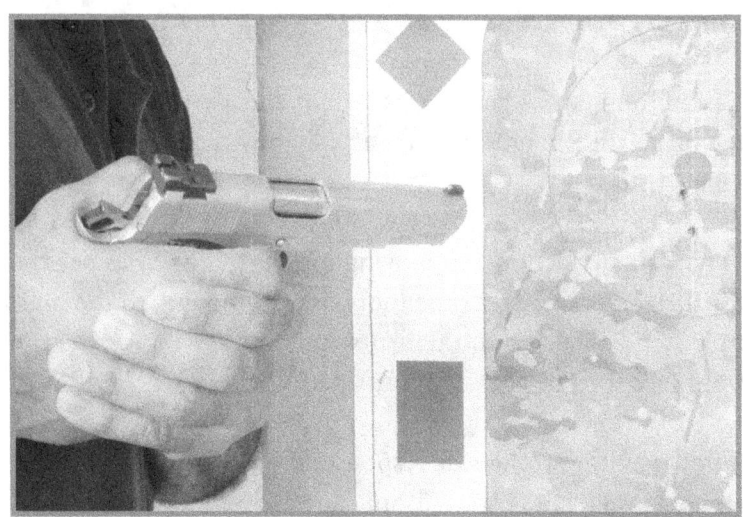

At such confined areas of operation sighted fire is not necessary (and in fact becomes an operational liability at bad-breath ranges). By appropriately training to deliver rounds downrange quickly and accurately from the Weapon Retention position, your gun handling and marksmanship skills at extreme close quarters will increase measurably.

Bringing a Gun to a Knife Fight

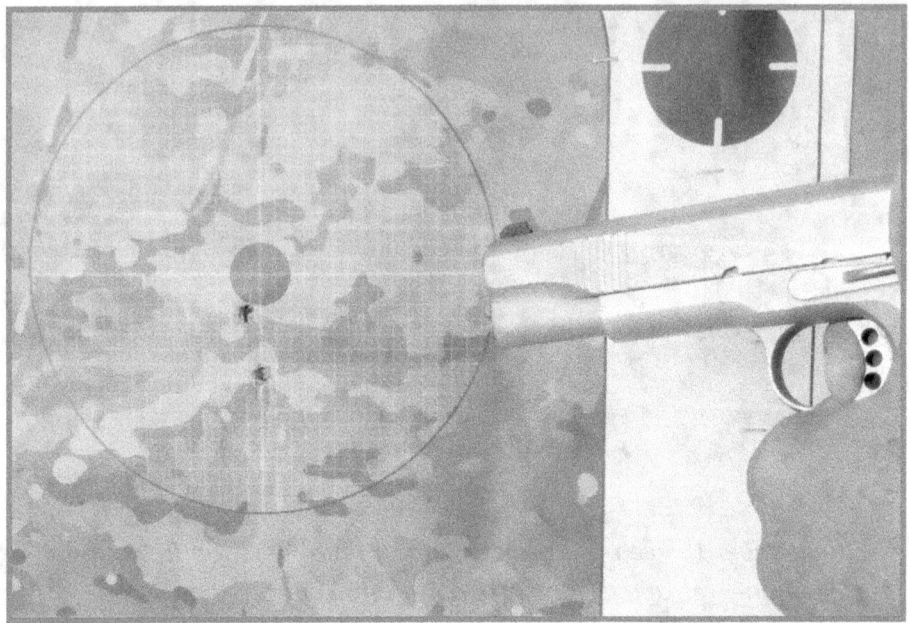

Presentations While Moving off LOA—Support Side

If environment or conditions do not allow you a 45 degree angle-step off to the strong side, then it may be necessary to move to the support side.

The step are identical to moving to the *strong side* as per above, except for the very first step of the footwork. In moving to the *support side*, simply step laterally with the first step and then a *pivot away from the threat* to face it from your support side.

Similar to the strong side response, if you remain stationary and *then* go to guns well you've wasted time and if you move your SFP from position A to position B and *then* go to guns you've also wasted time. Optimal usage of time and space is to execute your presentation on the move and toward an optimal direction.

How to move toward a POD in a 45 degree angular movement while executing a perfect handgun presentation:

Part IV: Bringing a Gun to a Knife Fight

1. Starting from the Hands Above position, face the threat and prepare to move 45 degrees off the LOA to the support side.

2. **Step One:** Referring back to our light switch analogy again, we're going to hook on one more light to the circuit. Imagine that there is an imaginary string tied from your support side foot to your weapon hand wrist. When you move your support side foot laterally 90 degrees and away from your attacker (keep in mind that he's still at NCR) this is the light switch that pulls your strong hand into the "Grip" step of the Presentation Cycle *(step one)*, your support hand to your center mass and places your foot in a deep lateral step and back from the incoming attack.

The very first step (first half of a shuffle step as per above) in this process immediately draws your center mass (location of all your vital organs) of the LOA and way from the blade in the best possible physical POA. It simultaneously creates space, which increases your response time, decreases your SOI, puts you halfway into a SFP, pulls your support hand out of the path of the blade, and places your strong hand firmly in place at Step 1 of the Presentation Cycle—total time cost : about a half second.

Pivot your strong side foot under your body weight away from the threat and into a solid SFP (now re-facing the threat) and while that's happening simultaneously execute the remainder of the Presentation Cycle up to the point of look and assess the situation (step 5.)—total time cost: about a half second.

By completing this simple *gross-motor* two-step movement, you have effectively *Controlled Mobility*, literally stepped off the LOA, completed your *Presentation Cycle* (to the point where it needs to go), changed your physical position in time and space, which in instantly gains you control of the *Power Curve* thus forcing your opponent to react to your new position and all of this in less than 1.5 seconds.

If the scenario starts out with even more space between you and the assailant, then this same movement off the LOA support side may also be executed resulting in *sighted fire*. The following sequence illustrates moving off the LOA to the strong side and due to increase in Reactionary Gap, ending up with the firearm in the *sighted fire* position.

Same as above begin with a Stable Fighting Platform and in the Hands Up position facing the threat.

Bringing a Gun to a Knife Fight

2 Same as above simultaneously move support-side leg laterally 90 degrees away from the attack while executing first step of Handgun Presentation Cycle. Notice lower center of gravity and vital CL / CM moved off LOA.

3 Now with an increased Reactionary Gap this allows you full sighted fire position strong hand supported and in a Position of Advantage.

Part IV: Bringing a Gun to a Knife Fight

Live Fire off LOA—Support Side Drill

If you're interested to see for yourself how this technique works on the support side this time, go ahead and try this simple live-fire square-range drill you can run to test your ability to respond at NCR by moving 45 degrees off the LOA to your support side.

Set Up: Be sure you are at a secured range and you are cleared hot from the RM and RSOs. Following all safety and range rules, set up paper targets and stand at the three yard line. Wearing additional garment to simulate concealed carry, face down range, make ready to a full load and holster. Remain facing downrange in the *hands below* position ready to follow range commands.

Drill: The RM / RSO will issue commands and run shooting string first by the numbers and then all as one motion dry fire and then lastly using live rounds. The first set, stand directly in front of your target and upon range commands, make ready and come to a full load. Upon audio command, you will step off the LOA 45 degrees to the support side and deliver two rounds to the center mass of the target from a sighted fire position (arms extended).

Facing downrange starting out from NCR, stand greater than arms length from the target in a Stable Fighting Platform and in the Hands Up Position.

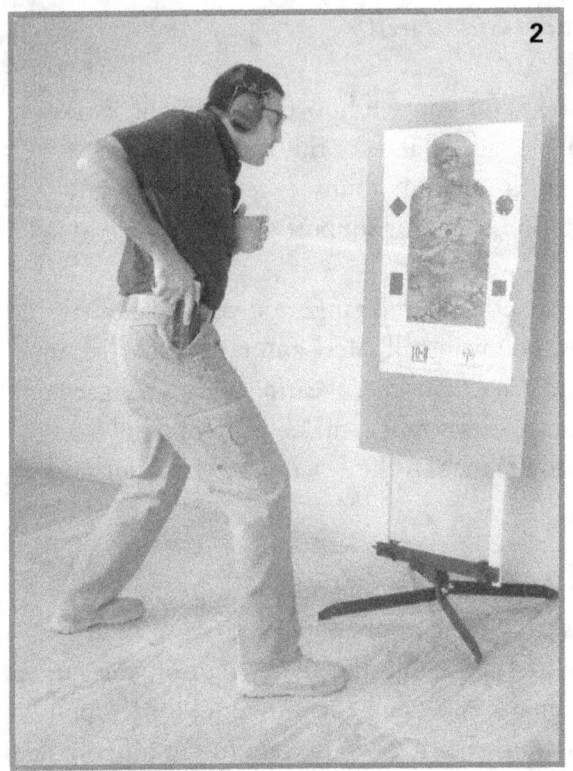

Execute first part of lateral shuffle step plus "Grip" step of Handgun Presentation Cycle immediately followed by

Execution of second half of pivot step including two rounds to the body from a sighted fire (hands extended) position.

Part IV: Bringing a Gun to a Knife Fight

The second set, the RM will issue the exact same commands, however, this time go ahead and try delivering those same two rounds from weapon retention position.

Facing downrange starting out from NCR, stand greater than arms length from the target in a Stable Fighting Platform and in the Hands Up Position.

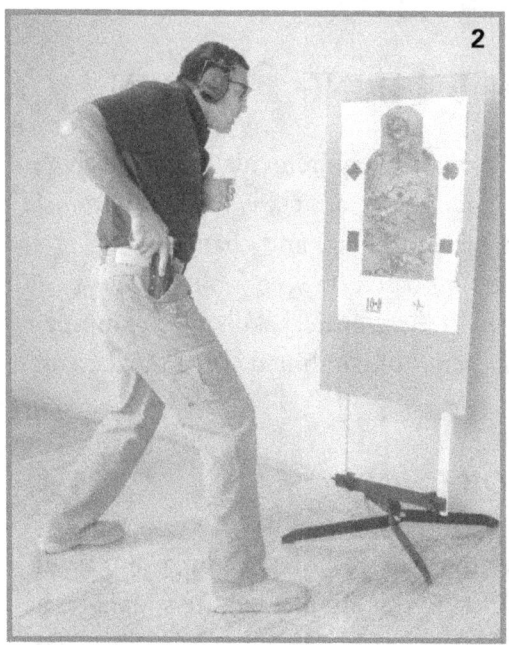

Execute first part of lateral shuffle step plus "Grip" step of Handgun Presentation Cycle immediately followed by

Execution of second half of pivot step including two rounds to the body from weapon retention position.

CHANGING RANGE AND FIRING POSITION

One of the most important performance requirements in effectively handling a surprise and rapid contact range attack, is the ability to change ranges (take and keep control of range) and change firing positions (sighted and unsighted fire) based on scenario conditions. An excellent live fire drill to develop these critical skills is to combine all of the above basic skills into a series of combined CQB movements.

Live Fire Range Position CQB Drill

If you're interested to see for yourself how this range and firing position transition sequence works try this simple live-fire square-range drill you can run to test your ability to respond by moving 45 degrees off the LOA to your strong side utilizing both a range change as well as changing from unsighted fire to sighted fire.

Set Up: Be sure you are at a secured range and you are cleared hot from the RM and RSOs. Following all safety and range rules, set up paper targets and stand at about the three yard line. Wearing additional garment (if applicable) to simulate concealed carry, face down range, make ready to a full load and holster. Remain facing downrange in the *hands above* position ready to follow range commands.

Drill: The RM / RSO will issue commands and run a shooting string first by the numbers and then all as one motion dry fire and then lastly using live rounds. The first set, stand directly in front of your target and upon range commands, make ready and come to a full load. Upon audio command, you will step off the LOA 45 degrees to the strong side and deliver two rounds to the center mass of the target from an unsighted fire position (weapon retention position), followed by continual movement (moving the stable fighting platform) 45 degrees back and away from the target while simultaneously moving to a sighted fire position and deliver one round to the head. Final movement will include to two additional rounds to CM from the sighted fire (hands extended) position.

Facing downrange starting out from NCR, stand at arms length (or even closer) from the target in a Stable Fighting Platform and in the Hands Up Position. Placement of the hands on the target is preferable if allowed by RM / RSO.

Bringing a Gun to a Knife Fight

Move 45 degrees off the LOA to the strong side while simultaneously presenting the handgun to the Weapon Retention position and delivering two rounds to the body.

Continuing movement to increase the Reactionary Gap simultaneously move the handgun to sighted fire position and deliver one round to the head.

Continuing additional movement to increase the Reactionary Gap and keeping the handgun at sighted fire position, deliver two additional rounds to the body.

Part IV: Bringing a Gun to a Knife Fight

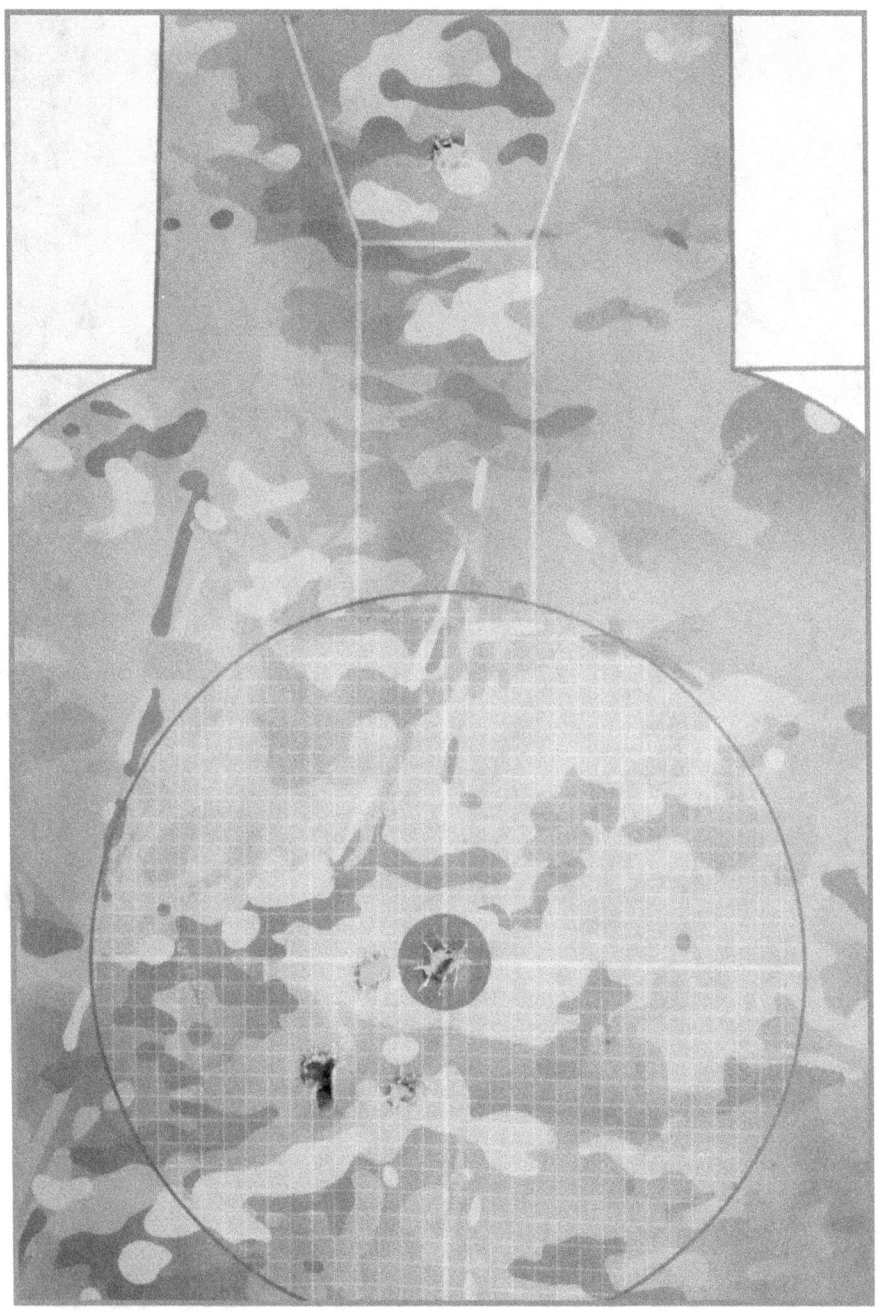

Upon completion of the drill there should be four rounds landed to the body and one to the head totaling five rounds on target.

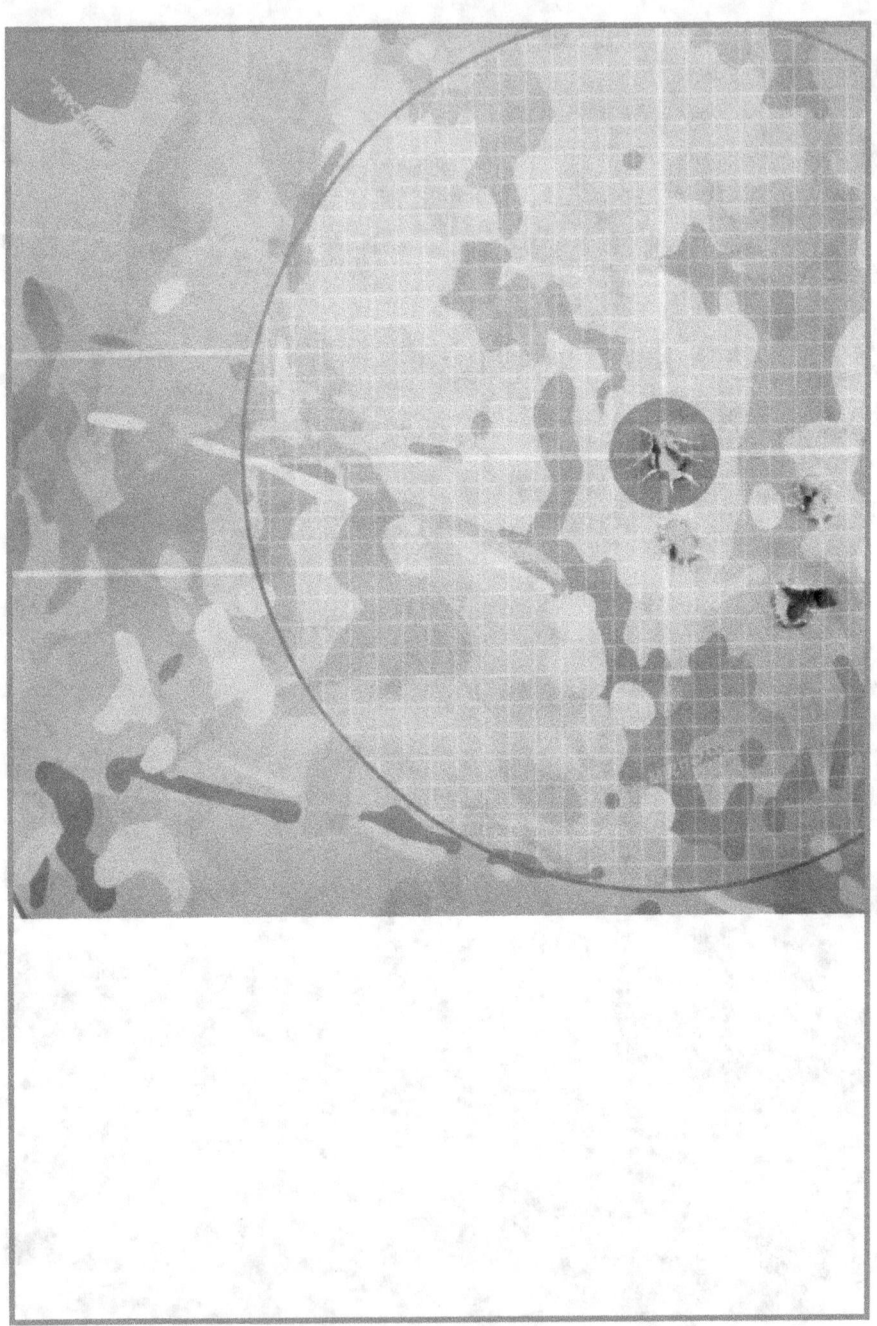

Net result strikes to the body are equivalent to an NSR.

LOW LINE ATTACK

If you draw an imaginary line across the body horizontally at about the belt line, the human body can be divided into two parts the upper half and the lower half. A knife attack to either of these two parts can be devastating.

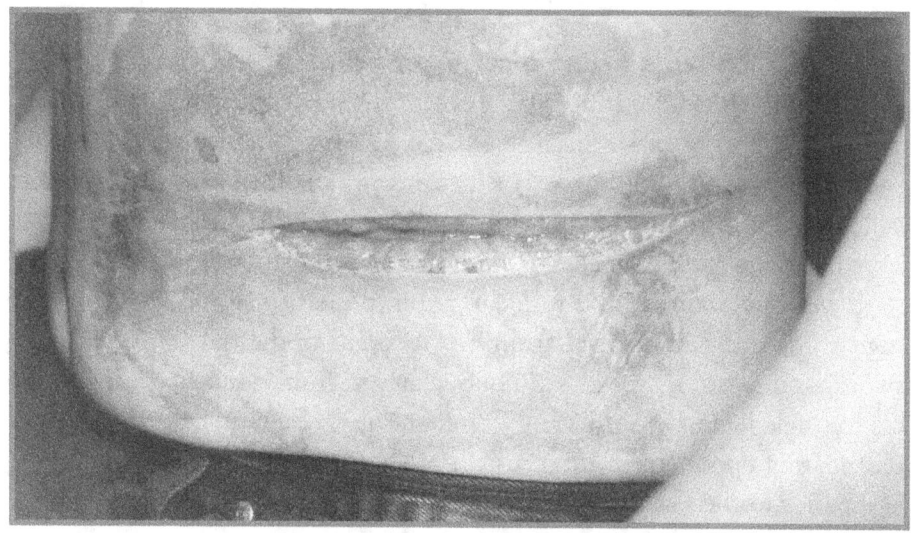

An edged weapon strike (slash) to a soft low line target.

An edged weapon strike (stab) to a soft low line target.

As covered earlier the human body is comprised of both soft and hard targets. A knife strike to any soft target will cause more physical damage than a knife strike to a hard target. Of the soft targets on the human body none will bleed out quicker (aside from the heart itself), than the inferior vena cava and the abdominal aorta.

The inferior vena cava and the abdominal aorta are the two major ascending and descending circulatory pipelines of the human body.

The most debilitating attack to these pipelines is a thrusting motion with the knife. Influential 16th century European fencing masters Giacomo DiGrassi and Vincentio Saviolo published their discoveries that the thrust was found to be vastly superior to the slash. These discoveries validated the ancient Roman writings of Flavius Vegetus Renetus who noted that the Roman generals found that the thrust was superior to the slash and thus was the basis for adaptation of the Roman *Gladius* (thrusting sword) and validated yet again by Procopius in the 6th century. Thus, swords and sword fighting techniques changed from double-handed slashers to single handed thrusters as a direct result to their effectiveness in terminating opponents. The thrust throughout history, including today, is superior to the slash.

The primary targets are the abdominal aorta and its branches, which lie behind the visceral organs and supply them with blood. Branches of the abdominal aorta also supply the abdominal wall with blood. Knife thrusts to the kidneys, liver, and spleen can also lead to rapid exsanguinations. At the level of the navel the abdominal aorta divides to form the common iliac arteries that supply the legs with blood. This was the traditional target for the Japanese seppuku suicide (hara kiri)—found to be the most humane method of self termination in ancient times.

The common iliac arteries divide into internal and external iliac arteries. The iliac veins run parallel to the arteries, returning blood to the heart. The external iliac arteries lead into the legs where they become the femoral arteries.

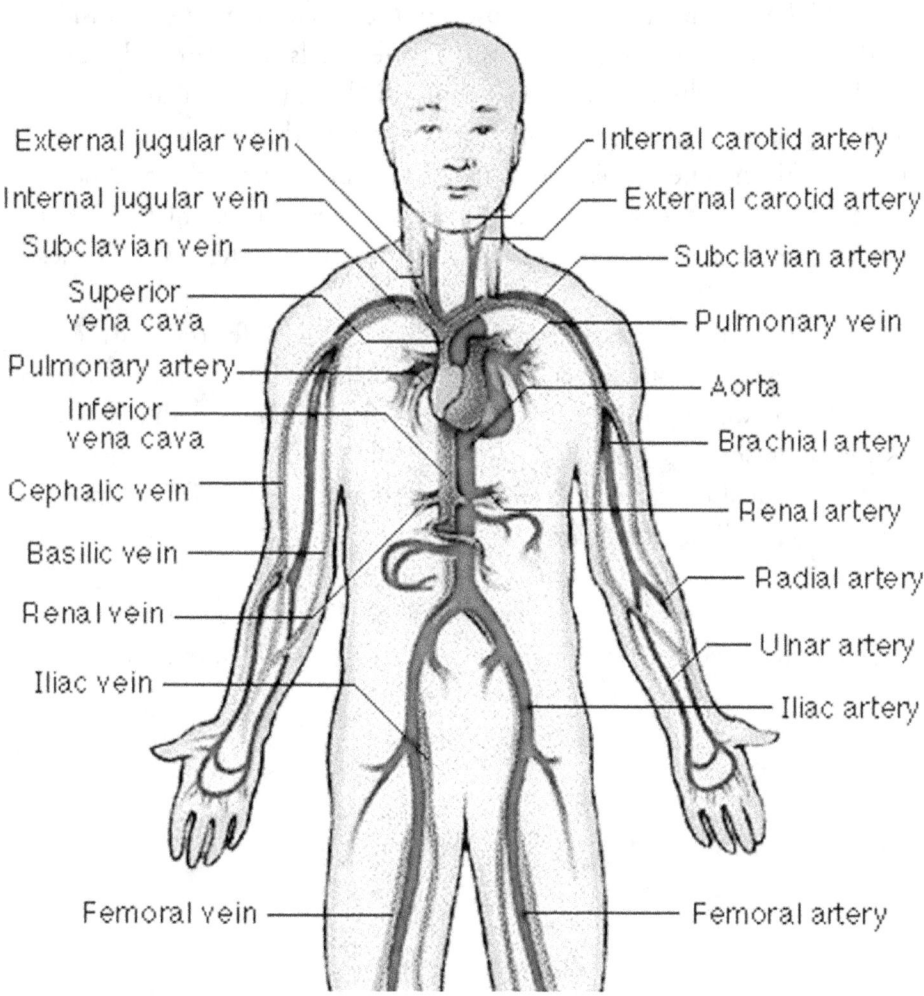

Illustration of inferior vena cava, abdominal aorta and connecting arteries.

The femoral arteries are closest to the surface high on the inside of the thighs, just lateral to the groin. The femorals spiral around the thigh and a branch passes directly behind the knee (popliteal artery). Thus a well-placed (or even "bad guy gets lucky") thrust anywhere from the navel to the kneecap can be as lethal as a thrust above the beltline. It is no secret why these low line soft target areas remains popular (and just as effective) to this day with various "knife fighting" systems worldwide.

The remaining two scenarios will analyze a knife attack at the toughest distance—at contact range, the toughest position—in the Red Zone, at the worse possible disadvantage—surprise attack with a knife, as well as at both high-line and low line attacks with the knife. These scenarios will also take a close look at the common "what ifs" that may occur in such difficult scenarios.

Given above, let's first start with a low-line attack and save the high-line attack for the final scenario with a couple of options.

Part IV: Bringing a Gun to a Knife Fight

Scenario 4—Low Line Attack at CAE and CR

Beginning with the conditions of the environment, we'll start with a *confined area of engagement (CAE)*, outdoors (narrow walkway between your house and fence), late at night (low-light), no noticeable bystanders or pedestrians in the vicinity but houses are close enough that someone looking out the window is definitely in range of a stray 9mm round in *your* neighborhood. Along the pathway between your house and the fence, you are on foot on your way from your vehicle to the back door and traveling down a long, dimly-lit narrow walkway, and, yes, carrying a concealed and loaded firearm (handgun) accessible to your weapon hand and on your person. Thankful to finally be home after a very long-ass day at work you unwittingly drop to *Condition White*. You have your keys in one hand and a newspaper in the other. You're very tired and thinking of nothing but that comfortable couch and the crisp taste of that first beer. Such thoughts keep you from your normal *Condition Yellow*.

You hear a sound next to you in the walkway—but it's too dimly lit to positively identify. You have *observed* something with your audio senses at which point you have entered into the *OODA Cycle* (Observe) and have switch from *Condition White* to *Condition Orange (skipping Condition Yellow)*. Your senses heighten, and you move quickly to then next step on the *OODA cycle* (Orient). Utilizing your knowledge of *Control of Position, Range and Mobility* determine your time and distance from the narrow walkway to open space. You then decide to move toward a POA to one side of the walkway in such a manner as to prepare for engagement of threat in a SFP and then finally *act* out your plan physically, all the while monitoring the *condition of your threat, the condition of the environment* and *the condition of your weapon system(s)*.

Suddenly and without warning, coming at you from a short distance at CR *(contact range)* is a menacing-looking large athletic male wielding what appears to be a sharp and pointed metallic object, identified by you as a knife, capable of delivering severe bodily injury and, of course, death. This change in the *condition of the threat* causes you to switch to *Condition Red* and run another *OODA loop*. You have *observed* that this threat at CR is heading straight toward you with his blade com-

Scenario 4—An assailant hides behind a low wall with blade ready to strike at a time and place of his choosing.

Part IV: Bringing a Gun to a Knife Fight

ing in straight at your low line for a stabbing and his gaze fixed. Gaining speed and closing the *Reactionary Gap* rapidly he is now preparing to thrust into your abdomen just inches away.

Now *oriented* to this new set of circumstances your heart starts pounding faster and your palms sweating as you register and process important data: Threat is already at CR (*Contact Range*), in motion, closing extremely quickly, armed with a dangerous weapon, I'm in pretty bad shape here deeply behind the *power curve* and no time or space to run without getting skewered, I remember that my gun is loaded and I'm pretty sure there's one in the tube, but there's not a snowball's chance in Hell that I can get to it in time because of this CR distance, plus he's moving PDQ and man, there's no choice but to deal with this hand-to-hand first and then go to guns.

With palms sweating, you make an important *decision*: He's on me at *Contact Range*, one more step and I'm toast, believe me I *want* to go to guns but there's absolutely no time, gonna have to make the call here—I'd really like to step out of the way but he's just placed me in the Red Zone and no time for anything but pure hand-to-hand defense.

Your mind is processing at light speed—movement forward or backward no longer an option, guns not an option, your primary threat is that incoming blade toward your midsection. You need to make safe that inbound weapon. You finally *act* upon that decision.

Relying on your CQB training, you respond to the incoming thrust pushing down and away with both hands on his weapon forearm (only one of your hands actually makes contact because of the blinding speed of the attack and you forgot all about the newspaper in that hand), nonetheless you have succeeded in diverting the incoming blade by smashing it down and away from your centerline, push off his body, which creates enough space which creates enough time—you now have the curve—you are in the process of dropping everything in your hands and although in the middle of the OODA Cycle you check off all 28 boxes *(Real World Reasons)*, change your physical posture from unstable to an SFP, you immediately move off the line of attack (LOA) to 45 degrees angled back to your strong side to a POA establishing a known backstop and simultaneously (while moving your SFP from point A to point B) commence the 8-Step cycle of handgun presentation.

Right smack in the middle of your *handgun presentation cycle:* 1. Clear away your concealment garment(s) and simultaneously grip the firearm while defeating any retention devices on the holster system. 2. Clear from your carry position and Cant to Retention Position. 3. Hands come together. 4. Punch and Look. 5. Assess the situation. You stop mid-cycle here and start a new OODA Loop *observing* that the bad guy is now recovering from your initial defense and turns to move toward you with a full *committed attack*. Moving to the *retention position,* instantly and due to proximity of threat, while he's trying to catch up (his reaction slower than your action—by your simultaneous 45 degree step plus firearm presentation you have placed him behind the *power curve*) you apply *unsighted fire* from the *retention position* and hammer two rounds toward *center mass* of the assailant. He freezes for a spilt second. It appears to be the case that at least one of the rounds maybe hit, but you can't tell if it was (and if it was then was it a hit to a vital or not) and your *OODA cycle* kicks down to *orient* to this new *condition of the threat, condition of your environment and condition of your weapon system.*

He drops away rapidly and staggers backward into the darkness to full NCR holding on to his belly while you maintain control of the firearm and since the range changed you switch back to the superior *sighted fire* position with your arms now extended. Unable to attain good sight alignment and a good sight picture as your target has changed physical position in such a manner as to impair your visual acuity, you can't really take another shot, but hang tough at the "and fire again if necessary" part of the presentation cycle Step 5, when he, apparently wounded, staggers back and away, dropping the knife and tries to slip back into the darkness. You reacquire your sights, move to an alternate POD and angle your body in such a manner as to deliver rounds downrange with a sound backdrop (in this case the foundation of the house) as he reaches again for the knife you empty the remainder of your entire magazine, shoot to slide-lock and perform a tactical re-load. By now your neighbors, hearing

Part IV: Bringing a Gun to a Knife Fight

gunshots, have dialed 911. You maintain front sight on threat and observe that there is no movement from an apparently lifeless body bleeding all over your walkway.

Your score an SOI Level 1 possibly a bruise (SOI Level 2) due to the hand-to-hand contact while your opponent apparently is at an SOI Level 5. Clearly you are the victor in this gunfight with a knife.

Play by play: You really didn't have any time or space to operate—zero *Reactionary Gap*. He started out the gate at *Contact Range*. You were operating in a *confined area of engagement* and in the *Red Zone* the entirety of the incident, which lasted maybe around two seconds. Man it was shocking how fast it went down.

You were fully aware of the ever-changing *conditions of the threat, the condition of the environment* and the *condition of your weapon system*. You made the best decision possible to utilize your hands versus his hands as you had no space to use your legs and no time to go to guns. Pushing down and away at the incoming knife strike you managed to make safe the incoming weapon, push off his body, simultaneously move off LOA and complete the *Presentation Cycle* (as well as all the other Cycles of Action) and in a timely manner. You were fortunate to have handled the threat in a forward, aggressive and effective manner by emptying the contents of your entire magazine in an effort to stop this life-threatening situation.

You were doubly fortunate to end this scenario without anyone getting injured (yourself and your neighbors included) except for the bad guy. You sustained little or no injuries and although sweating profusely and a little shaken up—you won.

Close-up Replay 1: Get In or Get Out. In close Quarter Combat—especially with regards to a deadly contact weapon attack such as with a knife (or other dangerous weapon) there are only two response options, simply put "Get In" or "Get Out." There are no other options.

"Get Out" is a term that describes moving away from CR toward NCR with a quickness effectively creating distance, which instantly creates time and simultaneously lowers your potential for injury. "Get In" on the other hand, immediately allows you to go on the offensive and attack the attacker—forward, aggressive and effective. Depending on the condition of your threat, the condition of your environment and the condition of your weapon system(s)—only you can "read the need" on this and determine which of the two (Get In or Get Out) is the more viable option. It is strongly recommended to either "Get In" or "Get out" as indecision causes stoppage of cycles and will eventually bring you to lose control of Position, Range and Mobility, thus placing you behind the curve and the fight in control of you as opposed to you controlling the fight. Get In or Get Out—you need to make that decision in a billionth of a second because *indecision kills*.

If you have the time and the space to "Get Out"—well, that's the safest option as it immediately gains you POA at the Green Zone and of course lowers your SOI considerably. However, rapid physical contact at these extreme close quarter ranges doesn't leave you many options other than to "Get In" and handle it on the "inside" of the fight. Trying to "Get Out" when the "A" choice is to "Get In" makes little or no change in your position or range, buys you no advantage and spells certain disaster.

One can make an attempt to either Get In or Get Out. As was mentioned earlier, everything has a price tag. If you move out then you give up valuable real estate but you gain distance (space) which buys you time which instantly lowers your SOI and further allows you more options as well as opportunity to make the next decision to solve this particular problem.

In this particular case, the correct choice was to engage the threat at CR, "Get In" and handle the attack first with your bare hands. Clearly this scenario permitted no other options, nowhere to turn, no way to move, going to guns would have given him time to cut you to pieces mid-way through your presentation cycle.

Speed and Surprise

Try this simple drill: stand directly in front of a buddy (don't say anything about what you're about to do) and while in mid-conversation and completely unexpectedly place your trigger finger straight on his sternum. He will look at you and wonder if you've been smoking a crack pipe, but this mini-drill will clearly demonstrate both the power of a surprise attack as well as the directness of the shortest distance between two points.

Bringing a Gun to a Knife Fight laws of physics:

1. action is slower than reaction

2. shortest distance between two points is a straight line

One of my favorite quotes from the masters that directly applies to going from Condition Yellow to Condition Red while simultaneously (and flawlessly) executing all the required cycles of action to present a firearm and delivering accurate rounds down range in a decisive and rapid manner:

"Speed is the absence of all unnecessary movement."

Hands versus Hands

Instead of taking my word for it, there's a quick drill that you can run with your training partner to test the "Get In" and Get Out" theory. Ask your role player to stand at contact range again with his / her trusty plastic training knife. You stand facing your training partner with only a holster and blue / red gun (be sure to follow every safety procedure in the book here and ask your partner to again check a second (and third) time that you have a blue / red gun in your holster. Now, without using your hands try and either go to guns or use your legs or both or whatever you want to come up with *without* using your hands. What does your experience tell you?

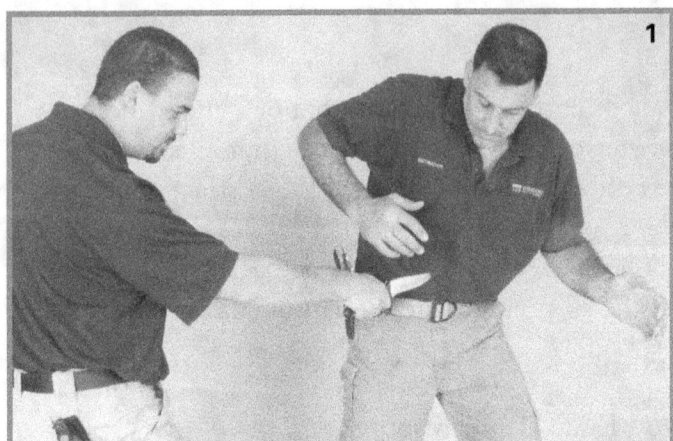

Try using "legs only" at CR against an inbound low-line thrust.

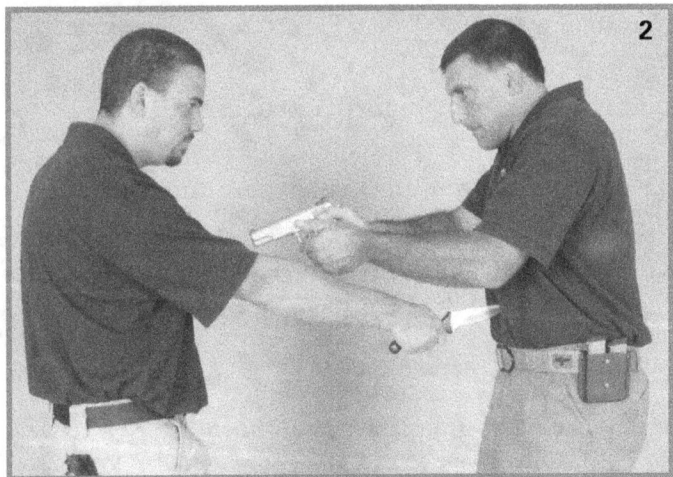

Try using "gun only" at CR against an inbound low-line thrust.

Down and Away

The best way to train for such low line CR attacks at CAE is to work with a training partner every once in a while to keep your skills up. One of the best drills is a "down and away" drill that goes like this: ask your training partner to stand at CR and with a plastic training knife in his / her strong hand. In a slow and controlled manner the role player thrusts a low-line abdominal strike toward your beltline.

Executing the below options about ten repetitions, you may then ask the role player to switch to the opposite hand and run the same exact series utilizing the role-players support side.

Part IV: Bringing a Gun to a Knife Fight

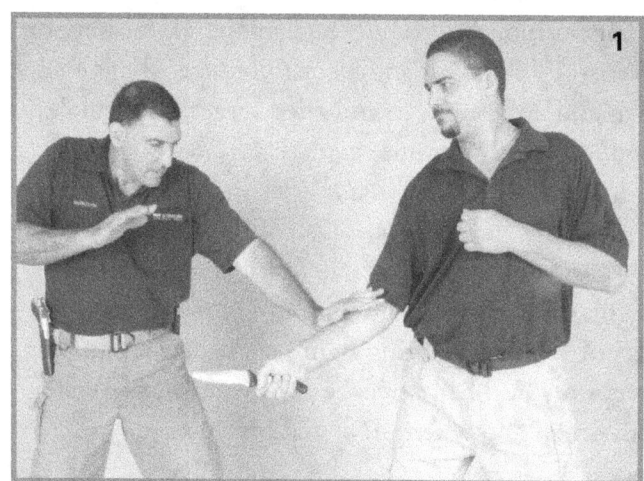

Optimal Support Hand Response— Down and Away

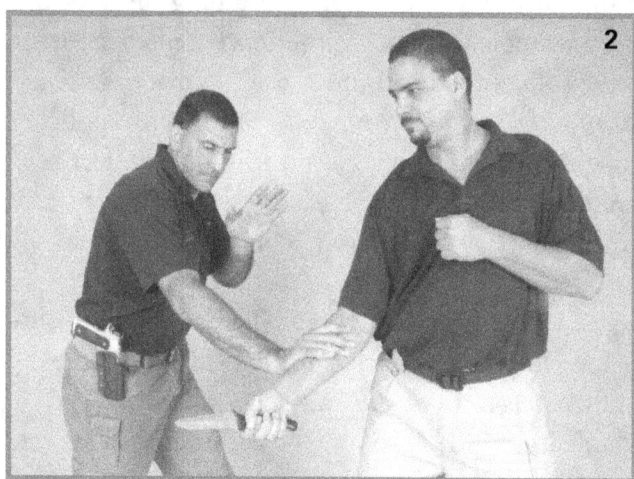

Optimal Strong Hand Response— Down and Away

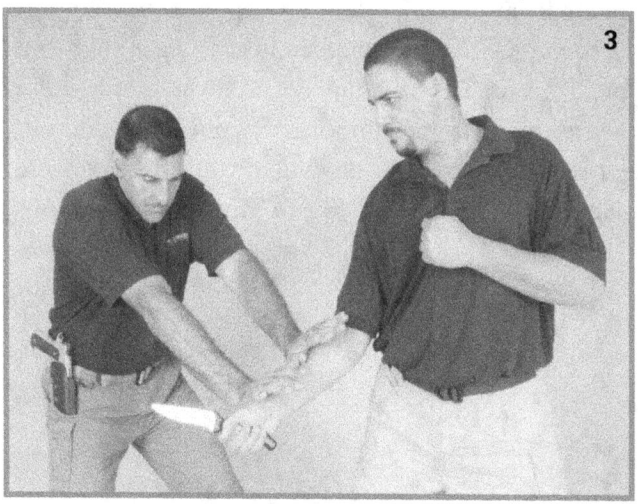

Optimal Response with both hands— Down and Away

Regardless of your position, utilizing the strong hand, the support hand, both hands or even your elbows is sufficient to redirect the incoming low-line attack down and away from its intended target. Most males will agree pushing straight down is not quite enough (as the tip will be directed straight into your ball bag), *down and away* remains the optimal choice.

When running this drill, don't get hung up on "correct position" or "fingers pointing left" or "fingers pointing right" or "using the support hand only because it keeps my gun hand free," etc. as you will NEVER be able to predict exactly when and where an attack may occur.

The masters of antiquity had an old saying regarding this type of CR at CAE with an edged weapon that was as true from the depths of pre-recorded history to the split second you finish reading this page: "*First make safe the weapon—then make safe the body.*" It directly applies to this technique. Although very simple in concept, it is highly effective in practice and a great rule of thumb in keeping sharp weapons away from your body and creating enough space/ time to go to guns.

Close-up Replay 2: Push off to create space. The only viable solution at such immediate and close range attack is to first "make safe the weapon" (accomplished by *hands versus hands* and *down and away*) and then to "make safe the body," again this can only be accomplished via the hands. Due to the close proximity of this range of engagement it is critical that you go immediately from making safe the weapon to making safe your body. This can be accomplished by immediately after pushing down and away on your opponent's *weapon arm* your second gross-motor skill is to push directly at the center mass of your opponent's *body*. It could be his shoulder it could be his back it could be anywhere you can make contact to keep him off balance long enough for you to move to a POD.

Push Back

Again, instead of taking my word for it, there's a drill that you can run with your training partner to test the "Push Back" theory. Ask your role player to stand at *contact range* again with his / her trusty plastic training knife. You stand facing your training partner with only a holster and blue / red gun (be sure to follow every safety procedure in the book here and ask your partner to again check a second (and third) time that you have a blue / red gun in your holster.

The role player will thrust in a slow and controlled manner with the plastic training blade in either his / her strong side or support side hand. Executing a "Down and Away" movement first make safe the weapon and then execute a "Push Back," clear to a POD and go to guns smoothly and with "the absence of all unnecessary movement" as possible. As you get more proficient ask your role player to move at you faster and faster until he / she is attacking at full speed. What does your experience tell you?

Begin the training drill at Contact Range and from the Hands Up position in a Stable Fighting Platform.

Bringing a Gun to a Knife Fight

First, make safe the weapon (slamming incoming weapon along low attack line Down and Away).

Then make safe the body (Push Back) rapidly making forceful positive forward–aggressive–effective contact with upper body of the attacker.

Part IV: Bringing a Gun to a Knife Fight

Be sure to gain full extension and create an optimal Reactionary Gap.

Make safe your body by moving of the LOA 45 degrees to either the strong side or support side (direction determined by environment) and simultaneously initiating the handgun presentation cycle.

Sufficient time-space allows for full presentation of the handgun with good sight picture and subsequent trigger control should the scenario demand. Notice shooter now positioned in a **Position of Advantage** *(in a green zone)*.

Grabbing the Knife Hand

What about grabbing the attacker's knife hand or arm? A very good question and one frequently asked at many edged weapon defense courses (both SAI and DTI). In any fight, there are no rules. In any fight there's never a "never" and never an "always," but there are certain considerations that need to be pondered. Consider that by grabbing your opponent's hand that you are at *contact range*, in the *red zone* and fighting for your life at the very highest potential SOI and with zero *reactionary gap*. He may be bigger, stronger, younger, higher level skill, juiced up on drugs (see 28 Real World Reasons), he may have an accomplice or accomplices and with one—or possibly two of your hands tied up in the fight you cannot get to your gun.

Further, you are now engaged in a stand-up grappling match with a knife—which, according to Greg Dossey (a very highly-respect retired Los Angeles Police Dept. Sergeant who conducted numerous studies, collected, documented and published the findings of hundreds of actual incidents involving law enforcement professional), about 86% of all stand up fights end up on the ground, odds are most certainly stacked against you that it will end up on the ground.

Consider that you could end up on the ground grappling with a brutally fierce opponent wielding a knife who may be bigger, (recalling the admonition of Bill Hall—"fightin' ain't easy, fightin' ain't pretty and size does matter"), younger, stronger, desensitized, well trained (in a federal penitentiary), and in better physical condition who is intent on ripping your throat out with his bare hands. Then consider that in addition to this life and death struggle on the ground with a knife, that *you* brought a gun to a "knife fight" and the terrifying possibility that gun could easily be taken away from you and used against you (while you're worried about the knife). No rules remember, he could even have a gun himself.

Regardless of the involvement of guns and knives, your very best option is keep him off balance and reacting (behind the curve). Although it may appear very tempting to close in and grab that knife hand (a plausible short-term objective), your primary objective is to take and keep control of the overall fight.

HIGH LINE ATTACK

The only remaining attack line that has not yet been covered is an attack on the high line. Again referring to the imaginary horizontal line located at about the belt level, any area located above this line of demarcation is considered a "highline" target. The most vulnerable of these highline targets are the soft targets such as the internal and external jugular veins, the internal and external carotid arteries, the subclavian arteries, brachial arteries, inferior vena cava and abdominal aorta. A knife strike (slash, thrust, puncture, etc.) to any one of these exposed and vulnerable hydraulic pipelines can bleed out a human body in a matter of minutes and depending upon the severity and exact placement of the cut or stab wound—a matter of seconds.

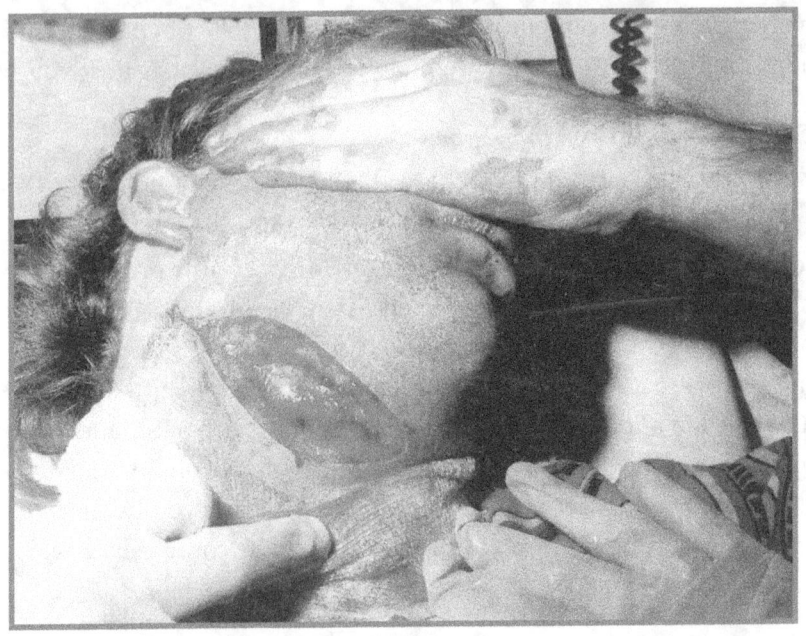
An edged weapon strike (slash) to a soft highline target.

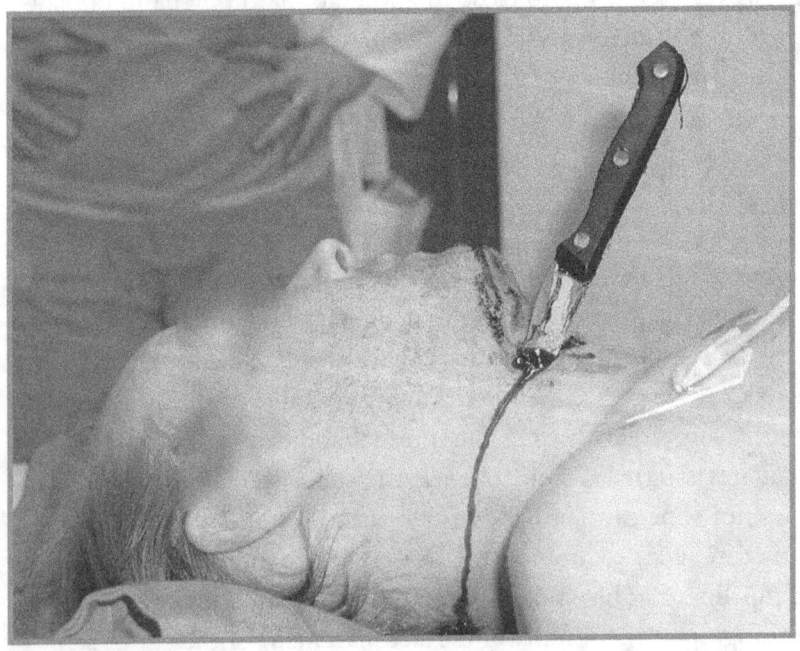
An edged weapon strike (stab) to a soft highline target.

Part IV: Bringing a Gun to a Knife Fight

Attacks on the high line can have devastating results. There are two problems with evading a highline attack. One is that it is usually coming in from above—which places you at a tactical disadvantage right from the start and two is the fact that all untrained shooters are of the mindset, "Well, I'll just shoot him."

Untrained response for high-line slash to the throat (vulnerable high-line soft target)—go immediately to guns.

Again, don't take my word for it. The following test is for those shooters who would like to test their reactionary skills at Contact Range and in the Red Zone. Keep in mind that all handicaps are removed as the shooter knows what to expect, already has his response prepared in his mind, is training with a blue / red gun and from an open holster (unconcealed and with no retention / safety issues). Even given all of these concessions, here's the drill:

Bringing a Gun to a Knife Fight _____

You stand facing your training partner at Contact Range (no cheating—make sure he can reach out with his training knife and at least be able to make contact with your throat with either the point or edge of the training knife). Your hands can be in any of the three fighting positions covered. On the command of "go" he simply attacks on the high line. Your objective is to reach for your handgun, execute a clean presentation, place muzzle squarely on target and get your finger onto the trigger all before he makes contact with your throat. After trying it a few times, what does your experience tell you?

What's the difference in end result between taking it for the team (illustrated) and the above training drill?

If you're interested in an optimal solution to the problem of a surprise, contact range, red zone attack with an edged weapon from the highline to your throat then read on.

SCENARIO 5—HIGH LINE ATTACK AT CAE AND CR

Beginning with the conditions of the environment, we'll start with a *confined area of engagement (CAE)*, indoors at your home (in a small garage attached to your house), at night (low-light), no noticeable bystanders or pedestrians in the vicinity but buildings are close enough that someone looking out the window is definitely in range of a stray 9mm round sailing through *your* neighborhood.

Thankful to finally be at your home after a very long-ass day at work you turn the key to the front door lock, walk in and close the door behind you. Walking to the kitchen you have your keys in one hand and newspaper and mail that you just scooped up from the floor in the other. Safe and sound behind the locked door of your castle, you unwittingly drop to *Condition White*.

After only a matter of seconds after setting foot onto the kitchen floor you are still carrying a concealed and loaded firearm (handgun) accessible to your weapon hand and on your person. You're very tired and thinking of nothing but that comfortable couch sitting in the next room and the taste of that first beer calling your name from the fridge. Your thoughts keep you from your normal *Condition Yellow*.

Opening the fridge door and in mid-motion of reaching for that ice cold bottle of beer, you hear a noise coming from the vicinity of the garage—although unfamiliar it's too faint to positively identify. Nonetheless you have *observed* something with your audio senses at which point you have entered into the *OODA Cycle* (Observe) and have switched from *Condition White* to *Condition Orange* (skipping *Condition Yellow*). Your senses heighten, and you quietly close the refrigerator door, turn toward the direction of that unfamiliar sound and move quickly to then next step on the *OODA cycle* (Orient). Probably just the cat or something, but tough to determine what caused that sound so it warrants a visual confirmation. Slowly turning the garage door knob and breathing quietly you make entry with your gun still holstered (as it's really most likely the cat moving around out there). As you suspected you find nothing. Smiling at your paranoia you turn back toward the door.

Bringing a Gun to a Knife Fight

Scenario 5—An attacker waits at the top of the stairs ready to deliver an attack on his intended victim standing on the steps below.

Part IV: Bringing a Gun to a Knife Fight

Suddenly and without warning, coming at you from a short distance at CR is a menacing-looking large athletic male wielding what appears to be a sharp and pointed metallic object, identified by you as a knife, capable of delivering severe bodily injury and, of course, death. This change in the *condition of the threat* causes you to switch to *Condition Red* and run another *OODA loop*. You have *observed* that this threat at CR is heading straight toward you with his blade coming in rapidly—a backhand slash to your throat. Gaining speed and closing the *Reactionary Gap* rapidly with weapon arm raised overhead he is prepared to strike at a highline soft target (your exposed throat) just inches away.

Now *oriented* to this new set of circumstances your heart starts pounding faster, breath becomes shallow and your palms sweat as you register and process important data: There is an intruder in my garage. The threat is already at CR, in motion, closing extremely quickly, armed with a dangerous weapon, I'm in pretty bad shape here deeply behind the *power curve* and no time or space to run without getting skewered, I remember that my gun is loaded and I'm pretty sure there's one in the tube, and there's not a snowball's chance in Hell that I can get to it in time because of the CR distance, he's moving PDQ and man, there's no choice but to deal with this hand-to-hand first and then go to guns.

Through the adrenaline dump, you make an important *decision*: He's on me at *Contact Range*, one more step and I'm toast, believe me I *want* to go to guns but there's absolutely no time, gonna have to make the call here—I'd really like to step out of the way but he's just placed me in the Red Zone and no time for anything but pure hand-to-hand defense.

Your mind is processing at light speed—movement forward or backward no longer an option, going to guns not an option, your primary threat is that incoming blade toward your highline soft targets. You need to make safe that weapon. Finally you *act* upon that decision.

Relying on your CQB training, you respond to the incoming slash to your throat with both arms raised up in a quick-shield posture to protect your head, neck and torso from the incoming highline attack. It wasn't very pretty and barely blocked his tremendous striking force, but nonetheless your technique was successful in diverting the incoming blade by impeding its path to any soft target.

Successfully defending the highline and having made safe the weapon, your next course of action although operating in a *confined area of engagement*, is to make safe your body. Pushing away from your centerline, open palm striking violently against his center mass with both hands, creates enough space which creates enough time—you now have the curve—you are in the process of dropping everything in your hands and although in the middle of the OODA Cycle you check of all 28 boxes (*Real World Reasons*), change your physical posture from unstable to an SFP, you immediately move off the line of attack (LOA) to 45 degrees angled back to your strong side and simultaneously (while moving your SFP from point A to point B) commence the 8-Step cycle of handgun presentation.

Right smack in the middle of your *handgun presentation cycle*:
1. Clear away your concealment garment(s) and simultaneously grip the firearm while defeating any retention devices on the holster system.
2. Clear from your carry position and Cant to Retention Position.
3. Hands come together. 4. Punch and Look. 5. Assess the situation.
You stop mid-cycle here and start a new OODA Loop *observing* that the bad guy is now recovering from your initial defense and turns to move toward you with a full *committed attack*. Moving to the *retention position*, instantly and due to proximity of threat, while he's trying to catch up (his reaction slower than your action) by your simultaneous 45-degree step plus firearm presentation you have placed him behind the *power curve*.

You apply *unsighted fire* from the *retention position* and hammer an *SDR* toward *center mass* of the assailant. He freezes for a spilt second. It appears to be the case that at least one of the rounds may have hit the assailant, but you can't tell (and if so was it a hit to a vital or not) and your *OODA cycle* kicks down to *orient* to this new *condition of the threat, condition of your environment and condition of your weapon system.*

He drops away briefly but again your assailant resumes his attack. With your ears ringing you empty the remainder of your entire magazine

Part IV: Bringing a Gun to a Knife Fight

(NSR), shoot to slide-lock and perform a speed re-load. By now your neighbors, hearing gunshots, have dialed 911. You maintain front sight on threat and observe that there is no movement from an apparently lifeless body bleeding all over your garage floor. The smell of burnt gunpowder fills your nose, ears still ringing, a drop of sweat falls from your right eyebrow in the deafening silence. You blink and it's over.

Your score is an SOI Level 1 possibly a bruise (SOI Level 2) due to the hand-to-hand contact while your opponent apparently is at an SOI Level 5. Clearly you are the victor in this gunfight with a knife.

Play by play: You really didn't have any time or space to operate—zero *Reactionary Gap*. He started out the gate at *Contact Range*. You were operating in a *confined area of engagement* and in the *Red Zone* the entirety of the incident, which lasted maybe around two seconds. Man it was shocking how fast it went down.

You were fully aware of the ever-changing *conditions of the threat, the condition of the environment* and the *condition of your weapon system*. You made the best decision possible to utilize your hands versus his hands as you had no space to use your legs and no time to go to guns. Executing a *Quick Shield* against the incoming backhand strike with the knife you managed to make safe the inbound weapon, *Push Back* his body, simultaneously move off LOA and complete the *Presentation Cycle* (as well as all the other Cycles of Action) and in a timely manner. You were fortunate to have handled the threat in a *forward, aggressive and effective* manner by emptying the contents of your entire magazine *(NSR)* in an effort to stop this life-threatening situation.

You were doubly fortunate to end this scenario without anyone getting injured (yourself and your neighbors included) except for the bad guy. You sustained little or no injuries and although sweating profusely, hard of hearing and a little shaken up—you won.

Close-up Replay 1: Quick Shield: The strike came directly toward your throat on angle and at high speed. Pinned in the *Red Zone* at *Contact Range* and in a *confined area of operation* with a high-probability of injury potential and with no space and no time to move or to go to guns, your only option was to utilize your bare hands in an immediate *forward, aggressive and effective* defense. The most important part of this personal defense maneuver is to first make safe the weapon.

Quick Shield

Specifically designed for application at the dangerous Contact Range, this technique provides the operator with a simple gross motor skill to protect CL / CM against a high line attack and can be executed in less than one second.

Referred to as a "Quick Shield," this technique is employed primarily as a temporary insurance program in response to a high-line attack at CR in order to move to a POA or POD. Used in conjunction with the Push Back technique, the Quick Shield provides an effective personal defense option at Contact Range.

First "make safe the weapon." The Quick Shield technique is a rapid personal defense response which allows temporary immobilization of an incoming strike at Contact Range. In this example the Quick Shield is applied to an incoming back-hand strike to the head.

Part IV: Bringing a Gun to a Knife Fight

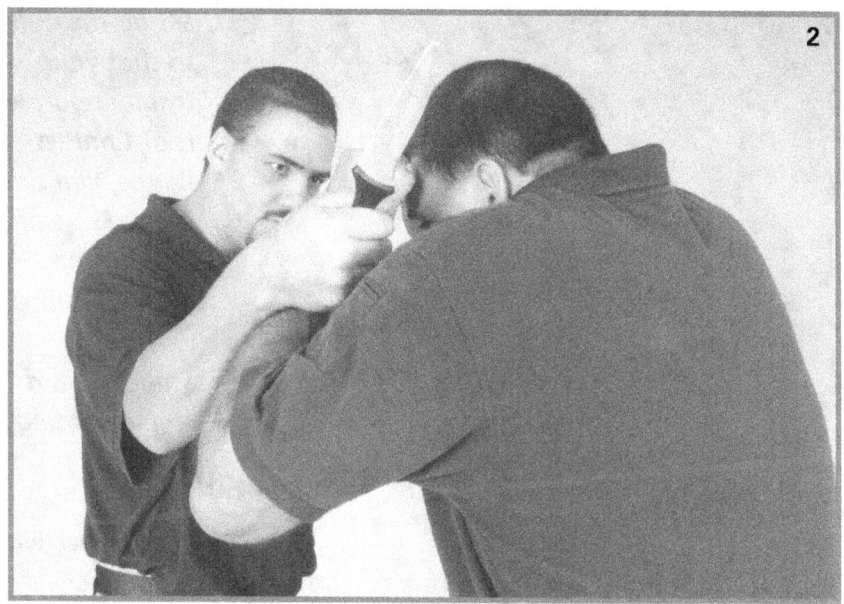

In this example the Quick Shield is applied to an incoming forehand strike to the head. Note that the closed fist is attached to the forehead and the chin tucked in for additional structural support from the shoulders. Remember to keep your eyes open and, of course, on the threat at all times.

In this particular case, the "A" choice was to engage the threat at *CR* and handle the attack first with your bare hands. This scenario permitted no other viable options, no where to turn, no way to move to a *POA* or a *POD*, going to guns would have given him time to cut you to pieces before you even started your presentation cycle.

After completing the *Quick Shield* (and having made safe the weapon) you immediately decide to lower your *SOI* potential and "*Get Out*" by executing a *Push Back* technique (make safe the body) and go to guns.

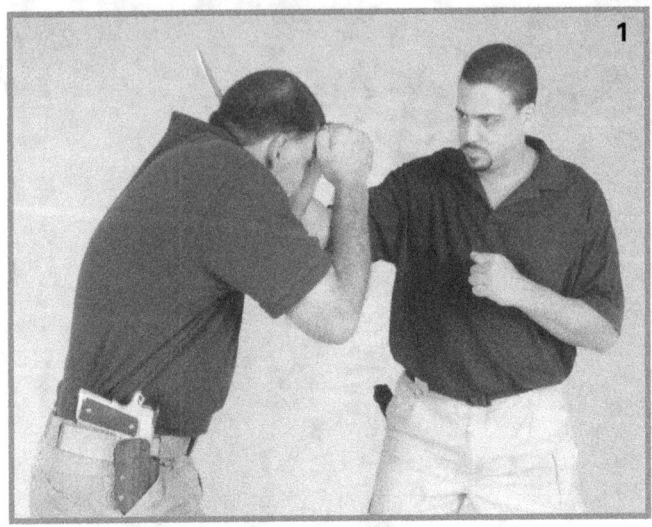

Set up the drill so that your training partner is at Contact Range, you are in the Red Zone and he's prepared to move with speed. Standing in a stable fighting platform in the hand position of your choice with a holstered training gun face the threat who should already have a training knife in his hand poised in the highline position about to deliver a forehand slash to your throat at speed. On the command of "go" the role player attacks with a forehand strike to your throat at speed. Utilizing a Quick Shield response temporarily yet rapidly impedes the highline attack.

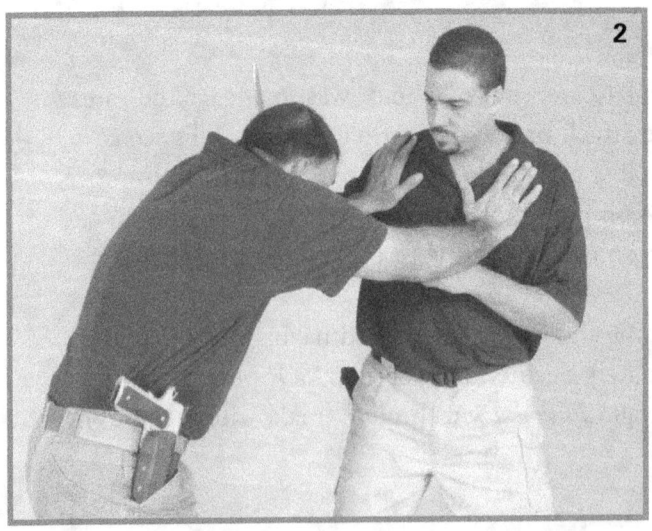

After making safe the weapon, the next objective is to make safe your body. Using both hands and in a forward, aggressive effective manner, push with both hands to increase the Reactionary Gap.

Part IV: Bringing a Gun to a Knife Fight

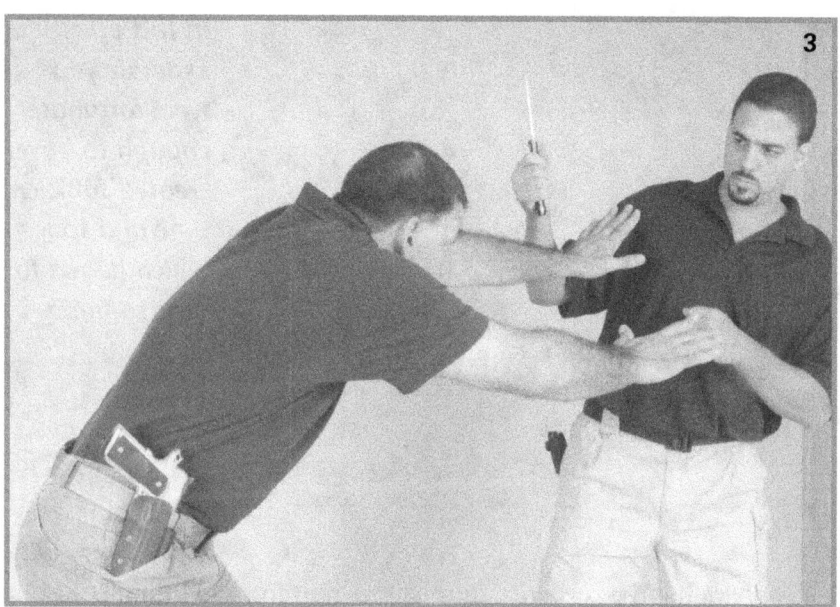

Remember, the focus here is on forward, aggressive, and effective. This guy just tried to kill you. Feel free to knock him into the next zip code.

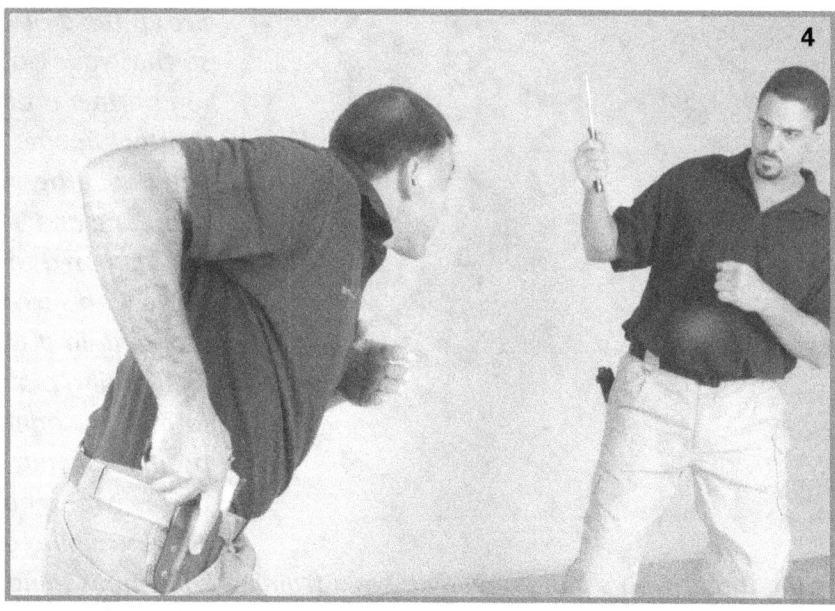

Now with an increased Reactionary Gap, this allows you to step off the LOA while simultaneously initiating the handgun presentation cycle.

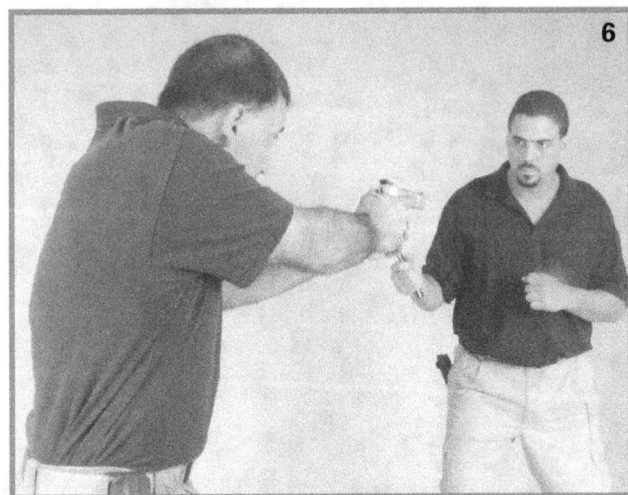

6 In this particular example you were fortunate enough to have created sufficient time and space which allows for sighted fire.

Changing the scenario, in this next training evolution, the attacker will now deliver a backhand slash to your throat and purposely not allow you to go to sighted fire. In this example you will be forced to respond from the Weapon Retention Position.

1 Set up the drill so that your training partner is at Contact Range, you are in the Red Zone and he's prepared to move with speed. Standing in a stable fighting platform in the hand position of your choice with a holstered training gun face the threat who should already have a training knife in his hand poised in the highline position about to deliver a backhand slash to your throat at speed. On the command of "go" the role player attacks with a backhand strike to your throat at speed. Utilizing a Quick Shield response temporarily yet rapidly impedes the highline attack.

Part IV: Bringing a Gun to a Knife Fight

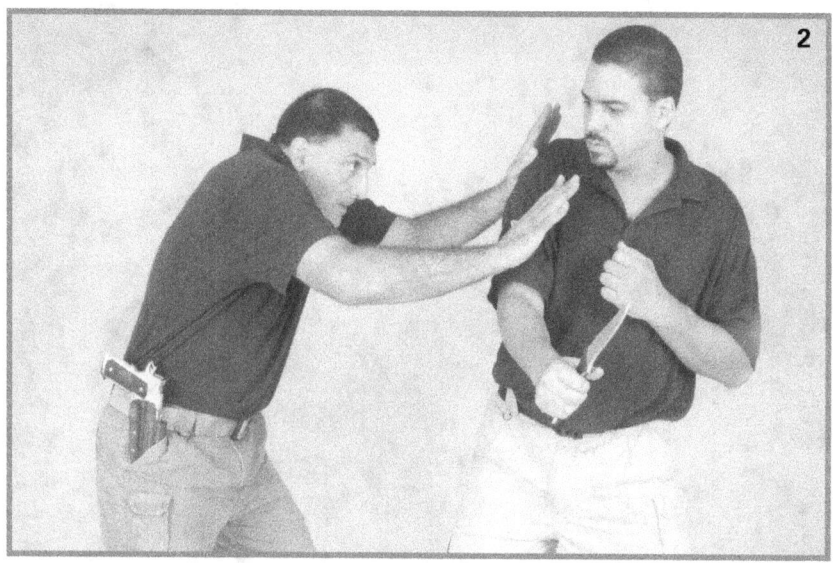

After making safe the weapon, the next objective is to make safe your body. Using both hands and in a forward, aggressive effective manner, push with both hands to increase the Reactionary Gap.

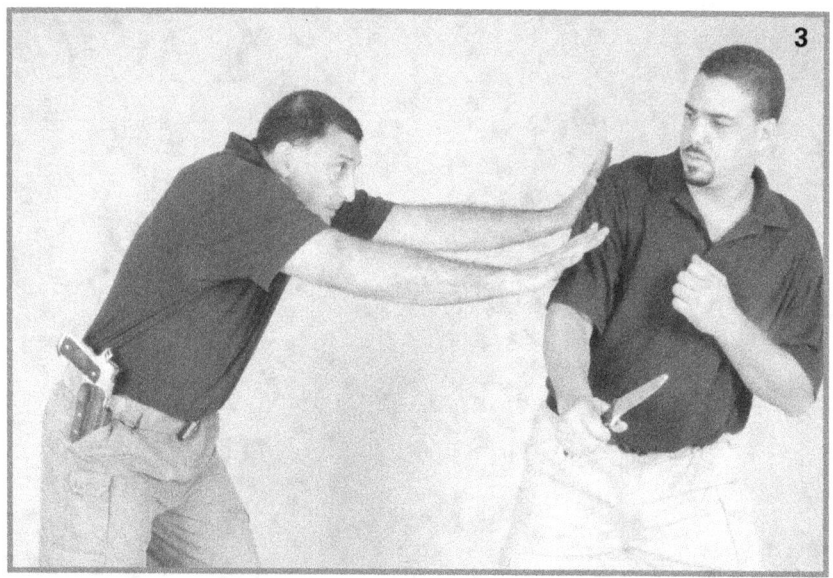

Remember, the focus here is on forward, aggressive, and effective. This guy just tried to kill you.

Bringing a Gun to a Knife Fight

Now with an increased Reactionary Gap, this allows you to step off the LOA while simultaneously initiating the handgun presentation cycle.

In this particular example you were not permitted sufficient time and space allowing for sighted fire. Your only remaining option is moving to Weapon Retention Position.

It is important to note that the Quick Shield is a highline hand response option only. If you had the time and space for a leg response option then you would use your legs to break from the attack and go to guns—no need for a highline hand response if you have the time and space to move off LOA.

The Quick Shield is designed specifically as a last ditch effort (since you can't use your feet for defense and not enough time and space to go to guns) to at least get an obstruction or some sort of cover up around your brain box and with a quickness prior to the blade edge or point reaching its intended highline target.

When training this technique there is no need to step into the strike. Stepping into your opponent with a Quick Shield when you can simply step back and go to guns is unrealistic training. If you find yourself stepping in then you are starting the drill at *too great a distance* and your role player is allowing an unrealistic amount of time and space. Again at NCR you have sufficient time to utilize the legs and simply step off the LOA and go to guns. The idea here is to create a worst case scenario attack with a knife at CR and in the Red Zone. Ask your role player to start the drill at CR and place you in the Red Zone for reality-based training.

Quick Shield Push Back Live Fire Drill

If you're interested to see for yourself how this technique works, go ahead and try this simple live-fire square-range drill you can run to test your ability to respond at *CR* by executing a *Quick Shield* followed by a *Push Back* moving 45 degrees off the *LOA* to either the *strong* or *support side* and shoot an *NSR* to *CM* of the target from the *Weapon Retention Position*.

Set Up: Be sure you are at a secured range and you are cleared hot from the RM and RSOs. Following all safety and range rules, set up paper targets and stand at your arm's length from the target. Be sure to check the area around you that there are no obstructions to your footwork as well as backstop and beyond. Wearing additional garment to simulate concealed carry (if applicable), face down range, *make ready* to a *full load* and holster. Remain facing downrange in the *hands below* position ready to follow range commands.

Drill: The RM / RSO will issue commands and run the shooting strings first by the numbers and then all as one motion dry fire and then lastly using live rounds. The first set, stand directly in front of your target at arms length and upon range commands, make ready and come to a full load. Upon audio command, you will execute a *Quick Shield* followed by a *Push Back* moving 45 degrees off the *LOA* to either the *strong* or *support side* and deliver an *NSR* to the *center mass* of the target from the *Weapon Retention Position*.

Facing downrange and starting from a stable fighting platform (and with RM / RSO permission) place at least on hand on the target to simulate Contact Range and stuck in the Red Zone with little or no time to respond.

Part IV: Bringing a Gun to a Knife Fight

Execute Quick Shield. Be sure that your hands are trained up high enough that your thumbs both touching your temple area. Keep your eyes down range and focused on the threat throughout the entire drill.

Simulate a Push Back movement utilizing both hands simultaneously.

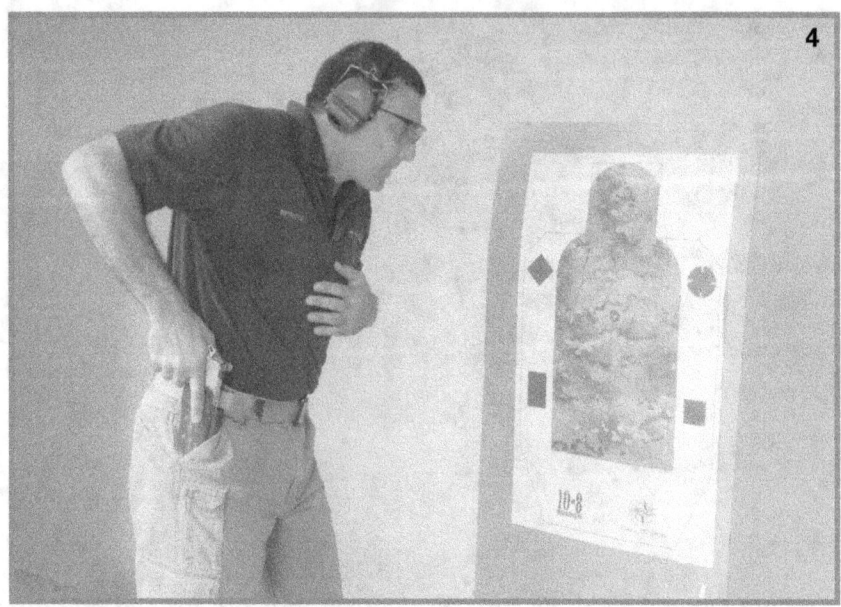

Execute stepping of LOA first step plus "Grip" step of **Handgun Presentation Cycle** *immediately followed by*

Execution of second half of "moving off LOA" step including delivery of an NSR to center mass of the target from the Weapon Retention Position (with both hands retracted).

Part IV: Bringing a Gun to a Knife Fight

If the shooter chooses to develop additional range / position skills as previously covered, an additional step of increasing **Reactionary Gap** *and moving to* **sighted fire** *position (delivering two additional rounds to the body) can be added.*

Knife Assault Grips

As a full-time training instructor, it is often the case that I am frequently asked to field questions about what to look for if someone is coming at you with a knife. Near to the end of our study here the majority of these key observational items referencing assault with a knife have already been covered such as range (NCR / CR), position (safe / unsafe—red / green zones), mobility (stationary, forward movement, etc.), committed and uncommitted attacks, low line and highline attacks, confined and open areas of engagement and others. All of these although applicable to a knife attack are additionally applicable to any handheld "other dangerous weapon."

However, a remaining and beneficial defensive (proactive) observation specific to assault with a knife is the attacker's knife grip. How is your attacker holding the knife in his hand? There are basically only two general positions—the blade tip is pointing up (or forward) or the blade tip is pointing down (or backward).

Example of assault with a knife tip up and edge forward.

Example of assault with a knife tip down or backward and the edge facing forward.

Part IV: Bringing a Gun to a Knife Fight

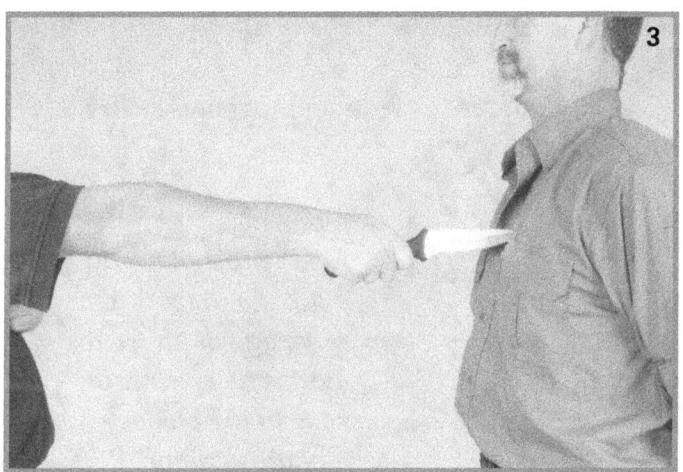

If the blade tip is pointing upward or forward this gives you less distance to react which in turn reduces your response time which limits your reaction options.

It additionally and rapidly closes the reactionary gap from NCR to CR and in doing so raises your potential for injury.

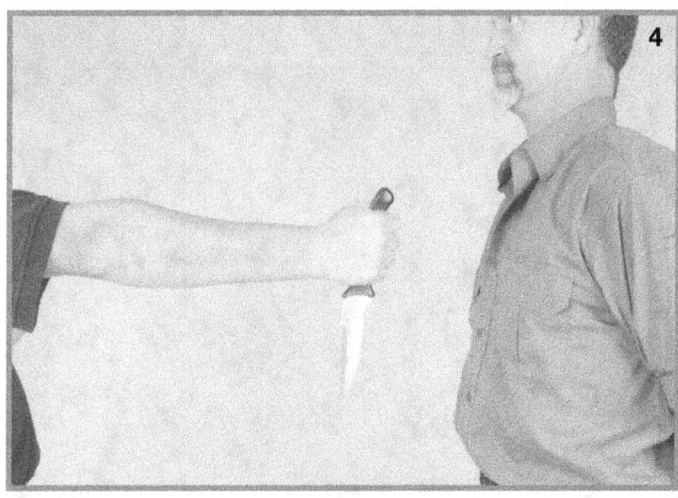

On the other hand, if the blade tip is pointing down or backward (away from your CL / CM), your assailant would need to be at Contact Range in order to deliver effective strikes (raise your SOI) with his knife. The need for him to further close the gap in order to be effective, **mechanically** allows you more space, which allows you increased response time which may improve your reaction options as it would take longer for your attacker to reach deeper into CR with this particular grip.

Assault Grip Range Familiarization

Again, don't take my word for it, test it out for yourself. Try this simple range familiarization drill:

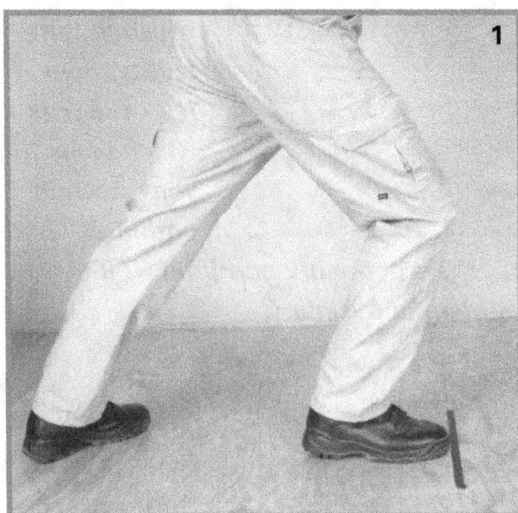

Ask the role player to place a marker at the very edge of his front foot as he extends the knife in the blade forward position as far as he can possibly reach.

Standing directly in front of him, extend one of your arms so that the tip of the blade barely touches (the very edge of CR) and mark your front foot position.

Part IV: Bringing a Gun to a Knife Fight

Now ask the role player to reverse his grip and without moving his feet from their previous position to extend the blade tip as far as possible.

Standing directly in front of him, and without changing your foot position, extend one of your arms. What do you notice about range based on assault grip?

Highline Attack at CR in CAE—"Get In" Option

A common remaining "what if" is, "What if the attacker moving *PDQ* at *CR* in *CAE* swings the inbound knife at your head with a forehand as opposed to a backhand as in the previous example?" The exact same technique can be applied. As a matter of fact there are (as previously covered) two options—"Get In" or "Get Out." The safer of the two is, of course, to "Get Out" as previously covered.

Utilizing a training handgun while your role player has a training knife, set up this next drill at Contact Range with you (as the operator) at the Red Zone. Ask your role player to deliver a rapid forehand highline strike to your throat.

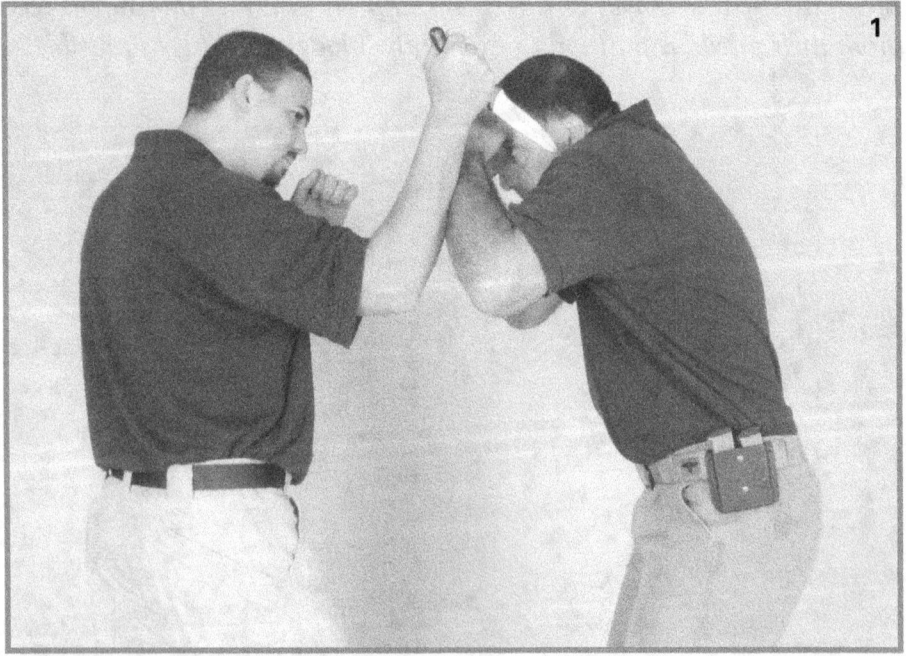

First "make safe the weapon." The Quick Shield technique can be reinforced by tucking in your chin behind your shoulder to provide temporary cover for vulnerable highline targets. Remember to keep your eyes on the threat.

Part IV: Bringing a Gun to a Knife Fight

Then make safe the body (Push Back) and...

Get Out (move to a POA / POD) and go to guns.

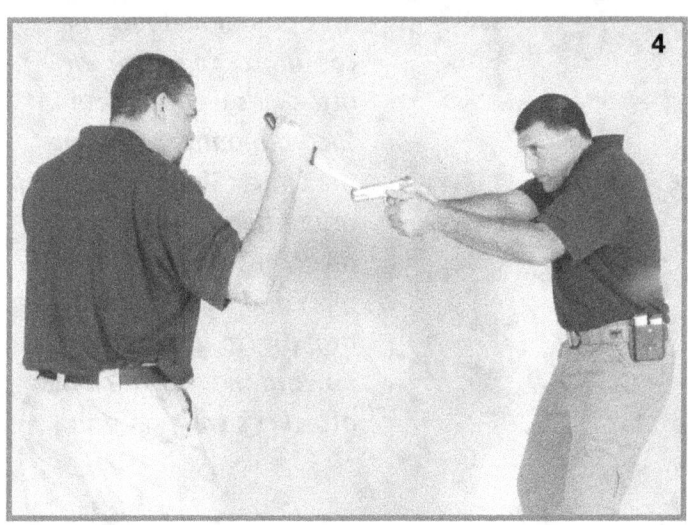

However, it may be the case that *condition of the threat, condition of the environment and condition of your weapon system(s)* may dictate otherwise—you may need to "Get In." If it ends up being a requirement to "Get In" the same advice of the masters apply—first make safe the weapon and then make safe your body.

The decision has been made to "*Get In*." First rule of thumb is to "make safe the weapon" which is accomplished by temporarily securing the weapon arm in such a manner as to impede movement of the weapon in all four directions (up, down, left and right).

An optimal method one can utilize to secure the attacker's weapon arm in such a manner following the **Quick Shield** *is to wrap around and firmly lock the attacker's weapon arm up high and tight against your arm pit (to impeded any upward movement of the attacker's weapon arm).*

Part IV: Bringing a Gun to a Knife Fight

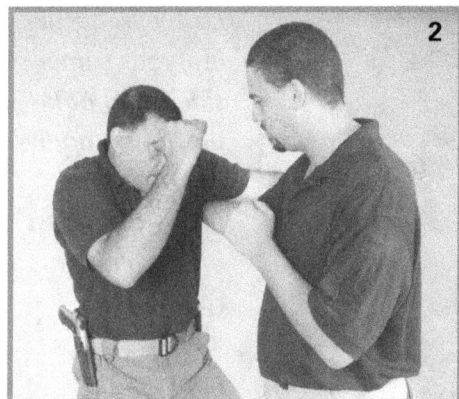

Next "drop your chicken wing" slamming your elbow toward your rib cage firmly pinning the attacker's weapon arm in such a manner as to prevent (albeit temporarily) lateral movement (left and right).

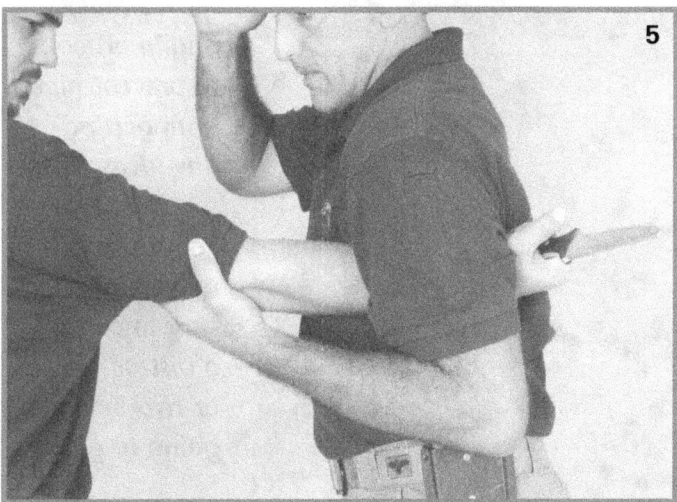

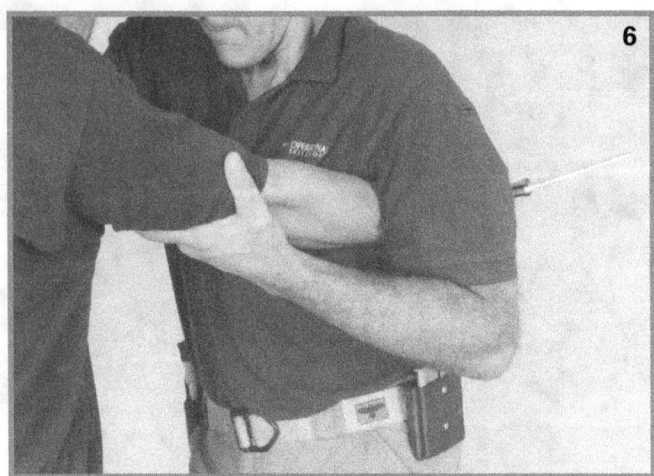

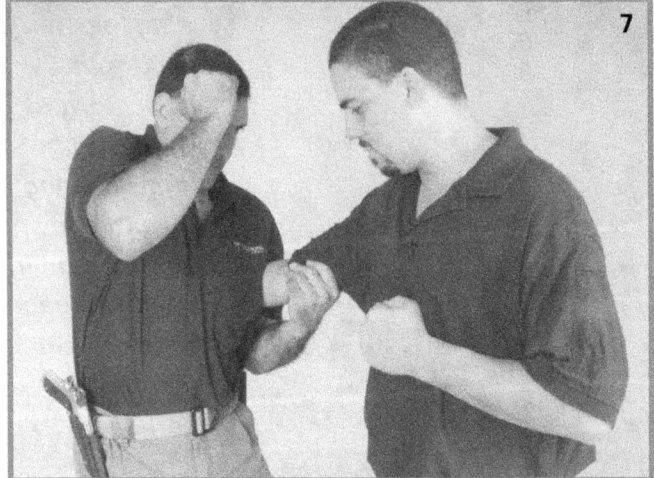

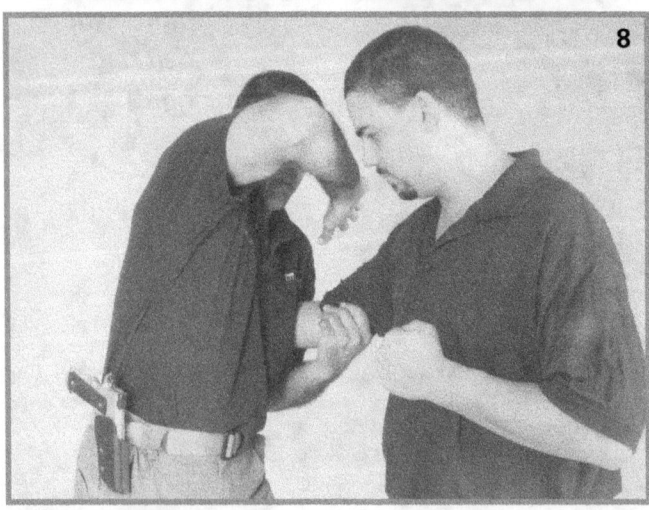

Lastly, by securing your same-side hand palm up tightly applying pressure upward against his upper arm (above the elbow) this impedes not only downward movement of the attacker's weapon arm but also secures a temporary mechanical compliance of preventing his trying to pull his hand out from under your arm. At this time, and in order to prevent him from getting any ideas about reaching for your gun, it may be necessary to deliver a distraction or two before going to guns.

Part IV: Bringing a Gun to a Knife Fight

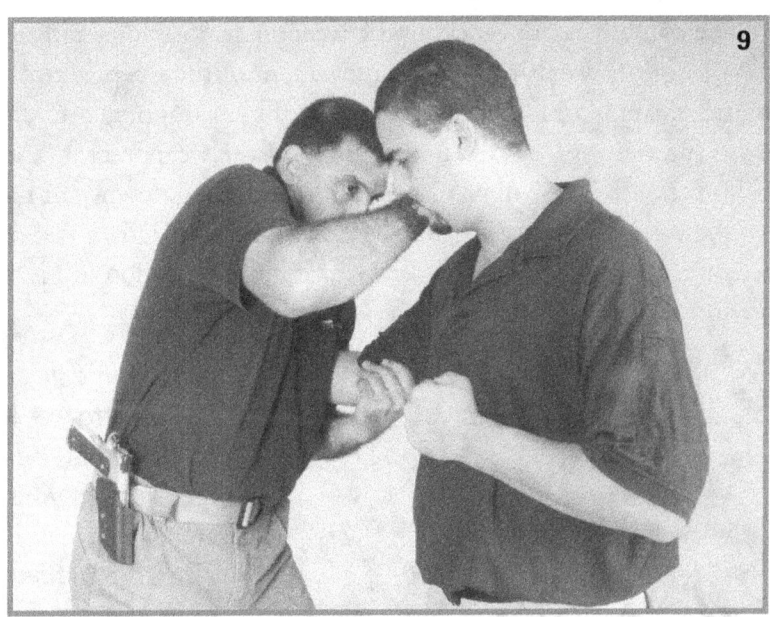

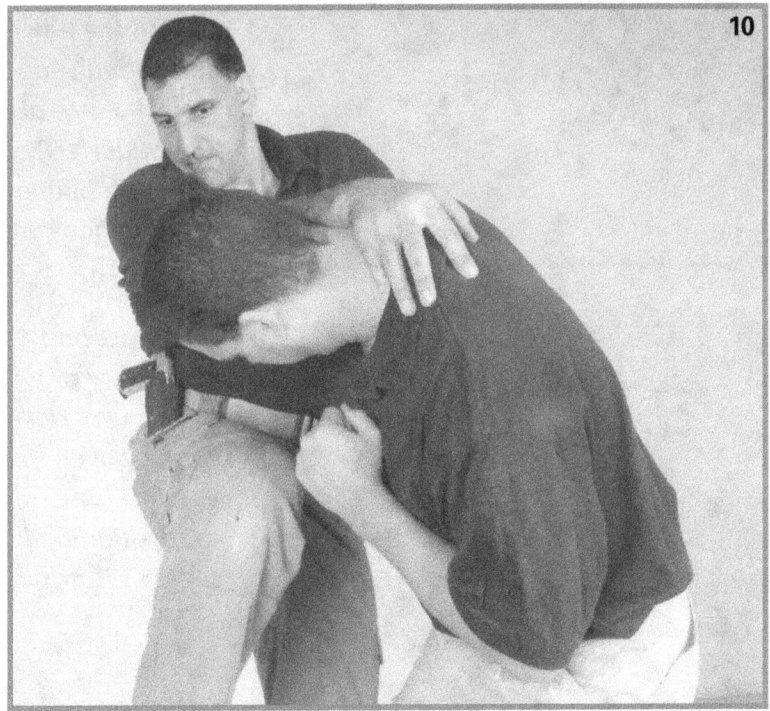

Given very little response time you may not have the option to go immediately to your gun. Your only remaining option may be to briefly continue with elbow and knee strikes to create the opportunity to get to your gun.

The combination of locking the weapon arm up high and tight into your armpit (preventing upward movement of the weapon arm), plus pinning the weapon arm between the inside of your trapping arm and your torso (preventing any lateral movement of the weapon arm) and your palm pressure in the upward position (preventing downward movement of the weapon arm), plus a little Old School Beat Down (OSBD) all mechanically contribute to the temporary immobilization of his weapon arm.

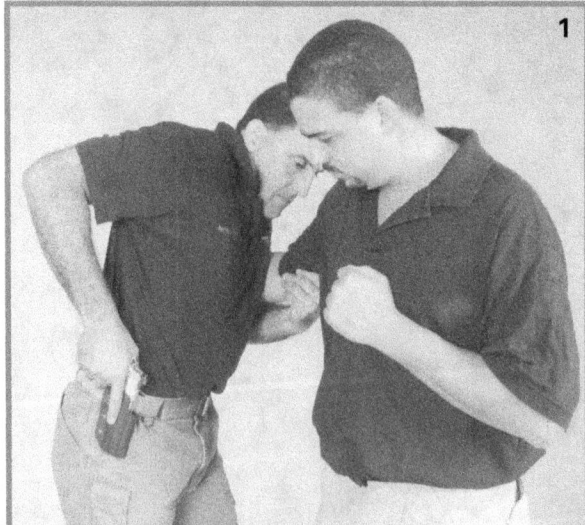

Following delivery of OSBD, attacker will be placed off balance, reacting (to your forward–aggressive–effective actions) and remain firmly behind the power curve long enough for you (even at such close quarters) to initiate a handgun presentation cycle.

A contact body shot or delivery of an NSR at this very close range will cause discomfort, alter his motivation and loosen his grip.

Part IV: Bringing a Gun to a Knife Fight

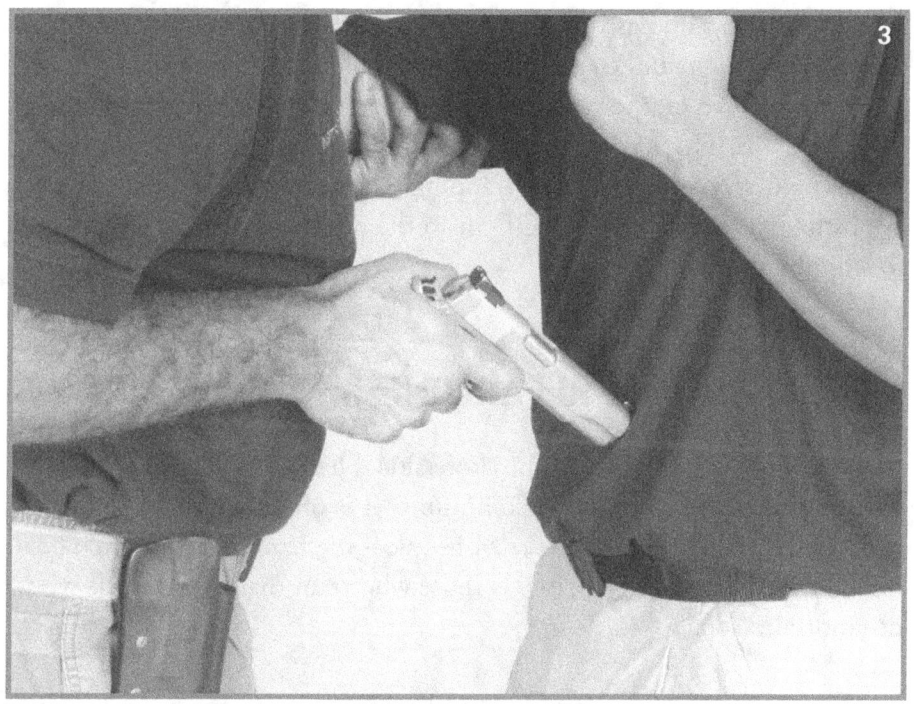

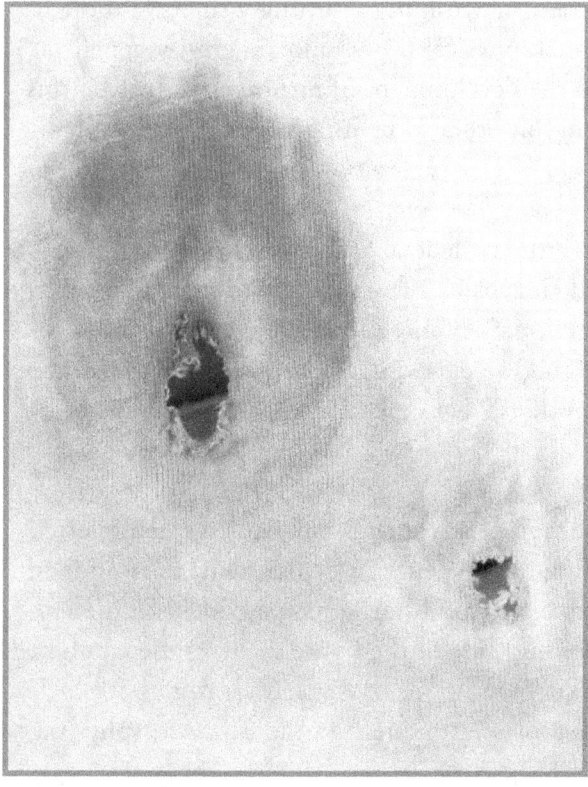

Close up shot of actual result on a t-shirt of two live fire body contact shots. The top round was fired about an inch away from the surface of the shirt. The bottom round was fired about three inches away. The reader may notice the burn-blast marks caused by the exploding gases as well as particles of fouling especially accompanying the top round.

Keep in mind as was previously covered, that there is a counter for every technique under the sun. Is it possible for a well-trained (or lucky) attacker to escape your temporary weapon arm trapping technique? Of course it is. That's why it's strongly recommended by the masters that you do not "stay and play" after trapping the weapon arm and as quickly as possible move to a POA / POD or to the next level of force necessary to stop the threat.

CONDITION OF PREPAREDNESS

In working predominantly in the professional hard-skills (combative shooting and defensive tactics) community it is often said that the world is divided up into only two types of people—the hard and the soft. The only difference between the two is those who train (hard) and those who do not train (soft).

Used in the context of hard-skills development, the word *training* does not refer to going to the gym, running or lifting weights (although these do in fact assist in overall physical fitness and are greatly beneficial to overall readiness), but to the development of *tactical* skills (small arms and defensive tactics training) in order to maintain a condition of preparedness.

What can we do as military, federal and law enforcement professionals and defense-minded citizens of a free republic to remain hard? The answer is two fold—the development and continued maintenance of software (combative concepts) and the development and continued maintenance of hardware (physical skills). Let's take a closer look at these two critical pieces.

The operating condition of any quality operator is often referred to in the industry (depending upon agency or department) as an individual's "condition of preparedness." Condition of preparedness on the *software* (mental skills conditioning) side of the house includes the combined Defensive Mindset (including Conditions of Awareness) from both SAI and DTI. Whereas condition of preparedness on the *hardware* (physical skills conditioning) side of the house includes the combination of pretty much everything else that's covered in this manuscript.

Conditions of preparedness also include physical conditioning also known as physical training (PT) which includes cardio and strength training. Ask any professional fighter and he will tell you that all skills, experience and size being equal, the fighter that runs out of gas first will lose. In other words, if you're in better physical shape than your opponent, then the odds are stacked in your favor right from the start. PT is important and there are minimal physical requirements wherever you look throughout the professional training community. Some of these requirements are tougher than others such as those of a US Marine Forced Reconnaissance, US Navy SEAL, US Army Ranger, SWAT, CRT or other special operations personnel. Regardless of agency or department each of these requires some PT minimum requirement for a reason and that reason is that if you don't meet a minimal standard of physical fitness, then you are not physically prepared to do the job. The very same requirements apply to those of us who wish to remain prepared for any lethal altercation— general physical conditioning is a huge factor.

Another critical factor in the development of hard skills is *desensitization*. Those of you who may not know him or have not read any of his outstanding books or attended any of his superb seminars, Lt. Col. David Grossman (US Army, Ret.) Director, Killology Research Group, (click on www.killology.com) is an internationally recognized scholar, author, soldier, and speaker who is one of the world's foremost experts in the field of human aggression and the roots of violence and violent crime.

A West Point psychology professor, Professor of Military Science, and an Army Ranger, Col. Grossman has combined his experiences to become the founder of a new field of scientific endeavor, which has been termed "killology." Col. Grossman is an Airborne Ranger infantry officer, and a prior-service sergeant and paratrooper, with a total of over 23 years experience in leading U.S. soldiers worldwide. He retired from the Army in February 1998 and has devoted himself full-time to teaching, writing, speaking, and research. Today he is the director of the Killology Research Group, and in the wake of the 9/11 terrorist attacks he is on the road almost 300 days a year, training elite military and law enforcement organizations worldwide about the reality of combat. If you have not attended his outstanding seminar "The Bullet Proof Mind," (see www.Killology.com for more info) then you are remiss in acquiring phenomenal tools for your mental conditioning.

Col. Grossman delves very deeply into the desensitization component. The meat and potatoes of this concept are what any professional war fighter (soldier, Marine, etc.) does (subconsciously) through their years of training—they become acclimated as a result of their training. As an example, if you've never fired a gun before in your life, then odds are you're not accustomed to an explosion occurring at the end of your arm followed by recoil. No doubt you would most likely react adversely to these effects of firing (e.g. blinking, little or no muzzle control, etc.). Over time any shooter will become acclimated or, more accurately stated, desensitized to these effects and learn to overcome them as the number of repetitions is increased.

The overall desensitization mechanism works similar to the telling of the same funny joke over and over again. It may have made you double over with laughter the first time you heard it, but the second time it wasn't so funny, and the third time you heard the same exact joke it had even less of an effect on you than the first two times. The more you hear the same joke, any reaction you may have had prior eventually "goes flat" and you become completely inoculated from any effects of hearing that same joke. The very same applies to a first-time boxer. When hit in the face by an opponent's boxing glove he winces and closes his eyes (less than optimal when you're in the ring). However, the more times he gets hit in the face by his opponent, the more he becomes desensitized to getting hit in the face and therefore becomes less and less affected.

The terminal objective of any training is to develop a conditioned response by which both conceptual and physical skills development, combined with desensitization and physical conditioning (results of PT) can give you the edge (no pun intended) in any fight—with a gun or a knife or even your bare hands.

Getting to the shooting range and actually training (running drills and getting quality repetitions—*by the way, this is very different than going to the range only once a year to re-qualify*), hammering out a few pushups, some sit-ups, a little cardio and developing your defensive tactics—is all about preparedness. The whole key to creating and sustaining combat readiness is to be better trained and better prepared both *mentally* and *physically* than your opponent.

PERISHABLE SKILLS

Regardless of where your background falls in the spectrum of experience—all skills are perishable. We've all heard the common admonition "keep your skills honed." Not unlike the sharp edge of a quality knife, over time and without sharpening, hard skills can rust and become dull.

All skills are perishable, both mentally and physically. One of my masters relayed a story about a high-school buddy of his who was a championship swimmer back in the day and competed in the Olympic Games when he was in his twenties. After that time he stopped swimming completely as his lifestyle changed and as is the normal course of life's events with a wife, kids and a full-time job barely got any time to train at all. Later on in life, this same guy (now in his early forties) at some party jumped into an Olympic-sized pool and about killed himself. Everyone at the party was shocked as here was this championship Olympic swimmer who just about drowned in a backyard swimming pool.

As he was recovering in a nearby emergency room, my master visited him and asked him what had happened. "Well," he said, "in my mind I was still 21 years old and training for the Olympic Games, but my body is now 42 years old and my mind was writing checks that my body wasn't able to cash!" The moral of the story is that if you don't keep up with your physical skills training, they diminish over time.

Diminished skills occur both physically and *mentally*. How many years has it been since your freshman year of college? Go ahead and try to pass a freshman-year collegiate math or calculus final exam. How would you score fifteen or twenty years later? Unless that particular mental faculty is utilized on a regular basis—*mental* skills are subject to the same natural peril of *physical* skills—"If you don't use it you lose it." The masters advise, "Endeavor to keep both a sharp mind and a hard body."

The answer is consistency.

As an instructor at Gunsite Academy in Arizona, I often get the opportunity to work with shooters from all walks of life—the full gamut from seasoned professional military operator to civilian soccer mom Mrs. Johnson who had never held a gun in her hand in her life and everyone in between.

One example of consistency is the true life story a down-home country farm boy who attended one of the intermediate pistol classes with no particular background other than working out on the farm and his dad teaching him some pointers about shooting.

Attending this particular class were a handful of law enforcement officers (two of whom were SWAT Team Leaders) a couple of active military personnel a few pilots and some other civilians including this kid from out in the sticks who was maybe in his late twenties. All throughout the week of training, this kid was for five days straight consistently hitting the highest scores in no matter what drill we were running. Finally at the end of the week, there was a man-on man competition held to find the best shooter in the class. If memory serves it was a full class of sixteen shooters.

The drill called for two students at a time to stand along side their competition opponent both facing down range with pistols holstered, facing five steel targets and a split steel target in the middle. The first one to hit all five targets, complete a speed reload and drop his half of the split steel target was the winner. Each winner would then be paired off with the winner of another bout until only one winner remained.

As you could well imagine when this farm boy ended up the overall winner in the man-on-man competition that there were a few bruised egos—especially from the military and law enforcement folks. They were understandably upset and confused as to why this civilian kid handed them their ass. It wasn't even close—he smoked them all by a huge margin.

The answer is simply consistency. I asked him later on after graduation what his training regimen was and he replied sheepishly, "Well, every night I come home after work and just shoot a few magazines to stay sharp and keep my skills." Nothing spectacular, he would occasionally attend a shooting school maybe once a year or so and each night when he came home from work, sauntered out to the north forty and hammered through a couple of magazines to keep his hard skills up.

Professional operators and competitive shooters share this same secret—continued training and refreshing of both *soft* and *hard* skills. Professional shooters, when training for a competition on average hammer about 1500 rounds a week down range. Some agencies train their high-end operators roughly on the same numbers based on top tempo. The real high-profile competitive shooters may burn through anywhere from 1500 to 2500 rounds a week to stay in the game.

Unfortunately most cops, according to recent studies, maybe shoot less than 80 rounds a year and for most of them that's usually just to qualify. After a long-ass day on patrol the last thing you want to do is spend valuable off-duty time shooting. Right?

My good friend Bill Murphy, (a decorated 30-year law enforcement veteran—with military background and highly respected in the industry) did some extensive research on law enforcement professionals and training. Additionally, working as a consultant for Surefire Inc., as well as a Senior Gunsite Firearms Instructor, Bill is, in my opinion, one of the top-shelf firearms instructors out there today and a specialist in low-light training. His research concluded that only 5% of cops train on their own and on a regular basis. It is an unfortunate fact of life that most civilians who consistently shoot are better shots than most cops (not talking about specialty teams here). When general law enforcement management is approached to increase training programs for their employees such responses as "Well, that's not budgeted," "We can't afford to take the guys off the line," "They can go train on their own," etc. come up (if you can even get an answer out of them at all). Believe it or not there are some departments who allocate less than sixty rounds a year to their officers for carry and qualification. Keep in mind that qualification *does not* qualify as *training*.

In the example of gun-toting professionals who receive little or no training from their department or agency and who do not train on their own, where do you think their level of skill and proficiency with a handgun may be? Now if it's the case that these individuals receive little or no SAI training can you guess as to how much DTI training these folks get? You guessed it—unless on their own—zero.

If you do the math and put together minimal or no training in SAI and zero training in DTI, then how would you imagine they would fare in a gunfight with a surprise knife attack at extreme close quarters? Now let's take this to the average concealed-carry permit law-abiding citizen. How many rounds a week, month, or year do they get in SAI training? How many hours a week, month or year do they get in DTI training? How would you imagine they would fare in a gunfight with a surprise knife attack at extreme close quarters?

The end game on winning any altercation is sustainment of these valuable yet perishable skills. All throughout this study, the training material has been presented in an easy-to-learn training method conducive to *familiarization*. If these training concepts and drills are followed as per above, then a level of *proficiency* in these tactical skills may be developed over time. As covered in great detail above, this training material familiarization and proficiency can develop valuable defensive shooting skills.

However, regardless of skill level, without *sustainment* and consistency of training, these valuable skills can and will diminish. Decaying alongside your diminished skills follows your ability to win.

Hard skills—you don't use them, you lose them.

Steve Tarani
July, 2007

GLOSSARY

AOT—Advanced Officer Training

ASAP—As soon as possible.

Center Line—It is the imaginary line drawn down from the crown of the head directly between the eyes, over the nose, along the sternum and through the groin. Along this 3-4 inch wide margin lay most of the body's major organs.

Center Mass—The heaviest part of the body and the largest surface area. Area of the human body containing the largest volume of internal organs.

CAE—Confined Area of Engagement (See Confined Area of Engagement)

CL—Center Line (see Center Line)

CM—Center Mass (see Center Mass)

Confined Area of Engagement—An area with little or no space to move your body and reposition to a better physical location. You may also be challenged with engaging a threat in this same area.

Contact Range—Distance which can be measured between the officer and business end of a contact weapon where it is not necessary for the attacker to move his bodily position in order to reach the officer.

CQB—Close Quarter Battle: Generally accepted term that refers to the usage of a firearm in a close quarters personal combat scenario. CQB can also include long gun (carbine) or sub gun as well as hand gun (pistol).

CR—Contact Range (See Contact Range).

CRT—Critical Response Team

Cycles of Action—In both DTI and SAI there are numerous cycles of physical activity which can also contain cycle within cycles. Some of these are the OODA Cycle (or loop) and the Shot Placement Cycle.

DEA—US Drug Enforcement Administration

DOD—United States Department of Defense

DOJ—United States Department of Justice

DT—Defensive tactics

DTI—Defensive Tactics Instruction

FAMS—United States Federal Air Marshal Service

FAQs—Frequently Asked Questions.

FBI—United States Federal Bureau of Investigation, aka "The Bureau"

Front Sight—There are two sights mounted on the top of the slide of a handgun. They are identified as the "front sight" and the "rear sight." The focal point of the shooter is (should be) on the front sight.

Full Load—The final carry condition of a firearm when it is fully loaded, that is the magazine is loaded to maximum capacity and there is a round in battery. To achieve a full load of a completely unloaded gun, insert a full magazine into an empty mag well. Cycle the slide to feed and lock a round into battery. Remove the magazine, top it off again and reinsert or simply insert another fully loaded magazine. The end result of this activity is referred to as a "full load."

Green Zone—A relatively safe physical position with regards to a threat.

Hard Skills—Those skills required by any law enforcement, military or specialized department or agency requiring proficiency in trained physical skills such as defensive tactics and firearms of its employees.

LEO—Law Enforcement Officer(s)

Line of Attack—An imaginary line drawn from the contact weapon to the officer's centerline. It is the most dangerous element in any contact weapon encounter. It is imperative that the officer be cognizant of this line.

LOA—Line of Attack. References the straightest line between two points—the attacker's weapon (or weapons) and your vital body part(s).

Glossary

Make Ready—A range command issued by either the RM or RSO which indicates that it is time to double check that your ear and eye protection is secured in place and functional, that it is now safe to remove your firearm from the holster and come to a full load. Common practice is to execute a press check prior to returning the gun to the holster barring any further commands.

Muzzle Discipline—The appropriate and safe control of the muzzle of a gun generally associated with tactical movement. Keeping the muzzle pointed safely down range as well as in such a manner to stabilize the front site allows for accurate shot placement.

NCR—Non-contact Range. Refers to that range where the attacker holding a knife or "other dangerous weapon" cannot reach out and make contact without moving his body closer and make contact with any part of your body or weapon. (see Non-contact Range).

ND—Negligent Discharge. Formerly referred to as an AD (Accidental Discharge) this updated terminology reflects the responsibility of the operator as guns just don't fire all by themselves.

Non-contact Range (NCR)—That distance where an attacker must move his physical position in order to reach the officer. In this situation, an officer has visual confirmation that a contact weapon attack has been deployed and it is identified as a clear and present danger. This is the safest of the two ranges.

N/S—A no-shoot. Situation in which it is determined that not shooting is the optimal response in a specific scenario.

NSR—Non-Standard Response. As opposed to an SDR (Standard Defensive Response) an NSR is any number of strikes up to the contents of an entire magazine in a very short span of time—usually not less than three rounds.

OAE—Open Area Engagement (see Open Area of Engagement)

Open Area of Engagement—An area with sufficient space to move your body and reposition to a better physical location. You are also challenged with engaging a threat in this same area.

OSG—Operational Skills Group, LLC—a California-based mobile training services company serving the Professional Training

Community since 1994, OSG offers vetted programs of instruction specific to military, federal and civilian law enforcement requirements. Source-reference ROE/UOF compliant, OSG exceeds industry standards as set by federal regulatory bodies. Such compliances include instructor/student ratios, safety and delivery protocol, outlines/hourly distributions, sustainment, and supporting documentation.

PDQ—Acronym for Pretty Darn Quick. Fast. Something executed with alacrity.

POI—Programs of Instruction.

Position of Advantage (POA)—An officer can gain position of advantage in one of two ways. The first method is through range and position where he places himself out of range of the attack and utilizes superior force options whereas the second method utilizes advantageous physical locations in the close quarter's altercation.

Position of Dominance (POD)—An officer can gain position of dominance in one of two ways. The first method is through range and position where he places himself out of range of the attack and utilizes superior force options whereas the second method utilizes dominant physical locations in the close quarter's altercation.

Position, Range and Mobility—Position, Range and Mobility are the three most important elements of controlling any fight.

Power Curve—Abbreviation for "Action-Reaction Power Curve"

Press Check—The physical action of manipulating the slide in such a manner as to expose the content of the chamber. It is strongly recommended (and good habit) to check both visually and digitally (using a finger) to ensure that a round is in fact in battery and that you have confirmed in your mind that you now have a loaded gun.

Primary Weapon System—Assigned Primary Weapon

PT—Physical Training (push-ups, pull-ups, running, etc.)

Red Zone—An unsafe physical position with regards to a threat.

RM—Rangemaster—the single individual who is ultimately responsible for all activities which transpire on the range.

ROE—Rules of Engagement

Glossary

RSO—Range Safety Officer. Assistant to the RM who enforces the rules of the range as well as assists with instruction as per the RM. There can be more than one RSO (and usually are) assigned to a range during most training or qualifications.

SAI—Small Arms Instruction

SDR—Standard Defensive Responses—two rounds delivered to center mass as opposed to an NSR (non-standard response).

Secondary Weapon System—Transitional Weapon / Back-up Weapon

SFP—Stable Fighting Platform

Shot Placement Cycle—Series of precisely timed sequential cycles of action (OODA Cycle, Gun Handling Cycle, Handgun Presentation Cycle, Trigger Control, Cycle (TCC), Trigger Break Cycle (TBC), Mechanical Cycle of Action (MCA), etc.) representing over fifty-eight individual processes (depending on specific firearm) all executed perfectly in sync with the intended result of accurate round placement.

SOI—Scale of Injury

SOP—Standard Operating Procedure(s)

SRT—Specialty Response Team

Strong Hand—Dominant hand—aka "Weapon Hand"

Strong Side—Side of the body where the dominant hand is located.

Support Hand—Non-dominant hand

Support Side—Side of the body where the non-dominant hand is located.

SWAT—Special Weapons and Tactics

TBS—The Basic School—USMC Base located in Quantico, VA.

TLO—Terminal Learning Objective(s). The purpose or "end goal" of the material of a particular course. What the student is expected to take home from training.

UOF—Use of Force

USMC—United States Marine Corps

USSS—United States Secret Service, aka "The Service"

STEVE TARANI—BRIEF BIOGRAPHICAL SKETCH

Author Steve Tarani lecturing on operational readiness.

Steve Tarani is an internationally respected authority within the law-enforcement and military training community. He is a full-time training consultant providing high-profile operational skills development programs for various agencies worldwide.

Tarani is unparalleled in the law enforcement training community as a master-level instructor and tactical subject matter expert specializing in use-of-force training. Steve is also the developer of well known Instructor Certification Programs which have gained both federal and Peace Officer Standards of Training accreditation throughout the continental United States.

His background includes:
- Instructor staff at the U.S. D.O.E. Nonproliferation and National Security Institute (Central Training Academy) Security Force Training Dept. at Kirtland Air Force Base (NM).

- Defensive tactics advisor to The US Federal Bureau of Investigation, US Transportation Security Administration (ISD ACSP) and the U.S. State Dept. Bureau of Diplomatic Security Antiterrorism Assistance Program. (ATAP)

- Sworn in the state of California and serves on staff as Senior Defensive Tactics and a Firearms Instructor for Del Rey Oaks Police Department in reserve capacity.

- Instructor staff as a Firearms Rangemaster at Gunsite Academy (AZ).

- CEO and Director of Training for Operational Skills Group, LLC as a full-time educator and training management consultant throughout the professional law enforcement and specialized military training community.

- Sworn in the State of Nevada as a Deputy for Pershing County Sheriff's Office.

- Federally certified Firearms Instructor (US DOE, US DOD, etc.).